Handbook on Interactive Storytelling

Handbook on Interactive Storytelling

Jouni Smed
University of Turku, Finland

Tomi 'bgt' Suovuo
University of Turku, Finland

Natasha Skult
University of Turku, Finland

Petter Skult
Åbo Akademi University, Finland

Registered Offices
John Wiley & Sons, Inc., 111 River Street, Hoboken, NJ 07030, USA
John Wiley & Sons Ltd, The Atrium, Southern Gate, Chichester, West Sussex, PO19 8SQ, UK

Editorial Office
The Atrium, Southern Gate, Chichester, West Sussex, PO19 8SQ, UK

For details of our global editorial offices, customer services, and more information about Wiley products visit us at www.wiley.com.

Library of Congress Cataloging-in-Publication Data

Names: Smed, Jouni, author. | Suovuo, Tomi 'bgt', 1974- author. | Skult, Natasha, 1984- author. | Skult, Petter, 1985- author.
Title: Handbook on interactive storytelling / Jouni Smed, Tomi 'bgt' Suovuo, Natasha Skult, Petter Skult.
Description: Hoboken, NJ : Wiley, 2021. | Includes bibliographical references and index.
Identifiers: LCCN 2021014074 (print) | LCCN 2021014075 (ebook) | ISBN 9781119688136 (cloth) | ISBN 9781119688150 (adobe pdf) | ISBN 9781119688174 (epub)
Subjects: LCSH: Video games–Authorship. | Video games–Design. | Interactive multimedia–Authorship. | Interactive multimedia–Design.
Classification: LCC GV1469.34.A97 S64 2021 (print) | LCC GV1469.34.A97 (ebook) | DDC 794.8/1535–dc23
LC record available at https://lccn.loc.gov/2021014074
LC ebook record available at https://lccn.loc.gov/2021014075

Cover Design: Wiley
Cover Image: © Inna/Adobe Stock

Set in 9.5/12.5pt STIXTwoText by Straive, Chennai, India
Printed and bound by CPI Group (UK) Ltd, Croydon, CR0 4YY

C9781119688136_160621

Contents

List of Figures

List of Tables

Preface

Imagine a group sitting by a campfire. The evening sky is getting dark and the first stars begin to appear. Everybody is getting cosy and warm, but something is missing. Then somebody starts telling a story.

This set-up could have happened at any time and anywhere in human history – it might have included even our hominid ancestors. There is something inherently human in the scene. The story and the process of telling it – they cannot be separated from each other. Telling stories is how we construct our memories, how we pass on our values, and how we communicate our experiences. It allows us to have a glimpse into another person's mind.

Just us, and the story.

This book tells a story, a story of how stories could be told using digital media. In many occasions, digital media is said to revolutionize or disrupt the way things have been done before. This is not what we are claiming here. Digital storytelling is not about disruption, breaking, or replacing old order. How could it? Stories will remain stories as before. Rather, this will bring stories back to where they once were. They will become alive and include our digital world in them. Someone will tell the story – human or computer – to somebody else – human or computer. This will be the new digital campfire.

Turku/Åbo, Finland
November 2020

Jouni Smed
Tomi 'bgt' Suovuo
Natasha Skult
Petter Skult

Acknowledgements

First and foremost, the authors would like to thank Harri Hakonen for his early involvement and initial work in analysing the material and his sharp views and insights into essential matters.

We would like to thank the team at Wiley for their efforts, especially our Editor Sandra Grayson and Managing Editor Juliet Booker. We are grateful to them for their flexibility during the trying times of the COVID-19 pandemic, which has also rattled our writing process.

Jouni. I want to acknowledge the important role that my late friend and colleague Timo Kaukoranta played 20 years ago in launching this expedition in the world of interactive storytelling. I would like to express my gratitude to the valuable inputs from my students over the years, and I am indebted to everybody who has attended my courses on interactive storytelling at the University of Turku in the period 2004–2020. My special greetings go to Lilia and Julian: I am always amazed at your fantastical storyworlds, and, now that I am done writing (at least for a while), I will be happy to spend more time hanging out there with Lord Kanther, D'opa, Härpats, and your other marvellous creations. And Iris, thank you for being there – living, laughing, and loving.

BGT. I wish to thank the hobbyist associations of Turun science fiction seura, Turun yliopiston tieteiskulttuurikabinetti, and Turun yliopiston rooli- ja strategiapeliseura for providing inspiration and insightful discussions related to storytelling and games. I also wish to thank everyone I have played role-playing games and live-action-role-playing games with, especially those who endured the most ridiculous and embarrassing clumsy experiments of mine in this field of interactive storytelling. Loving thanks also to my dearest wife and role-playing company, Riikka.

Natasha. I wish to thank fellow authors of this book; it has been an amazing journey and inspiring collaboration, which is one of many to come. I also want to thank IGDA Finland, Turku Game Hub, and MiTale teams for all the support and tireless discussions on the topics of interactive storytelling and 'industry' views. I wish to dedicate special gratitude to my family, Petter and Sara, for their endless support and inspiration.

Petter. I want to thank Åbo Akademi University for having me as a researcher after finishing my PhD during the writing of this book, my fellow authors for their patience and expertise, and, of course, my family and friends for their support.

1

Introduction

Humans are storytelling animals. We crave hearing stories at an early age, and as soon as we start telling them ourselves. The simplest life forms carry their legacy to their children as genetic instincts. More complex animals take this further by teaching their young through play and concrete examples. Humans are the only known species to bring up their young also with stories of imaginary and abstract examples. Take away stories and you would reduce humans to something else. As Barbara Hardy (1968) observes '[in] order really to live, we make up stories about ourselves and others, about the personal as well as the social past and future.' Alasdair MacIntyre (1981, p. 201) echoes this sentiment by concluding that 'man is in his actions and practice, as well as in his fictions, essentially a story-telling animal' because 'we all live our narratives in our lives and because we understand our lives in terms of narratives' (MacIntyre 1981, p. 197). Simply put, a human being is *homo narrans*, the 'storytelling human' (Fisher 1984).

When storytellers begin their story, there is a sense of wonder that the audience has. Out of a sudden, a new world is created in front of their eyes with characters and events that, at the same time, are relatable and familiar but are also new and strange. Who of us has not had that feeling when starting a book or a movie, a television series or video game – or simply hearing someone reiterate a story of what happened to them in the previous day. Story is a human way to connect with other people over the barriers of language, culture, or even time. *Epic of Gilgamesh* is almost 5000-year-old story, but we can still understand and relate its protagonist as he struggles through trials and tribulations.

It is not only that stories are used for entertainment or pastime but they are also records of our past, collections of wisdom and knowledge. They are a way to teach culture, values, norms, history, science to our children, to educate them to be a part of our bigger pack.

At the heart of this is the *storyteller*, the one who composes and collects the material into a presentable form to the public. In the beginning, they were doing all this by themself, but with time and technological advances they could use the latest inventions – writing, painting, printing, filming, computing – as an extension. Such advancements allowed them to store the stories, help to disseminate them, and bring them to the masses even on a global scale.

But this is not a story of the storyteller alone, because they would be nothing without the audience, the ones to whom the story is being told, who make the storyteller, lift them up or bring them down. Such popularity has become an essential aspect for many whose livelihood depends on the audience's goodwill.

Handbook on Interactive Storytelling, First Edition. Jouni Smed, Tomi 'bgt' Suovuo, Natasha Skult, and Petter Skult.
© 2021 John Wiley & Sons Ltd. Published 2021 by John Wiley & Sons Ltd.

The relationship between them has been a struggle of control. The storyteller cannot live in a vacuum and cut ties to the audience. Although there might be exceptions, many of them are now forgotten. There is *interaction* between the two that can take many forms. In oral storytelling, the bards would adapt to the audience's reactions and change the presentation whilst keeping the formula – the structure of the story. An author of a novel seems isolated from interactions, writing in solitude, a work that gets them printed and distributed, or a game designer working with a computer. None of them is working in a vacuum, but there is feedback, albeit slow and from a limited set. They have time to react and make changes. But what if the need for change is immediate and the range of possible choices is vast?

Digital media allows us to tell stories as well as any of the traditional ones. When we think about what is special about digital media, we have

- the possibility of combining different formats;
- the reproducibility (i.e. getting perfect copies in unlimited numbers);
- the ease, scale, and speed of distribution (e.g. by eliminating middlemen such as publishers); and
- permanence (at least in the short term).

The greatest concern with digital media is the long-term permanence. How many of today's digital stories will last as long as *Epic of Gilgamesh*? We are already witnessing deprecation or 'digital rust' due to outdated formats or devices. For example, the original assets and source codes of the video game *Blade Runner* (Westwood Studios 1997) were lost and had to be reverse engineered with great effort (GOG.com 2019).

New medium means that we have to refine our concepts. Traditionally, storytelling is seen as the author conveying the story to an audience via a medium. The author's story can be conveyed as a book to the reader, a film to the spectators, a play to an audience. *Digital stories* are not different, but digital devices are another medium. However, what is different is the possibility of *interactivity*. This allows the audience to affect the story being told. This is not anything new per se, but many non-digital storytelling situations retain this aspect. Imagine a bard telling a story orally, observing the audience's reactions and adapting the story accordingly. The same happens when a parent is inventing a good-night story to a child: the story changes and adapts. This requires a *second-person insight*. It is something that good teachers or tour guides can cultivate to capture their audience. The topics of a historical sight remain the same, but what the guide tells can be totally different for a group of bored teenagers than for a senior citizen on a holiday trip.

Computers thrive from interaction. The pace has got faster until we now expect to have a real-time response, the range is getting wider so that we can choose freely within the context, and interfaces have been getting clearer so that the users know what they are getting. This does sound like a perfect solution to the problem of providing interaction to storytelling – a storytelling machine. The idea is not that new but Ramon Llull proposed in *Ars Magna* from 1305 a machine to study the aspect of God with words, which influenced many thinkers such as Gottfried Leibniz to ponder the possibilities of a logical machine. Having left the analogue behind story generation became an aspect of study and creation. Since the 1990s there has been steady progress in research and development of interactive storytelling as a digital media.

The idea of interactive storytelling is an appealing one: what if I could change the flow of the story. Instead of being a passive recipient, what if I could actually have an impact on the way the story proceeds – but without the need of being the one who does the hard work and carries on the story. It is easy to see the lure of interactive storytelling because authoring itself is cumbersome and requires a lot of work and skills. It would be easier to just affect the story whenever one feels like, make little twists and changes so that the events would turn out how one wishes for.

This lost interaction is the key ingredient in the mix. We have become so accustomed to the ready-made worlds that many are craving an outlet for participatory action. It can be fanfic or cosplay or going to a themepark of our favourite storyverse. What if the story and its world (i.e. the storyworld) would be manageable enough to let you change it to your own liking. Naturally, you would say that we already have video games that allow us to fulfil our dreams (Adams 2014, p. 47). But think bigger. Instead of going through somebody's authored narrative, what if you could be the one in control, co-authoring (if you like) the story. This is the call of digital interactive storytelling where technology (i.e. algorithms) would be your tireless guide and bard leading you to a world that was designed to be experienced. You could play it, but you could have something else. Within these pages, we will get to know this world.

Before recounting that this chapter presents the basic terms and structure of interactive storytelling and how it differs from conventional (i.e. non-interactive) storytelling, we see how the four partakers – platform, designer, interactor and storyworld – are connected to one another, and in the subsequent chapter we look at each of them more closely. We also go through the history of interactive storytelling from non-digital to digital in various media to provide a historical perspective about the roles of interaction in storytelling. First, we need to clarify the terminology and basic concepts in Section 1.1. We provide a cursory glance on storytelling, narratives, interactivity, which we deepen throughout this book. Then, we take a look at examples of this in Section 1.2.

1.1 Interactive Storytelling

Storytelling is always interactive. Even an author working alone on an isolated island has the potential readers in their mind, and this interactive thought process affects how the story is being constructed. But we do not have to go so far because the sounding board is generally close to the author – family members, colleagues, the editor. Also, the reader of any book is not just passively having the same experience every other reader: there are personal contexts that make individual differences to the reading experience, and even those contexts change over time, so no two read-throughs are exactly the same (Falk and Dierking 2016; Mäyrä 2007).

But there is a difference between reading a book and attending a live-action role-playing (LARP) game. The interaction in larping is richer and more immediate than that in reading a text. In the former, the participants can affect how the story takes shape in real time, whereas a book gives you a readily formed story to enjoy.

If we look closely, we can recognize that the interactivity of storytelling forms a spectrum illustrated in Figure 1.1. On the one end, we have conventional storytelling (e.g. books

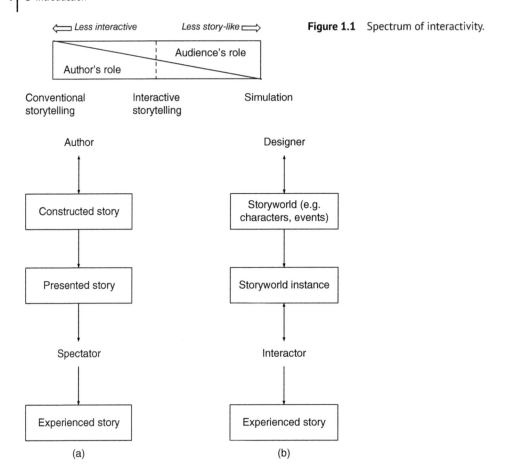

Figure 1.1 Spectrum of interactivity.

Figure 1.2 Comparison of (a) conventional storytelling and (b) interactive storytelling.

or films) where the author has full control over everything that happens in the story, but the audience has no control. On the other end, we have a simulation (or a sandbox) where the audience (e.g. spectator or player) is free to choose whatever they want to do, but the author has no control over the possibly emerging stories. One could say that in this case there is no author, but a member of the audience becomes their own author typically telling a story to themself.

When people are talking about interactive storytelling, they are usually referring to something that resides in the middle of this spectrum. Leaving aside the simulation, we can compare conventional storytelling and interactive storytelling (see Figure 1.2). In conventional storytelling, the author has a special place when constructing the story. One could argue that this construction phase is only a place where interaction (between the author and the storyworld) happens. Once the story is finished, it is ready to be presented to the spectators (or readers) who will form their own experienced story individually. All in all, the story is handed down without any real feedback loop or possibility to interaction.

In contrast, interactive storytelling puts the interactor in a key role. The designer is now providing the characters, props, and external events forming the storyworld. Based on this and the interactor's choices, a story instance is generated, which the interactor then experiences.

1.1.1 Partakers

We have now introduced two key partakers in interactive storytelling: the one who creates the work and the one experiences it. In the literature on interactive storytelling, the former is often called the author but – as one can discern from Figure 1.2b – we have opted for the term *designer*, which is also favoured by Adams (2013, pp. 8–9). One could even argue that 'author' is a special case of a 'designer' when the situation is limited to conventional storytelling and the designer has complete authority over the presented story. Moreover, within the game industry, 'narrative designer' is now established as a professional title, but, for the sake of conciseness, we omit the qualifier 'narrative' unless we specifically refer to the profession in question.

In the case of a person experiencing an interactive story, the situation is muddier. Terms such as 'player', 'actor', 'user', 'agent', and 'participant' have been used in the literature without a clear consensus (Smed and Hakonen 2008). Our choice here is *interactor*, which emphasizes being an interactive actor in a storyworld created by a designer; we use sometimes 'player' when it is more convenient or customary in the context but, generally speaking, 'interactor' can be used more broadly (e.g. when interactive storytelling is used in teaching or guiding). The interactor is the one who principally experiences the story as it unravels. We use the term 'audience' when we are more generally referring to a recipient of the story in any kind of storytelling, whether it is interactive or not. The interactor typically plays the role of the main character in the story, interacting with the other characters. Consequently, the interactor is a traditional type of an actor in the play as well (without the inter-prefix), and, as such, the interactor takes upon a role and is also a character in the storyworld.

Storyworld includes all the characters, props, scenes, and events set up by the designer for the interactor. Props are inanimate objects, which can be used in the storyworld, and events cause changes launched by fulfilling some criteria. Characters combine these two properties: they are both objects and agents of change. Scenes are the surroundings which the props and characters inhabit and where the events and characters can affect.

Although earlier the storyworld was built upon customary software, we would like to consider *platform* as a separate partaker. This follows the trend we have seen in other forms of software applications where the content production and the development environment get separated. For example, nowadays computer games are developed in dedicated platforms such as Unity or Unreal Engine, whereas earlier the development process included also creating the tools and runtime environment as well as the actual content.

This is in a similar fashion to how WordPress platform provides mechanisms for the user interface (UI) and visual layout for blogs. They are still versatile enough for each created site to have their own functionalities and individual appearances. The great majority of website developers no longer program everything 'from the scratch', but they apply pre-existing frameworks. The most significant exception is services, whose main content is tightly linked with mechanics such as Amazon and Facebook. Another example from the film industry is Charlie Chaplin – a pioneer in the field – who used to devise his own visual effects for his

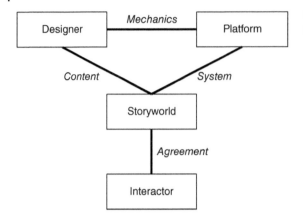

Figure 1.3 Partakers of interactive storytelling.

movies. In comparison, nowadays the most film productions use specialized companies for such purposes, which is analogous to how the software industry applies frameworks. At the moment of writing, we are seeing signs that interactive storytelling as software is maturing to this point of separation.

Figure 1.3 summarizes the four partakers and their interdependencies (Smed et al. 2018). Platforms provide the designer with mechanics to use with the content, and it acts as a system for running the storyworld. Designers' content fills the storyworld. The interactors agree to take part in the storyworld and play their roles in it.

1.1.2 Narrative, Plot, and Story

Narrative is a combination of *story* and *discourse*, where the story is a sequence of events (or action) and discourse is the selected events that are presented (Abbott 2002, pp. 16–17). Prince (1980) defines narrative as 'the representation of real or fictive events and situations in a time sequence', and according to him, the story is 'the content plane of narrative as opposed to its expression plane or discourse; the "what" of a narrative as opposed to its "how" ' (Prince 1987, p. 91). In other words, narrative is an actualization of the story. One could say that the 'presented story' in Figure 1.2a is a narrative as the 'storyworld instance' in Figure 1.2b. However, there is a difference regarding how these two get created (i.e. the process of storytelling).

The term 'narrative' has different definitions, but for this book, we have adopted the naïve view promoted by Adams (2013, p. 25), where *narrative* refers to the unchangeable material presented to the interactor. For this reason, Adams concludes that 'interactive narrative' is an oxymoron and it is better to use the term 'interactive storytelling'. However, many scholars prefer using 'interactive narrative' arguing that narrative can change, for example, when the interactor makes choices. This kind of terminological ambiguity is, unfortunately, quite pervasive in this field of study.

Our distinction here is that 'narration' belongs to traditional storytelling, whereas 'storytelling' is a process between the designer, platform, storyworld, and interactor – all the four partakers – that not only creates a story but also the resulting narrative that can be seen afterwards. To use another image, storytelling is like the lava pouring out of the earth – being

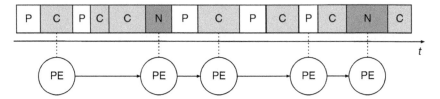

Figure 1.4 Interactor's perception of the sequence of events. P marks a player-generated event; C, a computer-generated event; and N, a narrative event. Plot events, marked with PE, are dramatically significant events and their sequence forms the plot.

liquid and malleable, following the surface and its contours, filling it, reacting to disturbances, whereas narrative is a solidified rock, possibly chiselled into a form.

Within the context of interactive digital storytelling, an *event* is any (possibly unseen) event that the computer can demonstrate (Adams 2013, pp. 26–27). A *narrated event* (following the above definition) is immutable and set by the narrative designer. A *computer-generated event* is the result of processing done on the underlying platform. A *player-generated event* is a response to the interactor's input. It is worth noting that narrated events are not necessarily needed in an interactive storytelling system. The interactor's perception of the sequence is illustrated in Figure 1.4. Events have three functions in a story: they can set a scene, reveal a character, or be a part of the *plot*, which is a causal sequence of events.

If an event is *dramatically significant*, we call it a *plot event*. This means that the event creates or releases the dramatic tension and that it is related (causally or by subject matter) to other experienced events. Figure 1.4 illustrates how plot events can correspond to narrative events (e.g. cutscenes), computer-generated events (e.g. a runtime decision by the platform to introduce a new character) or player events (e.g. the player choosing to save one of the characters from a zombie attack and letting others die). In traditional storytelling, the usual aim is to remove any insignificant events, whereas in video games – being partly a simulation of the real world – they may be included. How do we then distinguish the significance? As Adams (2013, p. 28) summarizes, it is subjective and context-dependent on the interactor's sense, which is why we cannot have a universal rule but have to rely on convention and common sense.

The plot is *advancing* when the interactor is experiencing more plot events, and it is stalled when this process ceases. If the interactor deliberately stalls the plot, we can say that they are obstructing the plot. This is related to the freedom we give to the interactor. We look deeper into this in Section 2.2.4.

A *plot line* is a manifestation of the plot. If the plot is defined in advance by the designer, we can call it a predefined plot. If the story can be different in each play, we can call it a *manifold story*. We make further observations on this in Section 4.1.

A *story* in Adams's naïve view means now all the events that the interactor can experience in the course of playing the work (Adams 2013, p. 29). For a story to be interesting to the audience, it must have a psychological buy-in by the audience, and the audience must engage in willing suspension of disbelief, which we address in detail in Chapter 5.

1.1.3 Interaction

Interaction can be seen as a reciprocal action, where entities' actions influence one another. Crawford (2013, p. 28) defines interaction as '[a] cyclic process between two or more active agents in which each agent alternately listens, thinks, and speaks'. Crawford uses this metaphor of a conversation to illustrate the phases through which the entities – whether they are controlled by a human or a computer – must pass in interaction. Adams (2013, pp. 29–31) agrees and sees interactivity as the user's ability to interact with any software. The *interactive range* (or freedom) of software – such as an interactive storytelling system – is simply the collection of choices made available to the user.

Interactivity should not be confused with *agency*, which means the user's ability to influence the system. In an interactive storytelling system, this could mean the interactor's ability to influence the plot line. Having a large interactive range (e.g. a vast array of options to choose from) does not imply that the interactor has also a stronger agency unless the options also have a meaningful and perceptible effect on the storyworld. We return to agency in more detail in Section 5.2.

Crawford (2013, pp. 37–41) lists that three factors affecting the degree of interactivity in storytelling are speed, depth, and choice. *Speed* refers to that the faster the turnaround is, the better the possibilities for interaction. For example, instant messaging has a short turnaround, whereas mailed letters can take days. Faster turnaround means that the communicating parties can react faster and see the result of their action faster. It creates a state of continuous 'motion' like individual film cells when played fast after one another. *Depth* is about the human-likeness of interaction (i.e. the deeper, the more human-like). Apart from simple cognitive modalities (e.g. hand–eye coordination or spatial reasoning), social reasoning would be the most important in interactive stories. *Choice* has a twofold focus. First, it is about the functional significance (i.e. agency) of the choices the interactor makes (i.e. how well they satisfy the interactor's wants or desires). Second, perceived completeness refers to the number of choices with respect to the possibilities the interactor can imagine. This does not mean that more is always better, but it is relative to the context.

Ryan (2006, pp. 107–116; 2015, pp. 162–164) recognizes two axes of interactivity:

- *Internal–external*: In *internal interactivity*, the interactor projects themself as a member of the virtual world, whereas in *external interactivity*, they are situated outside the virtual world – or to use the terms of Adams (2013, p. 270) the corresponding interaction model is avatar-based or omnipresent.
- *Exploratory–ontological*: In *exploratory interactivity*, the interactor can navigate inside the virtual world but cannot affect it, whereas in *ontological interactivity*, the interactor's decisions can send them into different paths.

These two axes are illustrated in Figure 1.5. The four quadrants that they divide represent different types of interactivity:

1. *Internal-ontological interactivity*: The interactor creates an avatar and interacts using it, which is typical in the majority of video games (e.g. first-person shooters, platformers, or adventure games).
2. *External-ontological interactivity*: The interactor observes a simulated world and has god-like controls over it (e.g. real-time strategy games or *The Sims*).

3. *External-explanatory interactivity*: The interactor explores a virtual world from the outside without any agency apart from choosing one of the ready-made paths (e.g. gamebooks or hypertext fiction).
4. *Internal-explanatory interactivity*: The interactor has an avatar but cannot affect anything but just observe (e.g. walking simulators or exploratory environments).

Naturally, we cannot make so discrete distinctions, but one should think of them as a continuum.

We can look at the diagonal from external-explorative to internal-ontological (i.e. from the bottom-right corner to the upper-left corner in Figure 1.5) and notice how the level of interactivity changes. Ryan (2015, pp. 175–185) differentiates these levels of interactivity. In the first level, *peripheral interactivity*, the interactive interface does not affect the story but rather makes the signifiers visible. The next three levels reside along the aforementioned diagonal:

- *Interactivity affecting the narrative discourse and the presentation of the story*: The material or content is predetermined, but the order of the story is highly variable (e.g. hypertext fiction).
- *Interactivity creating variations in a partly predefined story*: The interactors are typically a part of the storyworld and can alter their own story.
- *Interactivity leading to real-time story generation*: The story is no longer predetermined but generated. It is replayable and offers freedom to create different narratives.

Ryan concludes that the last one is superior to peripheral interactivity. Apart from these, she recognizes a fifth level, *meta-interactivity* (i.e. modding), where the platform is for modification (e.g. creating a new content, characters, or mechanics). This blurs the line between the interactor and designer, as we see in Section 3.1.4.

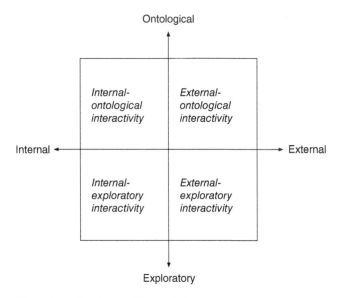

Figure 1.5 Four types of interactivity.

Ryan (2001, pp. 204) observes that interactivity 'was shut off by manuscript and print writing and reintroduced into written messages by the electronic medium, together with several other features of oral communication' such as real-time (synchronous) exchange, spontaneity of expression, and volatility of inscription. Digital systems are interactive and reactive by nature and that interactivity actually makes a difference between old and new media (Ryan 2006, pp. 98–99).

1.2 History of Interactive Storytelling

Storytelling originally meant telling stories to an audience. Most of the initial stories are based on learning about things that can harm us, both as individuals and groups. Stories can also give explanations and finding a reason for certain phenomenon or behaviour, which can give a basis for a religion – or even science. And, naturally, entertainment has always been a big motivator for storytelling.

Storytelling included an interactive part by default because the storyteller (e.g. bard) would have to adapt the story according to the audience (Murray 1997, pp. 188–194). If the audience did not respond favourably to the story, the storyteller would have to change the approach. Even epics such as the *Iliad* and the *Odyssey* started out as bardic tales and – regardless of whether they were composed by Homer – went through several centuries and countless generations of bards before they were first written down.

The change from orally told stories to written one was drastic. For example, Plato (1925, 275a–277a) expressed a critique on written word, which he asserts to be inferior to a human as a source of information (ironically, we know all this because Plato's story has been passed on to us in a written form). Apart from being an aid to the memory preventing one from truly knowing, it is non-dynamic and non-personal: you cannot make questions to a written text and it does not adapt to your needs. But this resilience to change and independence from the humans to carry it on have helped to save it, and we can still experience, for example, Bronze Age stories such as the *Story of Sinuhe* and *Epic of Gilgamesh*.

The introduction of the printing press in the fifteenth century made written word the preferred medium to distribute stories faster and to a wider audience. New inventions such as film and television meant the crafted narrative that would be reproduced in the same way – providing all spectators the same presented story; see Figure 1.2a. Literacy grew slowly and for many oral storytelling remained the main form of entertainment and passing wisdom. Further, murals and allegories in architecture (e.g. religious monuments and environmental art) provided a medium for visual storytelling (see Section 2.1.2).

Although the majority of literary works have been unicursal (i.e. offering one path to follow), there have also been examples – albeit rare – of multicursal works (i.e. offering critical choices to the reader). One of the earliest examples is *I Ching*, which is a Chinese book on divination dating back to between the tenth and fourth century BCE. The reader uses yarrow stalks (or special coins) to get six broken or unbroken lines, which together make a hexagram. The book has text for each of the 64 possible hexagrams and additional commentary for the individual lines, which can be changing or unchanging. Although multicursal works appeared as motifs after the Renaissance (Aarseth 1997, pp. 5–7), multicursal literature started gaining a foothold during the twentieth century (see Section 1.2.2).

Similarly, interactivity remained the fringes of other art forms such as theatre (see Section 1.2.1), cinema (see Section 1.3.3), and television (see Section 1.3.4). The advent of digital media from the 1940s onwards began to bring interactive forms of storytelling back to the limelight. It appeared in hypertext fiction (see Section 1.3.1), webisodics (see Section 1.3.2) and – most importantly – in video games (see Section 1.3.5).

1.2.1 Theatre

Western theatre has its roots in ancient Greece, where the plays were performed according to scripts. Some of those scripts such as Sophocles's *Oedipus Rex* and Aristophanes's *Lysistrata* have survived and are performed this day.

Interactivity and immersion are two facets of theatre, whose roles have varied throughout history. Ryan (2001, p. 295–305; 2015, pp. 216–222) recognizes four stage designs that arrange the theatrical space putting emphasis on either immersion or interactivity (see Figure 1.6):

- In a circular arena, the audience are surrounding the actors in the arena from all sides (e.g. a stadium). The audience are not only spectators, but they are also taking part in the experience interactively by commenting. Sports venues are typically based on this design.
- In a classical Greek stage design, the actors and audience are separated by the stage and the seats leading to a compromise of immersion and interactivity. The audience can still participate in the play, but it is becoming more a spectacle to be immersed in.
- In an Italian stage design of the Baroque era (the seventeenth century), the actors play on a lit and decorated stage, whereas the audience is seated in darkness, and they are further divided by the proscenium and an orchestral pit. All this leads to an immersive design that emphasizes spectacle and discourages interaction.
- In avant-garde theatre of the 1950s–1960s, the actors and audience were often intermingled, with some members appearing on the stage (possibly taking part in disciplined action) and some actors being outside of the focus among the spectators. This leads to high interactivity.

Interaction with the audience requires the actors to improvise. An early example of this is *commedia dell'arte* ('comedy of craft'), which started out in sixteenth-century Italy as a form of improvised performances based on sketches or scenarios. A typical *commedia dell'arte* performance would include characters from a roster including stereotypical features (some of which later evolved into modern-day circus characters).

Modern-day improvisational theatre formed in the 1970s from the improv theatre scene with likes of 'Too Much Light Makes the Baby Go Blind', followed later by the Frantic Assembly and the Viewpoints movement. Improvisational theatre is an intricate collaboration between the actors and audience. The actor should react believably and in an emotionally engaging way at every point of the performance. Based on the character-defining goal or drive, the actor should also create story opportunities that have an emotional impact. The other actors then strengthen or contradict this and offer new opportunities. The audience can also affect the performance by providing the actors cues on the situation, style, and their character's attributes.

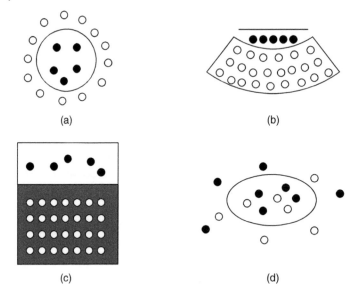

Figure 1.6   Stage designs in chronological order: (a) circular arena, (b) Greek stage design, (c) Italian stage design of the Baroque era, and (d) avant-garde theatre. The black circles represent the actors and open circles the members of the audience.

Another, more serious, strand of improvisational theatre is Forum Theatre, which aims at helping the audience to solve social problems through performances (Boal 1979). A typical Forum Theatre performance includes a preselected theme where first the actors begin an improvisational situation. At any point, members of the audience can shout and change the story – or even step on the stage to replace one of the actors.

Bertolt Brecht's epic theatre in the early twentieth century challenged the classical theatre (Ryan 2001, pp. 301–302). Brecht tried to prevent immersion and encourage interaction and critical thinking by applying a distancing effect (*Verfremdungseffekt*), where the play has a minimalistic stage and gets interrupted by songs and abstracts. Moreover, the actors can step out of their roles and engage the audience in a critical discussion.

1.2.2   Multicursal Literature

The twentieth-century literature explored the possibilities of multicursal storytelling. A list of some of these works includes the following:

- Doris Webster and Mary Alden Hopkins's *Consider the Consequences!* (1930) offers the reader a possibility to choose how the stories turn at various points. It is an early example of a genre that was later labelled gamebook.
- Ayn Rand's *Night of January 16th* (1936) is a play about a trial where the members of the audience are picked to be a jury. The work has two endings depending on the jury's verdict.
- Raymond Queneau's *Cent mille milliards de poèmes* (1961) includes 10 poems printed on cards, which allow to interchange the individual lines with any other card. Queneau

was part of the Oulipo movement, which was interested in combining mathematics and literature and experiment with the form.

- Marc Saporta's *Composition No. 1, Roman* (1962) is a novel with pages like a deck of cards to be shuffled and read in any sequence.
- Vladimir Nabokov's *Pale Fire* (1962) uses footnotes for multicursal storytelling.
- Julio Cortázar's *Hopscotch* (originally in Spanish *Rayuela*, 1963; English translation 1966) is a novel that can be read following two different sequences of chapters intended by the author or uniquely by the readers making their own sequence.
- Raymond Queneau's short story 'Un conte à votre façon' (1967) comprises 21 segments, of which 19 segments offer two alternatives for the readers to choose from (Queneau 1981, pp. 253–259).
- B.S. Johnson's *The Unfortunates* (1969) has 27 chapters where only the first and the last chapters are indicated, leaving the reader to choose the order for the remaining 25 chapters.

Gamebooks represent a genre of printed books that are not to read linearly but making jumps based on the reader's selection. One of the most known gamebook series is *Choose Your Own Adventure* (CYOA) series by Bantam Book. Between its launch in 1979 and 1998, they sold over 250 million copies. Three typical mechanisms are used in gamebooks:

- Branching plot novels include textual passages followed by a branch point where the reader has to decide the next move. Based on the selection, the reader is then referred to another page in the book.
- Role-playing game (RPG) solitaire adventures are based on the rule set of a pre-existing RPG (e.g. *Dungeons & Dragons*). This allows the player to play alone as the book acts as the game master by maintaining the story and controlling the non-player characters (NPCs).
- Adventure gamebooks use their own RPG system specially customized for the book.

The popularity of gamebooks started to dwindle in the 1990s as digital media (especially hypertext) allowed to implement them more easily.

1.3   Role-playing Games

Although many games include role-playing elements, the RPGs in their modern form evolved from fantasy wargames in the 1970s. One of the most influential RPGs is *Dungeons & Dragons* designed by Dave Arneson and Gary Gygax and published first in 1974. The subsequent RPGs are often variants or improvements of the original *Dungeons & Dragons* with more complex or simpler rule sets and themes varying from dystopian futures to everyday real life.

What is common to RPGs is the promotion of one of the participants into the role of a *game master*. The game master acts partly as a proxy for the original designers and partly as the author creating new content for the players. The game master maintains rules and leads the players through the game. Often, this includes using various storytelling devices to keep the players focused on the scenario as well as move them forward. The game master also controls the NPCs. Consequently, much of the entertainment value of RPGs relies on the game master.

The players of an RPG build a character and assume the identity of their character. This means, for example, when players are making a decision, it is based on what their characters might do in that situation and not what they themself might choose personally.

As the first computer RPGs emerged in the early 1980s, the role of the game master was modelled using algorithms. In many cases, these computer-driven game masters only maintained the rules and did not allow much deviation from the intended story.

RPGs also jumped from tabletop games to experiences in the physical world, which are called LARP. The earliest recorded LARP group started in 1977. LARPs include a predefined setting and backstory. The players create or receive their characters and adopt their behaviour accordingly during the play. As an LARP event can include hundreds of players, last for several days, and disperse into large areas, the role of the game master is often limited to making the initial set-up. Once the event is on its way, the players will act without any centralized control and the story will emerge from the players' interaction.

1.3.1 Hypertext Fiction

Hypertext fiction using digital media was pioneered by Judy Malloy's *Uncle Roger* (1986) and Michael Joyce's *afternoon, a story* (1987). The primary distribution media was CD-ROM, until from the mid-1990s onwards they were made available in WWW. The initial works were aimed at a literary audience, but they started to move towards conceptual art and performance (i.e. hypermedia fiction).

Some of the notable works in hypertext fiction are Stuart Moulthrop's *Victory Garden* (1991), Shelley Jackson's *Patchwork Girl* (1995), Robert Arellano's *Sunshine '69* (1996), and Mark Amerika's *Grammatron* (1997) (Rettberg 2015).

Despite of the attention that hypertext fiction received in the 1990s, it never lived up to expectations. It turned out to be difficult to write and maintain, and other forms (e.g. blogs and social networks) soon took its place (Johnsson 2013). However, new works of hypertext fiction have been appearing from time to time using, for example, the Web or Wikipedia as a medium (La Farge 2020; Truyens 2020).

1.3.2 Webisodics

The earliest instance of an episodic online story is Tracy Reed's *QuantumLink Serial*, which ran on AOL from 1988 to 1989 and is considered to be the first episodic online story. After each week's chapter, the audience wrote to Reed suggesting how they could be a part of the story, and she would select a few users and write them into the narrative and use their input to change the story.

The term 'webisode' was coined to describe Scott Zakarin's *The Spot*, which used the Web as a medium and ran on the site thespot.com from 1995 to 1997. It took its inspiration from television series such as *Friends* and *Melrose Place* and had characters (or 'spotmates') who were living in the same house. The spotmates, of whom some were portrayed by the writers and some by hired models, would keep an online diary (akin to blogs), respond to emails from the audience, post images and short videos on their life. Audience could become a part of the storyline and give advice to the characters.

Later webisodics used emerging digital media such as video streaming services and social media as a part of storytelling. For example, *lonelygirl15* (2006–2008) started on YouTube without initially revealing its fictional nature and evolved into a multi-character series, and *Soup of the Day* (2006) allowed the audience to interact with the main character via MySpace. Recently, an interactive horror story *#NeverAlone* has repeated this pattern on Instagram (Colburn 2020).

1.3.3 Interactive Cinema

Cinema provides possibilities to experiment with the limits of a medium. One class of these experiments is bringing the audience input into a part of the cinematic experience. Next, we highlight some of the milestones along this way. The reader interested in the history of interactive cinema is referred to Hales (2015) for more details.

William Castle's *Mr. Sardonicus* (1961) can be seen as a false start in interactive cinema. It included a 'punishment poll', where the members of the audience received a thumb printed on paper. Before the final reel of the film, the audience were prompted to vote whether the main character of the film, Mr. Sardonicus, was pardoned or not. This, however, was only a gimmick because only the punishment film was ever made and shown to the audience.

The first actual example of an interactive movie is Radúz Činčera's *Kinoautomat* (1967). It was originally made for Expo'67 in Montreal. The movie begins with a flashforward of the protagonist's apartment in flames. The movie consists of nine spots where the action stops and a moderator asks the audience to choose between two alternative scenes. After the voting, the movie proceeds according to the majority's choice. However, irrespective of the choices made, the end result is always the same: the fire.

The laser disc brought new possibilities for creating interactive films. In *The Aspen Movie Map* (1978–1981) by MIT Machine Architecture Group, the interactor can explore the town of Aspen, Colorado via the touchscreen interface. MIT Media Lab, founded in 1985, had Interactive Cinema (IC) research group led by Glorianna Davenport, which focused on poly-linear storytelling and reconfigurable video. On the commercial side, Vidtex released two interactive laser discs: *Murder, Anyone?* (1982) and *Many Roads to Murder* (1983) (Herman 2001, Chap. 10). They allowed the viewer to act in the role of a detective solving a murder case. The story was played by real actors. The interactive features of the laser disc allowed the viewer to look at evidence or solve the crime. Each disc featured 16 different plot lines.

The movie *Clue* (1985), based on the board game *Cluedo*, included three different endings. In the initial theatre release, each cinema got only one of the possible endings, which means that for the viewer there was no interactive element included apart from choosing the cinema where to see the movie. Later home video releases included all endings.

Bob Bejan's *I'm Your Man* (1992) is a short film, projected from a laser disc in a specially equipped movie theatre, which has seat-mounted joysticks with three choices. There are six selection points during the film, where the story can divert. The same technology was used in Bejan's film *Ride for Your Life* (1995), where the protagonist engages in a bicycle race to avoid alien invasion – and the audience has to make choices on his behalf every 10 seconds. Although these movies were intended to be a showcase for new technology, both the projection system and joysticks turn out to be too costly to gain wider popularity.

The film *Wax or the Discovery of Television Among the Bees* (1991) was the first movie streamed over the Internet in 1993. In 1994, a website called 'Waxweb' based on the movie was created (Blair and Meyer 1997). The original movie was cut into 80 000 pieces that could be pieced together akin to William S. Burroughs's 'cut-up' technique. The visitors could view the sequences in the order based on their choices along the story.

With the advent of DVD, moviemakers also dabbled with the possibility of creating interactive DVD films. David Wheeler's *Tender Loving Care* (1998) plays a story episode after which the spectators are asked a series of questions about their perception of what they have seen. The same method is used in David Wheeler's *Point of View* (2001). Morten Schjødt's *Switching* (2003) has no interface but is cyclic, jumping back and forth in time and place. *Final Destination 3* (2006) has a special edition DVD 'Thrill Ride Edition', which includes specific points where the viewer can choose the course of the story. *Late Fragment* by Daryl Cloran, Anita Doron, and Mateo Guez (2007) is a feature length film. The audience can click to change the scene or follow a character seeing the events from different viewpoints. Loops are also possible when the system is waiting for input from the audience.

Recently, there have been trials to use less invasive input technologies into an audience such as motion detection and mobile devices. However, they have not (yet) gained much attraction amongst the movie-goers or theatre owners alike. Instead, the possibility for interaction provided by streaming services (see Section 1.3.4) is gaining interest also in the movie industry. The animated short movie *Batman: Death in the Family* (2020) allows the viewer to make choices, leading to different sidetracks and endings. The movie is based on a 1988 story where the comic readers could choose the faith of Robin from two alternatives: die or survive. Another approach is to offer an app that allows the viewer to make selections in an interactive movie. For instance, *Late Shift* (CtrlMovie 2017) allows the viewer to choose in real time at decision points along the story, which then lead to one of the seven possible endings. In *The Complex* (Wales Interactive 2020), the decision points are also timed with an option to turn the timer off.

Although not truly interactive films, there are movies that have dabbled with having alternative stories. Krzysztof Kieślowski's *Blind Chance* (*Przypadek*, 1981) has three story lines about a medical student who has lost his call after the death of his father. Whilst running after a train for Warsaw, the outcome of each story depends on how he reacts to obstacles on the way. If he misses a drinking fellow and catches the train, he meets a Communist and joins the party. If he bumps into the drinking fellow but does not stop, he misses the train and hits a railroad guard and is arrested. In the end, he joins anti-Communist resistance. In the third storyline, he almost hits the drinking fellow, apologizes, misses the train but does not hit the guard. He then returns to medical school and stays out of politics altogether. In the end, he is going to a conference and meets people from the first two stories at the airport. Then he boards the aeroplane, which in the end explodes.

Kieślowski's movie inspired two less complex but more popular variants. In Peter Hewitt's *Sliding Doors* (1998), the protagonist misses the train in an underground station in the first storyline, whereas in the second she catches the train. In Tom Tykwer's *Run Lola Run* (*Lola rennt*, 1998), the protagonist goes through three alternative story lines depending on how she reacts to a dog in a staircase.

In Harold Ramis's *Groundhog Day* (1993), the protagonist relives the same day over and over. During the process, he gets to know the little town and its people, until he finds a way out of the loop into the next day. As we see in Section 4.1.2, this is an apt metaphor for a certain type of interactive story. Another good example of interactive storytelling, especially in the author-centric approach (see Section 3.2.1), is Marc Forster's *Stranger Than Fiction* (2006), which begins with a premise that the protagonist starts hearing a voice-over narrating his daily life. As he tries to avoid following the narration, he is forced to follow the story that is being told about him.

1.3.4 Television

On television, having multiple channels at the disposal has allowed creation of interactive stories, where the viewer can choose the viewpoint by changing the channel. Oliver Hirshbiegel's *Mörderische Entscheidung* (1991) is a crime story that was originally presented on two German TV channels ARD and ZDF. Zapping between the channels allowed the viewer to see the events from the perspective of the two main characters. A similar different perspective approach was used by *Noodles and 08* (1996) shown simultaneously on Swedish channels SVT1 and SVT2. The Danish production *D-dag* (2000) by Søren Kragh-Jacobsen, Kristian Levring, Thomas Vinterberg, and Lars von Trier extends the same principle and comprises four different 70-minute movies about bank robbery taking place on the New Year's Eve of the millennium.

Teijo Pellinen's *Akvaario* (2000) broadcast nightly over four weeks on the Finnish channel YLE1 starred two insomniac neighbours Ari and Eira. The audience could call on and vote from four impulses that would affect how the characters behave. The work had a library of about 5000 videoclips. Each week had an overall theme that allowed the story to progress: getting to know the characters, characters realizing they are hearing voices from the neighbour, discovery of a hole on the wall, and curiosity turning into an interest. At the final, Eira drops a scented note in Ari's mailbox as Ari opens the door, and the characters meet each other for the first time.

An interactive Web series *Try Life*, launched in 2012, presents episodes on teenage life, allowing the viewer to make decisions on behalf of the protagonists. A similar concept has been adopted by streaming services in developing interactive television shows. Netflix pioneered the genre and introduced to a wider audience shows such as DreamWorks' *Puss in Book: Trapped in an Epic Tale* (2017), *Buddy Thunderstruck* (2017), *Black Mirror: Bandersnatch* (2018), *You vs. Wild* (2019), *Carmen Sandiego: To Steal or Not to Steal?* (2020), and *Unbreakable Kimmy Schmidt: Kimmy vs. the Reverend* (2020). Also, Steven Soderbergh's *Mosaic* (2017) was made available first as an interactive app, before it was released as a non-interactive series on HBO. YouTube Originals produced an interactive episode 'A Heist with Markiplier' (2019), and dedicated interactive streaming services such as Ficto and Whatifi were launched in 2020.

1.3.5 Games

Apart from RPGs, there are several non-digital games based on storytelling. *Once Upon a Time* by Atlas Games (1994) allows the players to tell a fairytale out of cards. In *Dread* by

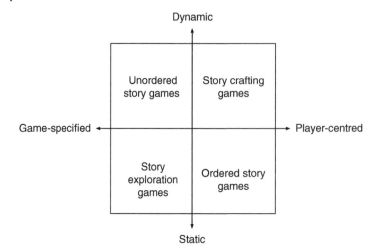

Figure 1.7 Classification of narrative-centric board and card games.

E. Ravachol and N. Barmore (2004), storytelling is connected to the game mechanics of *Jenga* to create suspense. In *Dixit* (2008) by Jean-Louis Roubira, the task of the players is to find cards matching the story among donated cards. *Fiasco* by J. Morningstar (Bully Pulpit Games 2009) directs the players to tell crime stories gone horribly wrong (in the spirit of the movie *Fargo*). *Rory's Story Cubes* (2010) by Rory O'Connor challenges the player to tell a story from symbols printed on the sides of dice.

Sullivan and Salter (2017) present a narrative taxonomy based on an examination of 12 narrative-centric board and card games. They divide the games along two axes (see Figure 1.7): the content of events and the temporal ordering of events. This leads to four categories:

1. *Unordered story games* are spatially centred and have random fragments to support the story creation (e.g. *Betrayal at the House on the Hill, Tales of the Arabian Nights, Agents of S.M.E.R.S.H.., Eldritch Horror*, and *Arkham Horror*).
2. *Story crafting games* have a general narrative structure with some evocative elements (e.g. *Gloom, Dixit*, and *Once Upon a Time*).
3. *Ordered story games* rely on that most of the events are created by the players (e.g. *Mysterium*).
4. *Story exploration games* put exploration in a central role (e.g. *T.I.M.E. Stories, Pandemic Legacy, Mythos Tales/Sherlock Holmes Consulting Detective*, and *Mansions of Madness*).

For the remainder of this section, however, we focus on digital games on various genres.

1.3.5.1 Interactive Fiction
Interactive fiction covers (text) adventure games played on a computer (Liddil 1981). One can argue that they are an evolved version of gamebooks – albeit gamebooks became popular later – that replaces the book with a computer program.

The first work of interactive fiction is *Adventure* (also known as *ADVENT* or *Colossal Cave*) by Will Crowther released in 1976. It inspired many to create their own text adventures, of which the most famous is *Zork* (1977) by Matt Blanc and Dave Lebling, who went on to found the company Infocom. Infocom released several games, sometimes working together with authors like Douglas Adams on a text adventure version of *The Hitchhiker's Guide to the Galaxy* (Infocom 1984).

Another pair inspired by *Adventure* were Roberta and Ken Williams, whose Sierra On-Line took advantage of the better graphical capabilities of the home computers in the 1980s and added a graphical user interface to assist with textual input. Sierra On-Line's roster of games include titles like *King's Quest* (1984), *Space Quest* (1986), *Police Quest* (1987), and *Leisure Suit Larry* (1988).

The emphasis on graphics continued with adventure games developed by LucasArts Games (later LucasGames) starting from *Maniac Mansion* (1987). Their user interface did not include anymore the possibility to input text, but all the players had to do is to select the desired action from a list of verbs and an inventory of objects. The list of verbs reduced from title to title during the 1990s until it included the trio hand (e.g. use, pick up, open), eye (e.g. examine, read), and mouth (e.g. eat, talk). Also, the genre got renamed as point-and-click adventures.

This strive towards graphical representation culminated in *Myst* (1993) by Cyan Worlds. *Myst* and its follow-ups used the encyclopaedic affordance provided by CD-ROMs by offering pre-rendered animation and voice-overs. Also, all player interaction was included into the game world without any additional user interface overlay.

During the late 1990s and early 2000s, interactive fiction as well as point-and-click adventures vanished from the limelight and remained in the hands of the hobbyists. One of the highpoints of this era is *Galatea* (2000) by Emily Short. Point-and-click adventures, however, got commercially resurrected when Telltale Games started publishing them on mobile devices, with *The Walking Dead* (2012) being their break-through title. *The Walking Dead* is also interesting from the viewpoint of interactive storytelling as it allows the player to have some agency when solving moral dilemmas.

Device 6 (2013) by Simogo hails back to text adventures by making the text and interacting with the text the focus of the game. The puzzles are a combination of visual and textual challenges that the player has to solve. Also, *Wanderlust Travel Stories* (Different Tales 2019) and *Wanderlust: Transsiberian* (Different Tales 2020) take their inspiration from text adventures and the slower pace of interaction that they required from the player.

Visual novels are similar to interactive fiction, but they put more emphasis on the story (Uusi-Illikainen 2016). They emerged in Japan in the 1980s but remained less known in the Western markets until the 2000s, when games such as *Phoenix Wright: Ace Attorney* (Capcom Production Studio 4 2001) started to be officially localized to English. Visual novels often include a branching story with multiple endings, offering a limited means of interaction. The main game mechanic is conversations, which includes reading dialogues and descriptive texts and answering them, for instance, via multiple choice questions. In addition, visual novels may include collecting items to be used later in a conversation and movement mechanics similar to point-and-click games.

1.3.5.2 Digital Games

If digital games provide a story, it is usually just a backstory or a linear story told in cutscenes (see Section 4.1.1). A classic example is *Dragon's Lair* (Sullivan Bluth 1989), which used laser disc technology to make the game more story-like by including animations. In the case of *Dragon's Lair*, however, the game story does not offer much brevity, but it is a linear story, where any wrong decision leads directly to a death scene. In this section, however, we review digital games that offer the player a chance to make choices that affect the unfolding or the outcome of the story.

The advent of CD-ROM in the 1990s brought about computer games that were sometimes marketed under the title 'interactive cinema'. For example, *Sherlock Holmes: Consulting Detective* (ICOM Simulations 1991), based on a board game, uses full motion video. *The Last Express* (Smoking Car Productions 1997) by Jordan Mechner is an adventure game that takes place on the Orient Express, days before the start of World War I. It attempts to simulate (speeded-up) real-time events and includes 30 characters. The story is non-linear and the player's actions and failures affect the outcome. In *Blade Runner* (Westwood Studios 1997), the protagonist Ray McCoy, a blade runner, chases replicants in the original movie settings and with voice-overs from the original actors. The game story has 13 different endings, which depend on the player's decisions during the game.

The founder and lead game designer of Quantic Dream, David Cage has argued strongly for maturation of video games to expand their range of expression and themes. Quantic Dream's *Fahrenheit*, titled *Indigo Prophecy* in the United States, (2005), *Heavy Rain* (2010), *Beyond: Two Souls* (2013), and *Detroit: Become Human* (2018) have been his answers to how to realize interactive video game storytelling.

In the 2010s, several experimental and avant-garde games tested the limits of storytelling in video games. In *The Stanley Parable* by D. Wreden (Galactic Cafe 2011), the player's avatar Stanley has to explore the empty building after his computer has broken down. The player can freely move around and influence the surroundings within the confines of the game world. The story is presented using a voice-over, which suggests where Stanley should go next and comments on his decisions, but the player is completely free to disregard the voice-over.

Dear Esther (The Chinese Room 2012) includes voice-over letter fragments from a woman called Esther. The fragments are distributed randomly on each game instance, which means that the story collected by the player is different during every gameplay. The developers continued the work in *Everybody's Gone to the Rapture* (2015).

In a similar manner, *Gone Home* by S. Gaynor (The Fullbright Company, 2013) focuses on an exploration of a mansion in Portland in 1995 by providing the player with any specific goal but piecing together the underlying story by examining the objects at the house. In *The Vanishing of Ethan Carter* (The Astronauts 2014), the player can use paranormal abilities to search the game world to find stories that a boy called Ethan Carter has written.

80 Days (Inkle 2015) draws inspiration from Jules Verne's novel *Around the World in Eighty Days* (with a steampunk twist), but allows the players to make their own choices selecting the route. Apart from the route selection, the generated story is affected by events and challenges that the player faces during the travel and whilst staying over in the cities.

Sam Barlow's *Her Story* (2015) puts the player in the role of an investigator solving a missing person case using snippets from old interrogation videotapes. By entering search terms, the player can find out new videoclips, which reveal more and more about the original story. A similar concept is used in Barlow's next game *Telling Lies* (2019), where the task is to find out why the four main characters have been subjected to electronic surveillance. Other mobile games trying out the possibilities of storytelling are *Florence* (Mountains 2018) and *My Child Lebensborn* (Sarepta Studio 2018).

RimWorld (Ludeon Studios 2018) is a base building game, where the basic story involves a group of space castaways stranding on a planet called RimWorld. The player commands the characters to construct a base, gather resources, and fight threats, such as pirate groups and native wildlife. The system has a strong concept of AI storyteller, which sets the rate and majority of random events. The game has a remarkable community of modders.

12 Minutes (2020) by Luis Antonio requires the player to play through the same events repeatedly in 12-minute intervals. In each repeat, the players learn more about the game world and its characters, which in turn helps them to find the way out of the loop. The premise resembles the movie *Groundhog Day*, which actually has a VR sequel called *Groundhog Day: Like Father Like Son* (Tequila Works 2019).

This list of games is by no means comprehensive but aims at pointing different approaches taken in incorporating interactive stories into digital games. As we can see, the game industry has been active in testing out ideas and pushing the envelope to provide new narrative experiences to the audience.

1.4 Summary

Our fascination with stories is immense. When we conquer new spaces and areas, among the first things we bring along are stories and storytelling. We can look at the endeavour of space exploration and, for instance, the Apollo moon project, and we will find different narratives: of the missions, of the construction, of surviving difficulties (e.g. Apollo 1 and Apollo 13), of the legacy, of the precursors and visionaries (e.g. Jules Verne or Georges Méliès).

Interactive storytelling presents a challenging environment for research and development. On the one hand, there is a requirement for interactivity (so common in many other areas) that allows the user (or interactor) to make independent choices from the given range of options. Also, giving the interactor a wide range of intuitively understandable options to choose from, we are, basically, giving them a freedom a choice and letting them have meaningful feedback from their choices. On the other hand, we are promising to give the interactor a story that is dramatically compelling and understandable by the interactors as a narrative, but heeding the choices at the same time.

We saw in this chapter how technology has affected storytelling over time from ancient theatre to cinema and, finally, to computers. Each new medium opened new possibilities for narratives, but computers offer the possibility to provide interactivity on a totally different scale that a book or a film ever could. We saw that there is a companionship with computer games that we discuss in detail in Chapter 2. Play and make-believe are essential parts of making an interactive storytelling system; it cannot exist alone as a crude mechanism.

In the following chapters, we look at the situation from different angles. We next go deeper into the theory in Chapter 2 to understand what constitutes a story and how it could be decomposed into smaller units and then possibly reconstructed as a story generating computer system. A review of the research done in interactive storytelling reveals the underlying challenges to be solved. After that we go through the four partakers presented in Figure 1.3, each in its own chapters. First, we take a look at the underlying platform in Chapter 3, where we focus on solving the most critical challenge, narrative paradox, to provide software where we can start building the content. This content is devised by the design, and we focus on the designer's role in Chapter 4. The interactors will take part in the process of story generation in their own part, which we discuss in detail in Chapter 5. Storyworld is the content and mechanism for this process, and we focus on it in Chapter 6. Finally, in Chapter 7, we broaden the scope and review the trends that can affect the way interactive storytelling might look in the future.

Exercises

1.1 Jorge Luis Borges writes in the short story 'The Garden of Forking Paths' from the collection *Labyrinths* (1941) as follows:

> In all fictional works, each time a man is confronted with several alternatives, he chooses one and eliminates the others; in the fiction of Ts'ui Pên, he chooses – simultaneously – all of them. He creates, in this way, diverse futures, diverse times which themselves also proliferate and fork.

In this and other short stories such as 'The Library of Babel' and 'The Book of Sand', Borges expresses the idea of infinite texts that could be read anew, and each time they would provide a new story according to the reader's choices.

Read these three short stories. Does Borges forecast interactive storytelling? What is his take on seeing the reader as an active, acting agent in a storyworld? Why has Borges been so influential to many seminal writers such as Murray (1997, pp. 30–32), Ryan (2001, p. 61), Aarseth (1997, p. 8), and Montfort (2004, pp. 45–46)?

1.2 MacIntyre (1981, p. 200) writes that unpredictability is a crucial characteristic of all lived narratives. Why is it important here? What is its relevance to interactive stories?

1.3 Recall the spectrum of interactivity illustrated in Figure 1.1 (p. 4). Why interactive storytelling cannot be a simulation? Why interactive storytelling cannot be part of conventional storytelling?

1.4 Let us think for a moment of the terminology:
  (a) What problems do you see in using terms such as 'designer' or 'author'? Are they loaded terms? What kind of connotation do they bring to your mind?
  (b) What about the terms 'interactor' and 'player'? What if we had opted for the term 'player' for this book?

1.5 We defined the plot events in Figure 1.4 (p. 8) to indicate 'dramatically significant' events, which can seem somewhat vague. What is the difficulty in trying to give a more precise definition?

1.6 Consider the 'interactive range' and 'agency' defined in Section 1.1.3. Can you see a use of making the interactive range broader? What would that entail?

1.7 What kind of situation could prompt the interactor to obstruct the plot? How to solve this situation (or is it a problem in the first place)?

1.8 Figure 1.5 (p. 10) illustrates Ryan's four types of interactivity. Try to come up with examples (e.g. games) for each quadrant. If you would move one of your examples to another quadrant, how would you have to change it so it would fit there?

1.9 The Oulipo (shortened from *Ouvroir de littérature potentielle*) group have tried to devise new structures and patterns for stories. Find out more about the group's ideas of potential literature and the works by its members. How do you see their standpoint with respect to interactive storytelling?

1.10 Looking at the stage designs of Figure 1.6 (p. 13), which one would fit to the following situations:
(a) Taking part in a real-world conference in a holiday resort
(b) Taking part in a virtual conference (e.g. Skype, Teams, or Zoom) with 5, 12, or 100 participants
(c) Following a chemistry lesson in a classroom
(d) Taking part in a physical education lesson in a sports hall
(e) Attending a meeting by Alcoholics Anonymous
(f) Attending a poetry recital in a bookstore
(g) Watching the World Cup Final from television with a group of friends
(h) Following an election debate while reading and making comments about it in social media
Would it be possible to change stage design in these cases and how would it change the dynamic of the situation?

1.11 Take the four stage designs illustrated Figure 1.6 (p. 13) and compare them with video game user interfaces (UIs). Which designs do they use? Which are underused or omitted? Could you come up with a design for the underused models?

1.12 Consider the role of a game master in an RPG. Define the qualities that they should have. How would they translate into a computer program?

1.13 Try to design a CYOA book (do not start writing the content but focus on the design). You can take an existing story (or a story universe) as a starting point. What can you say about the granularity of decisions? What do you observe? (*Hint*: You can limit yourself to one scene and use digital tools to help you.)

1.14 What are the main problems in realizing interactive cinema in a movie theatre?

1.15 How does streaming service change the situation for interactive television? Do you think that shows that allow the spectator to make selections will become more popular or will they remain as curiosities or technical demos?

1.16 Gameplay videos are a popular form of entertainment. Compare how interesting it is to watch
(a) an unedited and uncommented gameplay video;
(b) an unedited but commented gameplay video; and
(c) an edited and commented gameplay video.

1.17 Let us consider a situation where a player is streaming a live video from playing a game and the player is, at the same time, receiving live comments from the audience. If the player follows (live) the suggestions and wishes from the feedback, would this situation be an example of conventional storytelling, interactive storytelling, or simulation (see Figure 1.1, p. 4)? Why?

1.18 Trimming the stories by removing all dramatically insignificant events is sometimes exercised to such an extent that it starts working against the original intention. For example, the story can become too foreseeable because the introduction of any element means that it will be essential to the story at some point. Also, the story (e.g. a television series) might become difficult to follow if the viewer does not pay attention all the time to what is being told. Can you come up with examples of each of these situations?

1.19 Think about how you could use interactive storytelling (not necessary digital) in the following scenarios:
(a) Having a doctor's appointment for hearing test results and a diagnosis
(b) Going to a gasoline station to fill up the tank
(c) Having a loan negotiation
(d) Dealing with the death of a loved one
(e) Explaining to a child how the traffic lights work
(f) Planning where to go on a holiday

2

Background

Stories have been studied since antiquity. It is an elusive topic that has no clear-cut, general answers, but the studies offer some peeks of clarity. This chapter presents a selection of research work done in analysing stories in general and interactive stories in particular. This is not supposed to be a conclusive review of narrative theories as such but rather to provide a background and understanding of the matter, because the terminology, concepts, and sometimes even approaches are based on this work.

No matter what we humans do or observe, we also tend to become interested in learning how things work and why they work. This is also true for storytelling. Although it is difficult to say who was the first to do this, we do have written works from Aristotle onwards trying to understand how stories work and what makes a good story, which we review in Section 2.1. This is followed by a closer look on the research done in interactive storytelling in Section 2.2.

2.1 Analysis of Storytelling

We start our review by presenting some of the relevant theoretical work on storytelling in general. Our aim is not to provide a comprehensive study for analysing stories, but rather introduce concepts, models, and terminology that are often referred to in the scientific literature on interactive storytelling. One could – quite rightly – point out several omissions. Moreover, we focus on Western tradition and not, for example, Asian or African storytelling traditions (Jennings 1996).

We proceed in chronological order, because the later writers are usually expanding, criticizing, or refuting the earlier works.

2.1.1 Aristotle's *Poetics*

As with any scientific endeavour, one can always start with the Greek philosopher Aristotle (384–322 BCE), whose writings also include a treatise on drama called *Poetics* (c. 335 BCE) (Aristotle 1932). Although its analysis is based on ancient Greek theatre, it formed the basis of Western literary theory. Originally, *Poetics* included two parts, but only the first part focusing on tragedy has survived, whereas the second part focusing on comedy is lost.

Handbook on Interactive Storytelling, First Edition. Jouni Smed, Tomi 'bgt' Suovuo, Natasha Skult, and Petter Skult.
© 2021 John Wiley & Sons Ltd. Published 2021 by John Wiley & Sons Ltd.

In *Poetics*, Aristotle's intention is to dissect the attributes that make tragedies appealing to the spectators. It is not a tutorial on how to make a good drama per se, but a study of how a story told in a theatre play can affect people. He used a body of contemporary play as a basis. Of the wealth of material presented in *Poetics*, we would like to lift up here three concepts:

- Elements of tragedy
- Narrative forms
- The dramatic arch

Each of them has had a profound effect on Western drama and literature, and they can still be seen today in modern storytelling.

2.1.1.1 Elements of Tragedy
Aristotle (1932, 1450b8–12) recognizes six elements of tragedy – plot, character, thought, language, melody, and enactment – which he assigns to three classes depending on whether the question is about the represented objects, the means of representation, or the manner of representation (see Figure 2.1).

- Plot (*mythos*) describes the incidents of the tragedy and their order; it comprehends the whole action being represented. These actions should follow logically from what happened before and from the character's decisions. The plot is, therefore, a coherent and causal construction. Moreover, it should follow the principle of dramatic economy: if any incident is removed or changes its place in the plot, the unity of whole work changes. If it does not, then the incident is not an integral part of the whole and could be discarded.

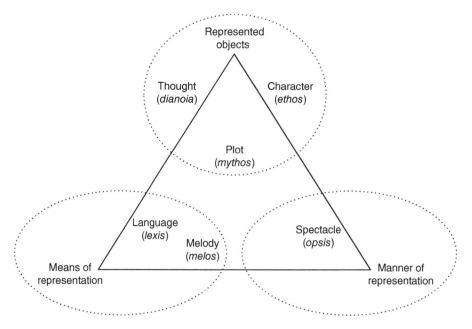

Figure 2.1   The elements of tragedy. Source: Heinonen et al. 2012, p. 88.

Apart from the logical order of incidents, the aesthetic value of the plot depends on its length (i.e. the wealth of material it presents) while still being condensed into a coherent and consistent whole.

- Character (*ethos*) reflects the moral choices that the character makes, which get revealed through the character's actions. Apart from traits and dispositions, this is the ethical nature or morality of the character (e.g. vices and virtues).
- Thought (*dianoia*) refers to the character's reasoning or rationality. It is 'the ability to say what is possible and appropriate' (Aristotle 1932, 1450b4–5). From this, we can infer the thought process and background of the character.
- Language (*lexis*) relates to the selection and arrangement of words and the use of language.
- Melody (*melos*) relates to the language, rhythm, and melody of speech.
- Spectacle (*opsis*) comprehends the whole appearance (e.g. costumes, props, and sceneries).

A good drama would pay attention to all of these attributes. It should not hide, for instance, the lack of characterization by clever dialogue or spectacles. It should start at the core from the plot, and every layer adds then something more on top.

2.1.1.2 Narrative Forms

Aristotle recognizes two narrative forms: epic and dramatic. In the *epic form*, events are represented through verbal narration (*diegesis*). The story focuses on the exploits of a solitary hero, and the story can be endlessly expanded. The motivations of the hero remain fairly simple. For example, the *Odyssey* is an epic story, which could be easily expanded with new adventures. This is also the form of the oldest stories or epics, which rely strongly on the plot – the audience expectations on what happens next.

In the *dramatic form*, events are represented through the imitation of action (*mimesis*). Here, the focus is on the evolving networks of human relations, and the action is mental rather than physical. Moreover, events follow the structure of the dramatic arc (see Figure 2.3), which we will look at closely a bit later. The dramatic form is obviously more mature than the epic because it adds a psychological layer to the characters as the thought becomes more complex. The action can now take place even in the same surroundings and the set of characters can remain the same during the play, but these characters are round (i.e. psychologically more lifelike) and not flat (e.g. one dimensional).

A third narrative form, not recognized by Aristotle, is the *epistemic form* (Ryan 2008, 2015, pp. 241–245). In this form, the story resembles detective stories (emerging in the nineteenth century), where we have a superposition of two stories: events that took place in the past and an investigation that leads to their discovery. These kinds of (mystery) stories are driven by the desire to know.

Ryan argues further that the fourth narrative form that emerged in the twentieth century is *soap opera*. In soap operas, the story is almost infinite, and the characters go through their own dramatic arcs, which can be partly overlapping and sequential.

2.1.1.3 Dramatic Arc

For Aristotle, change (*metabasis*), for example, from happiness to misery, is an elemental part of any tragedy. Simply put, it is the difference between the initial situation and outcome.

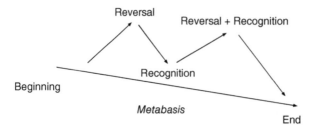

Figure 2.2   Changes in the plot of a tragedy. Source: Heinonen et al. 2012, p. 114.

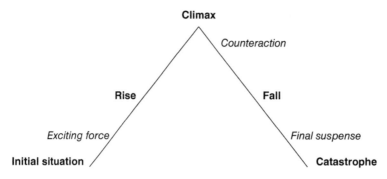

Figure 2.3   Freytag's dramatic arc.

Within this framework, the plot can change due to recognition (*anagnorisis*) and reversal (*peripeteia*) as illustrated in Figure 2.2. Recognition means a change from not-knowing to knowing, whereas reversal is a turning point in the plot. The general structure involves that the play has a central problem that divides it to halves: complication and unravelling. The problem causes complications, which then get solved.

Gustav Freytag (1900, pp. 114–140) provides an illustration and elaboration on the dramatic structure (see Figure 2.3). This formulation of the dramatic arc is widely known and used (and often mistakenly attributed to Aristotle). The complication increases after the initial situation has been exposed, often accompanied by an exciting force (or an inciting incident). The rising action increases the complication and drama, until it peaks out in a climax, which is followed by a counteraction leading to a fall. Before the end there is a final suspense that results in a catastrophe.

The dramatic arc has had a strong influence on the Western theatre. It has been seen as an ideal structure for well-formed plays and, consequently, films – and even video games. The idea of a three-act play has permeated even to an extent that the structure of a typical Hollywood movie can be pinned down to a structure shown in Figure 2.4. A two-hour movie has then a 30-minute Act I that sets up the story, introduces the characters, and ends with a challenge at Plot point 1 that starts Act II. The 60 minutes of Act II lead to a confrontation at the middle (or climax in Freytag's arc) dividing Act II into halves. Pinch 1 and Pinch 2 at the middle of each half are events that hold the halves of Act II together. Finally, the last 30 minutes or Act III then leads to a resolution and the end. In addition to this formula, there exist others offering their interpretation of the narrative arch and practical guidelines on how to use it for shaping up one's screenplay.

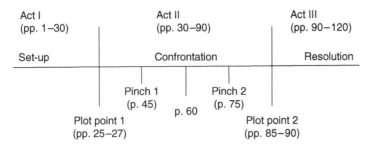

Figure 2.4 An example of a structure of a Hollywood movie script. A script for a two-hour movie has typically 120 pages (i.e. each page corresponds to one minute of the filmed movie). Source: Field 1984.

2.1.2 Visual Storytelling

Storytelling is a profound skill and associated with humankind that has been under evolution of its own, resulting in the notion of 'culture'. Having many connotations and shapes, culture is based on common knowledge with patterns of belief, behaviour, and social learning that continuously builds society. Potentially, all cultures have developed from the common grounds of knowledge, but each of them has an own ideal source(s) of allegories that facilitate communication among its members. Common customs and beliefs of each ethnic group are fused with a particular language and thinking modes of a single society. In other words, society without the assimilation of general knowledge would cease to be a society.

The act of copying and adaptation is most commonly seen as a means of cultural development. According to Luigi Pareyson, all human activity is invention and production of forms where everything that a human does – no matter is it intellectual, physical, or moral – has the same result, which is the form of creation that gains own comprehensibility and autonomy (Eco 1989, pp. 158–166).

When observing differences in cultures and their expressions, we often find similarities regardless of the obvious general diversities. What makes those similarities and yet differences in comprehension? If we compare early artefacts from the Far East, for example, areas of today's Europe, there are certainly different approaches in understanding the shapes and colours, structures, and purposes. Regardless of culturally specific expressions, certain forms can be commonly recognized as a tree, a plant, or a human figure. The question is: what shapes the differences in expressions along with time but also makes us understand those expressions irrespective of cultural or historical diversity? Hegel (1967, pp. 753–754) thinks that historical memory can be empathetically efforted to counteract the distancing aspect of time and that the act of recollection itself from the past would survive and connect itself again to the present. Historical works of art make us fitting observers and receivers of allegories. The spatial and temporal organization of the pictorial field conduct in which images tell us what they choose to reveal. However, receiving depends on the observer. Visual storytelling is a powerful method of teaching, emotionally engaging, and communicating – it is a timeless bond between the storyteller and the receiver due to culturally standardized patterns of approaching visual narrative.

2.1.2.1 Semiotics

When approaching the notion of visual storytelling, which obviously contains 'visual' and 'communicating' elements, the essence of any visual representation is to hold the *information*, the core meaning, and data which a visual form represents – a sign. Recognizing the information that a sign is carrying is the core principle of communication and storytelling. Semiology or semiotics refers to the science of signs with assumptions that cultural assets (such as language, visual art, or music) are composed of signs, where every sign holds the meaning beyond in its literal self (Eco 1978, pp. 182–188). The word semiotics derives from the Greek word *sema* – meaning 'sign'. The reason why it is important to include the theory of semiotics in visual storytelling, and particularly interactive storytelling, is because the development of semiotics which we have today, the essential role is to apply the model of language in the process of decoding the world by ideology only that which can be verbalized can be thought and which can be translated into words has a meaning. Challenges lie in the nature of the entity under study since images are not necessarily literary in concept.

The first semiotics treated everything as language, all images and objects were in fabrication of contents. Saussure understands language as a closed system whose purpose is communicating ideas and shaping the course of semiotics. The dichotomy language–speech is distinguished from language as a mainly written structure of verbal (as well as written) communication, and speech is, on the other hand, an individual and variable way of expression. In history, speech precedes language, while in cultural history, language precedes speech. Within Saussure's system, sign is constructed from signifier and signified. In that order, overpower of the spoken word can be seen in early times of human intellectual development, including the Old Testament and its many variables of the power of speech. Peirce's semiotics diverges slightly from Saussure's. He pursues the natural relation between signifier and signified. Peirce's sign is a tripartite consisting of an icon, index, and symbol (Lyons 1977, pp. 99–109). The iconic aspect of the sign is what relates it to something comprehensible (de Saussure 1966, 2006). Combining methods of Saussure with Marx and Sartre brings the possibility of taking unassertive objects as signs, as the bearers of accepted opinion and ideological trickery. When we ask what is a sign, most casually we can say that sign is a piece of an image, a fragment of something which can be recognized. As Barthes (1977) firmly puts, 'without recognition there is no sign'. Signs banish our grasp of the segmentations of experience, the numerous ways in which culture has made its experience permanent. This is why Goodrich says that a sign, properly understood, is not a substance but a relation between ordered sets of differences (Blonsky 1985). In that order, the study of semiotics questions not the sign itself but the system which will gather one set of features to another set, giving a sign. What is understood as signification occurs when chains of differences are conjoined and pass from one work to the other.

Jacobsson (1987, pp. Chap. 8) agrees with Saussure in supposing that messages are constituted by an axial relation in which metaphors (that correspond to associative substitutions) correspond to the vertical axios and metonymy (which is related to the syntagm and applied to the narratives set in linear time) to the horizontal. This elaboration laid a foundation for post-structuralism. Applied Saussure's linguistics can be found in Merleau-Ponty's (1964, p. 58) philosophy in relating the language–speech dichotomy to the phenomenology of perception. In relation between two media of expression such as text and image, can be found a remarkable symbolic application in which pictorial elements correspond to a written term. Iconographic methods achieve expression on the basis of textual reference. Merleau-Ponty associated language with painting and discussed their connection historically, regarding 'the painters and writers work for centuries without a suspicion of their relationship'. He observes that if in empirical language there is a hidden second-order language where signs give another implication of colours in which significations never free themselves from the intercourse of signs, it highlights the importance of looking at what is seen. In his understanding, all cultures prolong and challenge the past.

2.1.2.2 Work of Art

Regardless of what critics or art historians suggest, there are certain things which we expect from a work of art. Things that delight our senses, intellect, educate or excite us, enrich the experience and stimulate, intensify communication. These things usually vary from culture to culture and from era to era. They involve formal and affective as well as abstract intellectual properties. We admire and value properties such as balance, harmony, rhythmic, expressive or rather vivid because the tradition of criticism holds such relationships to be worth perceiving. The influence in perceiving is often connected to discussions of artists and the characteristics of their work providing recognition of certain traditions.

The concept of meaning has deep roots in the character of human nature that along with its changes also shapes general cultural progression. Forming and fastening new meanings to the phenomenon of nature, as well as to objects, behaviours, and relations, is an essential matter under query of human rational maturity. Furthermore, an interesting aspect in understanding human innovation urge is curiosity and a desire to find meaning of everything that surrounds us, to discover certain significance inside every individual event, item, or just a thought. In cultural growth, the essential role belongs to differences in approach of creating, understanding as well as accepting the various and yet unique systems of communicating within conceptions of belief, behaviour, and values. In diversity of cultures, important roles belong to development of the academic discipline and its approach as universal or common study of understanding. Furthermore, writing messages, stories, or histories by our usual standards and tradition are likely to change the concept once the method of recording the messages has changed. How does the method of communication affect the general understanding of the messages especially through a medium such as interactive storytelling?

2.1.2.3 Video Games as Visual Art

Video games are a new medium of creative expression which tackle multiple aspects in storytelling practices and empower both creators and players to build deeper relationships given by the medium itself. For a designer, a game is a way to interact and have dialogue with players – from getting players to understand the game to having them play the game in a way designers have intended them to do. Communication between the designer and player is one of the core elements of gameplay, which consists of conveying the information in more than one way. In other mediums, multiple elements convey the information to the viewer through visual and audio effects, emotion and anticipation of performers, composition, and dynamic view points. In games, the player is an active interactor with that environment, making an impact through actions and receiving feedback from these actions. Therefore, composing a game as a medium of entertainment carries more depth in its dialogue with the audience or players.

Unlike other visual media such as static images or paintings, animated or recorded videos, games break the static and one-way-directed messages into a dialogue form. The observer or player becomes a dynamic interactor with that message, making an impact through the actions and receiving feedback and responses from those actions. This dialogue is more successful as the game experience gives an expressive scope to the players, 'a choice' and variations in which players can respond to the given challenge in the game. This equips the players with the ability to choose how they wish to proceed the story and articulate a wide range of emotional engagements which are based on the choice of the gameplay actions. Creators provide the player with a set of actions to build a unique set of behaviors according to the rules of the world as its visual language for that particular game. Each game provides its own set of communicating tools through visual, audio, and special transmission, disregarding players' native language. This largely expressive 'vocabulary' is given to a player gradually, as the story and the gameplay unfold.

The role of visual narrative in setting specific aesthetics for providing interactive storytelling is to supply right visual clues that are responding to the complex structure of game mechanics and design of the 'desired game experiences' by its creators. Developers have their own goals about what the game should communicate and the way it should be received by the players; yet in practice we often see that players experience and interact with the gameworld in most innovative ways that even creators did not think of at first. This is the most interesting aspect of the visual storytelling inside the games, as designers provide the tools to experience the *fantasy*, while the players are the true creators of it.

Visual storytelling is based on familiarity of the concepts that it represents; the visual cues that are given to a player in each gameplay sequence must be comprehensive regardless of the possible interaction changes by

- gameplay modes – how players interact with the world (commonly changing throughout the game);
- camera modes;
- avatar or non-avatar modes;
- change of controls and inputs (followed by different gameplay modes).

The gameplay experience must consist of a stylistically unified visual language to keep the communication with the player intact. If any of the visual cues is out of balance with the rest of the designed experience, the risk to break the player's fantasy is higher. The methods of visual language of a game depends on a genre, type of story it is set to be told (e.g. linear, branching), choice of game mechanics, and the shifts of gameplay modes throughout the game. Regardless of the type of the gameplay experience one is developing, the visual narrative should follow the basic principles from the traditional art theory, which are also used widely in the film and animation industries such as the following:

- Building the authentic experience – this refers to the specific rules and characteristics of the world and interactions that player may conduct during the gameplay
- Relevant topics or situations in which the player can truly relay to, building the emotional engagement and relationship with the characters and the world inside the game
- Atmosphere – use of traditional visual storytelling practices such as composition and variety of view angles, colours and their values building the contrast and harmony, forms and shapes, perspective, and scale

The act of adaptation is that transforming the stories, especially written text, into another medium such as an image, film, or game. Regardless of the approach in distinction on the matters of fidelity is that an adaptation should be as faithful to the text as to the adaptation medium. Games are a new storytelling medium, and it is up to creators' vision to use that medium to tell a story. Each story is an individual experience and, as such, must be approached with the best practices and tools to create most immersive narrative experience with the resonating visual language.

2.1.3 Structuralism

After the Russian revolution in the 1920s emerged a new school viewing the structure of stories, called Russian formalism. It had later a major influence, for instance, in France, and it evolved to structuralism.

Russian formalism divides the story into three layers:

1. *fabula*: Logically and chronologically related series of events caused or experienced by the characters in the storyworld
2. *sjužet*: The finished arrangement (i.e. the plot) of the narrated events as they are presented to the reader
3. *media/text*: The surface of the story expressed in language signs

This structuralist approach led to different models, of which we review here three: Vladimir Propp's analysis of Russian folktales, B.N. Colby's analysis of Alaska Native's folktales, and David Rumelhart's story grammars.

2.1.3.1 Propp's Morphology of Russian Folktales

Vladimir Propp was a Russian structuralist, who was influenced by the Russian formalism. His special interest was Russian folktales, which he started to analyse to find a common structure in them. His book *Morphology of the Folktale* on the results of the analysis was published in Russian in 1928, and translated into other languages in the 1950s (Propp 1968). At the time, the book influenced many folklorists and encouraged the study of morphology, paving the way to, for instance, French structuralism.

The core of Propp's morphology are 31 narrative units or *narrathemes* that occurred in the analysed folktales. They are the basic primitives, which tend to occur in the same order in the stories (see Table 2.1). Each of these narrathemes has a symbol, which allows presenting the structure as a sequence of these symbols.

The narrathemes form spheres dividing the structure of the story into four phases:

1. *Introduction*: Introduces the situation and most of the main characters and sets the scene for the subsequent adventure.
   - β: A member of a family leaves home and the hero is introduced.
   - γ: An interdiction is addressed to the hero (e.g. 'don't go there' or 'don't do this').
   - δ: The interdiction is violated as the villain enters the tale.
   - ε: The villain makes an attempt at reconnaissance.
   - ζ: The villain gains information about the victim.
   - η: The villain attempts to deceive the victim to take possession of the victim or the victim's belongings.
   - θ: The victim is taken in by deception.

Table 2.1 A summary of Propp's narrathemes.

α initial situation	↑ departure	↓ return
β absentation	D the first function	Pr pursuit, chase
γ interdiction	of the donor	o unrecognized
ε reconnaissance	E hero's reaction	arrival
ζ delivery	F provision or receipt	L unfounded claims
η trickery	of a magical agent	M difficult task
θ complicity	G spatial transference between	N solution
A villainy	two kingdoms, guidance	Q recognition
B mediation, the	H struggle	Ex exposure
connective incident	J branding, marking	T transfiguration
C beginning	I victory	U punishment
counteraction	K resolution	W wedding

2. *Body of the story*: The main story starts here and extends to the departure of the hero on the main quest.
   - A: The villain causes harm to a family member or the family member lacks something.
   - B: The misfortune or the lack is made known (e.g. the hero hears the call for help).
   - C: The hero agrees to go.
   - ↑: The hero leaves home.
3. *Donor sequence*: The hero goes in search of a method by which the solution may be reached, gaining a magical agent from the donor.
   - D: The hero is tested to prepare the way for receiving a magical agent from the donor.
   - E: The hero reacts to the actions of the donor (e.g. faces a test set by the donor).
   - F: The hero acquires the magical agent.
   - G: The hero is directed to the whereabouts of the object of the search (e.g. by a helper).
   - H: The hero and the villain join in a direct combat.
   - J: The hero is branded (e.g. gets wounded or receives a special token).
   - I: The villain is defeated.
   - K: The initial misfortune or lack is resolved (e.g. the spell is broken or a captive is freed).
4. *Hero's return*: The hero returns home, possibly facing a final task in order to receive a hero's welcome.
   - ↓: The hero returns.
   - Pr. The hero is pursued (e.g. ambushed or ridiculed).
   - Rs: The hero is rescued from the pursuit.
   - o: The hero arrives home in an unrecognized form.
   - L: A false hero presents unfounded claims.
   - M: A difficult task is proposed to the hero.
   - N: The task is resolved.
   - Q: The hero is recognized (e.g. by a brand or by the possession of a special token).

- Ex: The false hero or the villain is exposed.
- T: The hero is given a new appearance (e.g. new garments).
- U: The villain is punished.
- W: The hero is rewarded (e.g. gets married or ascends the throne).

As these narrathemes collect the general structure of a story, a particular instance may lack some of them or even a whole phase (e.g. the donor sequence). The structure can be more complex having two or three sequences running parallelly or intersecting one another.

As we can see from narrathemes, stories have a set of characters, which are defined from the viewpoint of their significance to the course of action (i.e. the character roles are independent of the actual characters). Propp lists the following character roles:

- *Villain* who struggles against the hero (e.g. narrathemes A, H, and Pr)
- *Donor* who prepares the hero or gives the hero some magical object (e.g. narrathemes D and F)
- *Helper* who helps the hero in the quest (e.g. narrathemes G, K, Rs, N, and T)
- *Princess* (or her father) who gives the task to the hero and is often sought for during the narrative (e.g. narrathemes M, K, Ex, Q, U, and W)
- *Dispatcher* who makes the lack known and sends the hero off (e.g. narratheme B)
- *Hero* who departs on a search, meets the donor, and returns home (e.g. narrathemes C, ↑, E, and W)
- *False hero* who takes credit for the hero's actions (e.g. narrathemes C, ↑, E, and L)

A major critique against Propp's morphology is that classifies the character roles based on what they are (e.g. a hero, a donor, or a princess) and not what they do. The first semiotic role-based analysis of the narrative is the actantial model introduced by A.J. Greimas in 1966. Figure 2.5 illustrates the actantial model and the six actants. The protagonist of a story is the subject who is seeking for an object. The sender has dispatched the subject on this task, and the subject should deliver the object to a receiver. The subject gets aid from the helper, while the opponent acts as an antagonist to the subject's efforts.

As Propp's work was translated into English in 1958 (and later into French), his morphology gained recognition and began to influence Western narrative analysis. Moreover, the framework laid out by Propp has been very alluring to many computer scientists working on computer-generated stories. It offers an obvious implementation, where the system first recognizes what is the narratheme that suits the current situation and selects then the next narratheme in the sequence and creates a new content based on that.

2.1.3.2 Colby's Grammar of Alaska Natives' Folktales

Akin to Propp, Colby (1973) has studied the folktales of Alaska Natives to map out their narrative elements. In his model, the sequencing of narrative thought is eidochronic

Figure 2.5 The six actants of the actantial model.

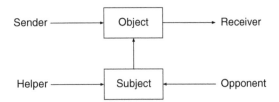

(*eidos* meaning 'idea' or 'image' and *chronos* meaning 'time' or 'sequence'). For Colby, the main unit in dividing the plot is an eidon. The plot is then a sequence of eidons, which forms the well-formed narratives. There are two types of eidons: primary eidons are rule-defined, whereas secondary eidons modify or accompany primary eidons, for example, as dramatic devices.

From the source material, Colby groups primary eidons into three categories: motivation, engagement, and resolution (see Table 2.2). A well-formed story must contain at least one move, which comprises a sequence of categories of motivation (M), engagement (E), and resolution (R). Using regular expressions (see Table 2.3 for the operators), we can state more formally

Rule 1: Move → M (Resp)*
Rule 2: Resp → E* R

The rules indicate that after motivation M, the sequence can contain several subsequences of engagements (E*) followed by a resolution (R). For instance, valid sequences would be M E R, M E R E R, M E E E R, or M E R E E R E R E R.

Each of the three categories can be divided into two subcategories. For motivation M, the subcategories are value motivation (VM) and immediate motivation (IM):

Rule 3: M → (VM) | (IM)

For engagement E, the subcategories are preliminary action (PA) and main action (MA):

Rule 4: E → (PA)? (MA)?

Table 2.2 Primary eidons.

Motivation	Engagement	Resolution
Fl food lacking	En encounter	Vc victory
Sl spouse lacking	Hs hospitality	Rl release
Ml maturity lacking	Ch challenge	Po possession
Vl villainy	Cn confrontation	Es escape
Bt betrayal	Pk provocation	Rs restoration
Sp separation	Ak attack	Re reunion
	Fh fishing/hunting	Mr murder
	Rv retrieval attempt	Gr group of reference
	Ps persuasion	Se settlement
	Tr transaction	At attainment
	Me magical engagement	
	Ma magical aid	
	El elimination	
	St struggle	
	Ds discovery	
	Dc deception	

Table 2.3 Regular expressions used in the rules.

Operation	Meaning	Example
|	Or	a|b matches either a or b
?	Zero or one occurrence of the previous element	a?b matches b or ab
*	Zero or more occurrences of the previous element	a*b matches b, ab, aab, aaab, …
()	Grouping of symbols	(ab)?c matches c or abc

For resolution R, the subcategories are immediate resolution (IR) or value resolution (VR)

Rule 5: R → (IR)? (VR)?

The main difference between Propp's and Colby's models is that the latter has intermediate categories that bring regularity to the structure of the story. These rules connect the six subcategories to the primary eidons of Table 2.2.

Rule 6: VM → (Fl) | (Sl) | (Ml)
Rule 7: IM → (Vl) | (Bt) | (Sp)
Rule 8: PA → (En)? (Hs)? (Ch)? (Cn)?
Rule 9: MA → (Ak)? (Fh)? (Rv)? (Ps)? (Tr)? (Me)? (Ma)? (El)? (St)? (Ds)? (Dc)?
Rule 10: IR → (Vc)? (Rl)? (Po)? (Rs)? (Es)? (Re)? (Mr)?
Rule 11: VR → (Gr)? (Se)? (At)?

The final set of rules listed in Table 2.4 define the type of the move, where the motivating eidon determines the resolution category.

The primary eidons seem to follow rules, whereas the secondary eidons have no rigid structure governing their location in the story (see Table 2.5). Their purpose is to make the story run smoothly by adding details and colour. In special cases, secondary eidons can substitute a motivating eidon.

Colby's system is clearly an improvement to Propp's system. However, Colby's work has not been known and, consequently, so influential in interactive storytelling research.

2.1.3.3 Story Grammars

The idea of story grammars is to give a general framework with hierarchical ordering of story elements, which are related causally or temporally. Apart from breaking down the

Table 2.4 Motivating eidons determining the resolution category.

	Type of move	Motivating eidon	Resolution eidon
Rule 12	Affective	Bt	Mr
Rule 13	Affective	Sp	(Po) | (Re) | (Mr)
Rule 14	Effective	Sl	Po
Rule 15	Effective	Ml	Po
Rule 16	Competitive	Vi	(Vc) | (Es)

Table 2.5 Secondary eidons.

Scene change	Dp	Departure
	Tf	Travel/flight
	Rt	Return
Conveyance of information	Pc	Perception
	In	Intelligence
Facilitation or prolongation	Fc	Facilitation
	Oe	Obstacle/evasion
	Ts	Terminal statement
Episodic transition	Ra	Routine activities
	Co	Comment

story into its constituent parts, a story grammar also gives rules for generating well-formed stories. The story grammar proposed by Rumelhart (1975) is based on syntactic rules, which generate the internal structure, and a corresponding set of semantic interpretations. The first five syntactic rules are as follows:

Rule 1: Story → Setting + Episode
Rule 2: Setting → (State)*
Rule 3: Episode → Event + Reaction
Rule 4: Event → Episode | Change-of-state | Action | (Event + Event)
Rule 5: Reaction → Internal Response + Overt Response

Rule 1 defines that a story consists of a setting followed by an episode. A setting consists of a set of stative propositions (Rule 2), and an episode is an occurrence of some event followed by the reaction of the protagonist. According to Rule 4, an event is either an episode, change of state, action or a sequence of two events. From Rule 5, it follows that a reaction consists of two parts: internal response and corresponding overt response. Each of these five rules is accompanied by semantic rules that help to interpret their meaning.

Rule 1': Allow(Setting, Episode)
Rule 2': And (State, State, …)
Rule 3': Initiate(Event, Reaction)
Rule 4': Cause(Event, Event) or Allow(Event, Event)
Rule 5': Motivate(Internal Response, Overt Response)

The semantic Rule 1' defines that a setting, which is conjoined propositions according to Rule 2', allows the reminder of the story. Rule 3' defines that there is a causal relationship between the event and reaction. A sequence of two events is interpreted as either the first event causing the second event or the first event allowing the second event to happen (Rule 4'). Rule 5' defines that a thought is related to its corresponding overt actions.

Rumelhart has presented in total 11 rules, but we can use these five basic rules to analyse the following simple story 'Margie's Balloon' (Rumelhart 1975):

(1) Margie was holding tightly to the string of her beautiful new balloon.
(2) Suddenly, a gust of wind caught it

2.1 Analysis of Storytelling | **39**

(3) and carried it into a tree.
(4) It hit a branch
(5) and burst.
(6) [sadness]
(7) Margie cried and cried.

Figure 2.6 presents the syntactic structure of the story and Figure 2.7 the corresponding semantic structure.

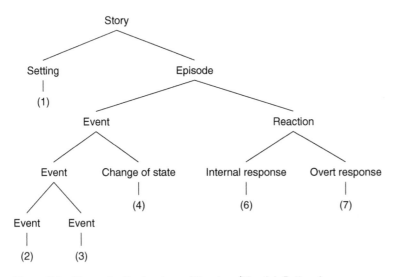

Figure 2.6 The syntactic structure of the story 'Margie's Balloon'.

Figure 2.7 The semantic structure of the story 'Margie's Balloon'.

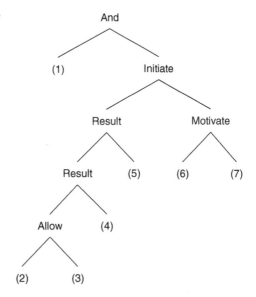

Thorndyke (1977) presents a simplified story grammar based on Rumelhart's. It stresses the importance of identifying structural elements common to all classes of stories:

(1) Story → Setting + Theme + Plot + Resolution
(2) Setting → Characters + Location + Time
(3) Theme → (Event)* + Goal
(4) Plot → Episode*
(5) Episode → Subgoal + Attempt* + Outcome
(6) Attempt → Event* | Episode
(7) Outcome → Event* | State
(8) Resolution → Event | State
(9) Subgoal | Goal → Desired state
(10) Characters | Location | Time → State

Mandler and Johnson (1977) also base their story grammar on Rumelhart, but they try to solve problems of limited scope (single or embedded episodes) and the dual structure (syntactic and semantic relations). Their grammar tree consists of terminal nodes (i.e. states or events corresponding to some surface expression) and connection between the nodes in one of three categories:

- and: nodes related by concurrence or temporal overlapping.
- then: nodes are temporally ordered.
- cause: first node provides a reason for the second one.

Figure 2.8 gives an example of the grammar tree based on the following 'Dog Story' (Mandler and Johnson 1977):

(1) It happened that a dog had got a piece of meat
(2) and was carrying it home in his mouth.
(3) Now on his way home he had to cross a plank lying across a stream.
(4) As he crossed he looked down
(5) and saw his own shadow reflected in the water beneath.
(6) Thinking it was another dog with another piece of meat,
(7) he made up his mind to have that also.
(8) So he made a snap at the shadow,
(9) but as he opened his mouth the piece of meat fell out,
(10) dropped into the water,
(11) and was never seen again.

The problem with story grammars is that they are applicable to simple stories with a single protagonist. Story grammars also omit the characters' beliefs about actions and the whole internal structure of their plans. Wilensky (1983) criticizes story grammarians that they are guided by the intuition that story grammars are similar to sentence grammars. Wilensky argues that this analogy is misguided because sentence grammars refer to linguistic objects, whereas story grammars refer to mental or conceptual objects. The existence of non-linguistic stories (e.g. pantomime or silent movies) further emphasizes this difference.

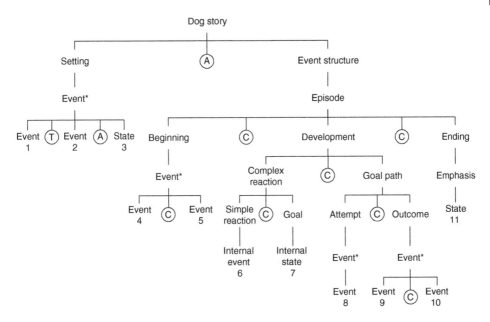

Figure 2.8 Underlying structure of 'Dog Story'. The connections 'and', 'then', and 'cause' are abbreviated and encircled. Source: Mandler and Johnson 1977.

2.1.4 Joseph Campbell and the Hero's Journey

Joseph Campbell proposed in the book *The Hero with a Thousand Faces*, published originally in 1949, the idea that all mythic narratives are variations of a single great story (Campbell 2008). This story, or *monomyth*, tells about the journey of an archetypal hero shared by world mythologies. It is a symbolic representation of the passage from childhood to adulthood through departure, initiation, and return.

Figure 2.9 illustrates the hero's journey as a cycle of 17 stages from the innocent world of childhood to the freedom to live at the end. The journey has three phases, of which the first one is initiated by a separation from the world of childhood when an adventure calls the hero. The hero initially refuses to embark on the journey, but with the help of a mentor (e.g. a supernatural aid) the hero finally leaves and faces the threshold of the known and unknown worlds. The hero is unprepared for this world and is caught in a 'belly of a whale' marking the separation from the known world.

The second phase begins with the initiation and descends into the unknown world. This will take the hero through trials (often occurring in threes). The 'meeting with the goddess' leads the hero into temptation, which threatens the progress. Having overcome the temptation, the hero is ready to meet the abyss (e.g. the actual villain) but is initially not yet ready and suffers a defeat, leading to the lowest point of the story that could involve some form of symbolic death. This point, however, is a turning point as the hero learns the lesson and survives the abyss. At 'apotheosis', the hero is ranked among the 'gods' and receives the ultimate boon to bring back to the inner world. However, the hero refuses the call to return, which concludes the initiation phase.

Figure 2.9 The hero's journey in the monomyth.

The third phase begins with a flight as the hero is chased by forces in the outer world towards the inner world. Reflecting the separation phase, an outside help rescues the hero and prompts the way to cross the threshold back to the inner world. As the story is closing to end, the hero has become a master of both inner and outer worlds. This finally grants the hero the freedom to live (and be free from the fear of death) – and the story to end.

Campbell's work has been highly influential in shaping Hollywood movies since the 1970s. For example, George Lucas has elaborated that when he was writing the script for *Star Wars* in the early 1970s, he was surprised to find similarities between the early draft and the monomyth.

The monomyth is also a pervasive story structure occurring in many video games. For instance, in *Horizon Zero Dawn* (Guerrilla Games 2017), the main character meets a mentor of a magically appearing VR device called 'Focus'. She crosses the threshold of her home village palisade to venture into the outer world. She enters the belly of the whale on several occasions, where the ancient technology has become buried underground. As the ultimate boon, she soothes down the corrupted monster machines and becomes master of the outer world, as well as is accepted as a proper member of her own village – the inner world.

2.1.5 Kernels and Satellites

Based on the work by Roland Barthes, Seymour Chatman (1978, pp. 53–54) separates the narrative content into two groups: kernels and satellites (see Figure 2.10). The term *kernel*

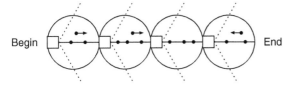

Figure 2.10 Squares present kernels and black dots the satellites. The circles illustrate the complete narrative blocks that kernels create. Apart from residing on the narrative path, a satellite can be an anticipator satellite of later kernels or a retrospective satellite of earlier kernels (marked with an arrow). The solid line marks the followed narrative path and the dotted line possible (but not followed) paths.

refers to the essential content of the story that is repeated when it is experienced anew. Basically, kernels form the identity of the story: if we change a kernel, we will destroy the narrative logic of the story and would end up having a different story altogether. In comparison, *satellite* refers to a content that could be omitted or altered without changing the identity of the story – although we might impoverish it aesthetically. For example, the identity of the story of Cinderella remains the same, whether she has one or two stepsisters or whether her chores include cleaning the house or peeling potatoes; however, the identity of the story would change, if Cinderella's father had died and her mother would have remarried instead.

This model is interesting from the perspective of interactive storytelling, because one can think of a kernel as a moment where the story could branch into different possible paths. These would be the moments when the interactor has to make important selections and form their own path to become the generated story. The satellites, on the other hand, are more malleable and allow easier interaction.

Espen Aarseth (2012) uses the kernel–satellite framework to differentiate stories and games by allowing the reader or player to have three kinds of influence: no, limited, or full (see Table 2.6):

- If the interactor cannot affect the kernels nor the satellites, agency is shallow and the story will reduce into a linear story (e.g. a novel or a film) that will take the same course in all instances. Such a structure is used, for example, in video games *Half-Life* (Valve 1998) and *Hellblade: Senua's Sacrifice* (Ninja Theory 2017).
- If the interactor can influence the satellites, we have a structure typical to linear games such as *Assassin's Creed II* (Ubisoft Montreal 2009) and *Final Fantasy VII* (Square 1997).
- If the interactor has the liberty to choose the kernels from a set of alternatives but has no influence on the satellites, we have a non-linear story (e.g. hypertext fiction).
- If the interactor can choose the kernels from a set of alternatives and can influence the satellites, we have deep agency, for example, in the form of a quest game such as *Star Wars: Knights of the Old Republic* (BioWare 2003) and *Star Wars: The Force Unleashed* (LucasArts 2008).
- If the interactor can influence both the kernels and satellites, we have a pure game such as chess and *Ingress* (Niantic 2013).

With respect to Figure 1.1, we could now fill in the gap between conventional stories and simulation by placing the labels from Table 2.6 into the spectrum.

Table 2.6 Using kernels and satellites to differentiate stories and games.

Kernel influence	Satellite influence	
	Not possible	Possible
No influence	Linear story	Linear game
Choose from alternatives	Non-linear story	Quest game
Full influence	N/A	Pure game

Source: Aarseth 2012

2.2 Research on Interactive Storytelling

Interactive storytelling, in the sense that we use in this book, began in 1986 when Brenda Laurel published her doctoral dissertation entitled *Toward the Design of a Computer-based Interactive Fantasy System* (Laurel 1986). She had worked in Atari in its heyday in the early 1980s, and then later in Activision, LucasArts Games, and Apple. Her research work stemmed from the idea that computers, especially their user interfaces, would be best seen as a stage governed by the rules of theatre. Her book *Computers as Theatre* (Laurel 1991, 2014) reflects this idea, and Laurel states: 'When we look toward what is known about the nature of interaction, why not turn to those who manage it best – to those from the world of drama, of the stage, of the theatre?' (Laurel 1991, p. xii).

Laurel's work inspired the first research work, the Oz Project (1989–2002), in Carnegie Mellon University led by Joseph Bates (Oz Project 2002). Initially, the research included studies simulating computer systems by the use of human actors and directors. Later on, the work continued with the systems like *Edge of Intention* and *Lyotard*. The interactive drama *Façade* by Michael Mateas and Andrew Stern (see Section 3.3.3) can be seen as the culmination of this line of research work.

Game designer Chris Crawford worked in Atari at the same time with Brenda Laurel. Crawford wrote the first book on computer game design (Crawford 1984) and founded the Computer Game Developer Conference. Game Developer Conference (GDC) – as it is called today – is the largest and most influential yearly event in the game developer community. However, its humble beginning was Crawford's living room which housed the first conference in 1988 with 27 attenders (including Brenda Laurel). In 1992, Crawford gave a keynote talk in the conference entitled 'The Dragon Speech' (YouTube 2014). In his talk, Crawford wanted to deepen the emotional impact of computer games, to tell stories that touch human beings, to make art. Being a game developer pioneer, he was saying goodbye to conventional games and welcomed a new task which he likened to pursuing a dragon. The years after that Crawford focused on creating an interactive storytelling system called *Erasmatron* and later *Storytron* and *Siboot* (see Section 3.3.2) as well publishing a book *On Interactive Storytelling* (Crawford 2005, 2013).

At the same time, another game designer was also tackling the problem of interactive storytelling. In 1995, Ernest Adams gave a lecture in GDC titled 'The Challenge of the Interactive Movie', where he lined out some of the challenges facing the realization of interactive storytelling. He continued writing and refining his views over the years, which were collected first in his doctoral dissertation (Adams 2013).

Just as Brenda Laurel approached computers from the perspective of theatre, Janet Murray looked at them from the perspective of literature. Her book *Hamlet on the Holodeck: The Future of Narrative in Cyberspace* (Murray 1997, 2017) focuses on the question whether the digital media can provide a basis for an expressive form. Her book and her subsequent work offered a new terminology for interactive digital media in general and interactive storytelling in particular.

Also in 1997, Espen Aarseth's *Cybertext and Ergodic Literature* was published (Aarseth 1997). He defines *cybertext* as centring the attention to the consumer of text so that the reader becomes more integrated in the process (Aarseth 1997, pp. 1–4). To differentiate this new type of 'reading' from the traditional, he uses the term *ergodic literature*. Ergodic combines the Greek words *ergon* (work) and *hodos* (path) to describe that traversing the text requires nontrivial effort (i.e. not just turning the page or pressing the play button) from the reader. Cybertexts belong to the ergodic literature, but they require calculation – usually by a computer – to produce the text. An important feature of the cybertext is that it keeps reminding the reader of the consequences of their choices: there are paths they have not taken – which might have even become inaccessible to them.

Marie-Laure Ryan's *Narrative as Virtual Reality* (Ryan 2001, 2015) and *Avatars of Story* (Ryan 2006) aim at explaining the concepts of immersion and interactivity and how they apply to narratives of all kinds. Her special interest is, naturally, in how electronic media (e.g. video games and VR) offers the potential for narratology. Ryan concludes that for a story to transcend culture and media, it has to present itself under multiple avatars.

Narrative Intelligence Reading Group started in MIT MediaLab in the autumn semester 1990 by graduate students Marc Davis and Michael Travers (Davis and Travers 1999). Their idea was to bring together students from artificial intelligence (AI) and literary theory to introduce work done in their respective fields and to find relevant research questions and a shared vocabulary for narrative intelligence (NI). The reading group comprising about 20 people met regularly until 1997, after which it continued as a mailing list.

In 1999, a conference on narrative intelligence was organized as a part of AAAI fall symposium series, with Michael Mateas and Phoebe Sengers acting as the program co-chairs (Mateas and Sengers 2003). Interestingly, after this point, the term 'narrative intelligence' vanished and was replaced by a variety of terms such as 'narrative technologies', 'interactive digital storytelling', and 'interactive narrative'. Also, after this point, the European researchers largely contributed to the research on interactive storytelling.

The narratology vs. ludology debate waged fiercely for a few years in the early 2000s. While narratologists analysed digital games in terms of story, ludologists rejected this approach and stated that narratives in games are incidental and they should be understood as formal systems and rules and analysed in terms of mechanics (Juul 1999, 2001). They argued that the notions derived from narrative theories are not effective to analyse games, and, simply put, games cannot convey narratives. After a while, ludology's position became more flexible (Frasca 2003). For example, Juul (2005) allows that digital games are 'half-real': they have a real part (i.e. rules and formal aspects) and a fictional part, which helps the player to understand the rules and interpret them. Finally, Murray (2005) declared that the battle is over.

The seminal texts to interactive systems and new media were first collected in *The New Media Reader* by Wardrip-Fruin and Montfort (2003). That was followed by the book *First Person: New Media as Story, Performance, and Game* edited by Wardrip-Fruin and

Harrigan (2004), presented a contemporary view on the topic. At the time in the 2000s, the website Grand Text Auto (Stern et al. 2003–2009) acted as a gathering point for many of the driving figures leading the discussion and shaping out the so-called new media research.

Research on interactive digital storytelling (IDS) was active during the 2000s, and the decade saw several doctoral theses, for example, by Mateas (2002), Osborn (2002), Riedl (2004), Fairclough (2004), and Louchart (2007). The academic research on interactive storytelling focused on three conference series. The biannual International Conference on Virtual Storytelling (ICVS) series was organized four times between 2001 and 2007 (Balet et al. 2001, 2003; Subsol 2005; Cavazza and Donikian 2007). The Technologies for Interactive Digital Storytelling and Entertainment (TIDSE) conference series was organized three times between 2003 and 2006 (Göbel et al. 2003, 2004, 2006). In 2008, these two conferences formed a joint conference series called International Conference on Interactive Digital Storytelling (ICIDS), which has been organized annually (Spierling and Szilas 2008; Iurgel et al. 2009; Aylett et al. 2010; Si et al. 2011; Oyarzun et al. 2012; Koenitz et al. 2013a; Mitchell et al. 2014; Schoenau-Fog et al. 2015; Nack and Gordon 2016; Nunes et al. 2017; Rouse et al. 2018; Cardona-Rivera et al. 2019).

Next, let us take a closer look at some of the aforementioned research work. This is by no means a comprehensive review of the literature, but aims at opening the development of thought since the 1990s.

2.2.1 Brenda Laurel and Interactive Drama

Most of Brenda Laurel's works are based on her idea in the invisibility of the computer. Accordingly, designing an interface is the real problem, and the aim is at creating a representational world that leaves the feeling of the interface behind.

At the heart of her work is, however, a neo-Aristotelian theory of interactive drama (see Figure 2.11). The following levels match the ones we saw earlier in Section 2.1.1, but Laurel (1991, pp. 49–65) uses different translations for some of them:

- *Action* (plot) comprises the whole action of the system. It is based on the interactor's collaboration with the system, and, consequently, the action may vary in each instance of the story.
- *Character* collects all the traits and dispositions of the interactor and computer-controlled characters alike.
- *Thought* represents the inferred internal processes of both interactor and computer-controlled characters.

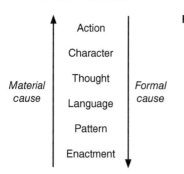

Figure 2.11 Neo-Aristotelian theory of interactive drama.

Figure 2.12 The flying wedge of possibilities.

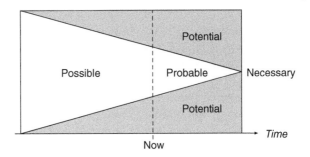

- *Language* focuses on the semiotics of all verbal and non-verbal (e.g. visual) phenomena.
- *Pattern* (melody) comprises the perceived, aesthetically pleasing patterns from the sensory phenomena.
- *Enactment* (spectacle) focuses on sensory dimensions of the presented story (e.g. auditory, visual, and tactile).

The levels are connected to one another via two causal chains: each level in Figure 2.11 is a formal cause for the level below it and a material cause for the level above it. For a further discussion on the neo-Aristotelian theory, see Mateas (2002, pp. 25–27).

Laurel (1991, pp. 67–73) illustrates the effect of choices with the *flying wedge of possibilities* (see Figure 2.12). When the story progresses, there are fewer possibilities that can be probable consequences to the history of events. This means that there is a more potential action that could have happened. Also, introducing new potential 'late in the game' can explode the structure of the action. The conclusion becomes more obvious over the course of the story, until only one necessary outcome is left, and at which point the story has come to its logical conclusion.

2.2.2 Janet Murray and the Cyberbard

Janet Murray's book *Hamlet of the Holodeck* ponders the question of whether a computer can provide the basis for an expressive narrative form. A digital medium provides the user with affordances, which are opportunities for the action made available by an interface. According to Murray (1997, pp. 71–90; 2012, pp. 51–80) a digital medium has four affordances:

- *Encyclopaedic affordance*: Digital medium can store a vast amount of (possibly semantically segmented) information in various formats.
- *Spatial affordance*: Digital medium can represent a navigable space.
- *Procedural affordance*: Digital medium allows us to specify conditional, executable instructions.
- *Participatory affordance*: Digital medium allows us to manipulate the content and processing.

These affordances make the digital medium a vehicle for literary creation: the procedural and participatory affordances make it interactive, and the encyclopaedic and spatial affordances make it immersive (see Figure 2.13).

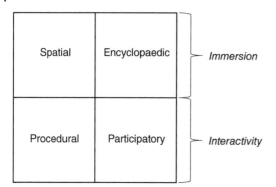

Figure 2.13 The four affordances of digital media. Immersion emerges from the spatial and encyclopaedic affordances and interactivity from procedural and participatory affordances.

Murray (1997, pp. 97–182) defines three aesthetics (or phenomenal strategies) of the digital medium: *immersion* which draws the interactor into the experience, *agency* which allows the interactor to affect the outcome, and *transformation* which allows the interactor to engage in roleplay. We study these closer in Chapter 5.

Murray (1997, pp. 185–213) also anticipates the coming of the *cyberbard*, which would exploit the properties of digital media and create procedurally multiform stories open to collaborative participation. Murray further claims that even densely plotted works like the *Iliad* and the *Odyssey* were collective efforts of a highly formulaic oral storytelling system. This bardic system is conservative, focusing on the underlying patterns where a particular performance can be created.

The most influential metaphor for interactive storytelling is the concept of the holodeck, which was the impetus behind Murray's book. The holodeck was first introduced in *Star Trek: The Animated Series* episode 'The Practical Joker' in 1974, but entered the public consciousness later in the series *Star Trek: The Next Generation* (1987–1991) and *Star Trek: Voyager* (1995–2001). Murray (and many others) regards the concept of the holodeck as an ideal model of interactive storytelling. Ryan (2008) collects lessons from Murray's vision of the holodeck as an ideal and proposes the following goals to pursue:

1. Natural interface (e.g. involving language and the human body)
2. Integration of user actions within the story (i.e. the user moves the story forward)
3. Frequent interaction (i.e. the user is not a spectator but can decide whenever)
4. Dynamic creation of the story (i.e. the plot is created as much as possible in real time)
5. Ability to create narrative immersion (i.e. engagement of the imagination in the mental construction and contemplation of a storyworld)

According to Ryan, the first four goals bring IDS close to life, and the last goal transcends it into art. Although Murray uses the holodeck as a motif, Koenitz (2018) summarizes that the essence of Murray's work is not the vision of the holodeck itself but the affordance and aesthetic qualities.

2.2.3 Models for Interactive Storytelling

We presented our model for interactive storytelling in Section 1.1.1. It includes the four partakers – platform, designer, interactor, and storyworld – that form the basis of this book. Other researchers have presented their own models, usually coming from different perspectives. Magerko (2014) introduces a model for analysing different kinds of interactive narratives. Its components include the processes employed, the content used and its structure, the system of control used in the system, and the social context in which the system is intended to be used. This PC3 (process, content, control, context) model can be used when analysing different kinds of interactive narratives such as theatre, games, and IDS systems.

- *Process* refers to the behind-the-scenes processes that enable the experience to occur. They are domain-independent means (e.g. the drama manager) of moving the story along.
- *Content* forms the surface of an interactive experience, which is a combination of story elements and story structure manipulated by the narrative process.
- *Control* is the gatekeeper of the story content. Here, we have a spectrum of story control from centralized to decentralized power structure.
- *Context* refers to the social elements of the system use and the intended purpose of the system.

Koenitz et al. (2015) present a chart of the ludonarrative field with semantic differentials as couples of significative opposing terms illustrated in Figure 2.14. Moreover, they propose that narrative artefacts could be located within a three-dimensional diagram, where the three axes are narrative complexity, dramatic agency, and agency.

Koenitz et al. (2013b, 2015) propose a specific theory of interactive digital narrative illustrated in Figure 2.15. A *protostory* refers to the concrete contents of the IDS system as a space of potential narratives. It comprises environment definitions, assets, and settings (e.g. user interface). The fourth component is narrative design, which is a structure within the protostory (e.g. plot) describing the flexible presentation of a narrative. This can be defined using narrative vectors providing a specific direction (e.g. plot points).

2.2.4 Narrative Paradox and Other Research Challenges

As we saw in Section 1.1, interactivity is the key difference between games and other forms of media, and game technology provides a new medium of expression where an essential

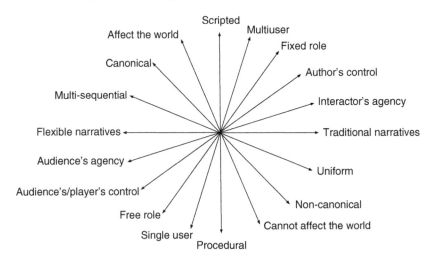

Figure 2.14 Semantic differentials in the ludonarrative field. Source: Koenitz et al. 2015.

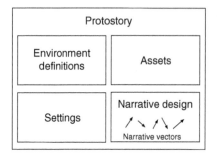

Figure 2.15 Protostory and its components. Source: Koenitz 2015.

part of experiencing the story happens through a direct participation with the story generation process. In order for the interactor to have agency in the storyworld, they must be able to make meaningful choices that affect the story's direction. This requires that the platform conveys information about the possibility of a choice to the interactor. Moreover, the interactor must, at the time of making the choice, have an idea of the possible consequences of that decision. Finally, to have agency, the ramifications of the choice in the story must be seen immediately and – to maximize the effect – they should also show an effect at the end.

The requirement of narrative agency – or freedom of choice – contradicts with the idea of a story being authored. Consequently, the core question at the heart of interactive storytelling is the *narrative paradox*, which happens when 'pre-authored plot structures conflict with the freedom of action and interaction characterics of the medium of real-time interactive graphical environments' (Aylett and Louchart 2007), which creates tension between the interactor's freedom and well-formed stories (Adams 2013). This can be seen from two ways (Louchart and Aylett 2005):

- The plot constrains the interactors' freedom, and
- interactive freedom affects the unfolding of the story.

Simply put, the more freedom the interactor has, the less control the author has, and vice versa. This can lead to the problem of internal consistency (Adams 2013) where the interactor can act inconsistently with respect to the author's intentions (e.g. plot, character, or storyworld). The interactor can refuse to follow the intended story and do something else instead. For example, imagine a game based on the film *Star Wars: A New Hope*. Now, the player controlling the character of Luke Skywalker could refuse to leave Tatooine, preferring to lead a life of a farmer. How could the author persuade the player to follow the intended story and leave the planet with Obi-Wan Kenobi and the droids? Or, as Ryan (2001, pp. 320) puts it, '[h]ow can the interactor freely choose her actions if her destiny is itself controlled by godlike authority of a world designer?'

The storyworld and its set-up limit the freedom of the interactor. For example, in *Façade*, the storyworld comprises a soirée of three people, and the theme is about a breaking relationship of two computer-controlled characters. If the player refuses to follow this set-up and decides, for instance, to act like a zombie (i.e. to march in and only utter 'Brains, brains!') or to act like having been shot and bleeding (i.e. to plead the characters to tie the wounds and to call an ambulance), the story is not progressing at all. The dissonance comes from the fact that the characters keep up their casual tone and try to invite the interactor in finding out their marital problems.

One possible answer is to increase the limits of the freedom of choice and forcing the interactor into a certain direction – either by hinting or even by coercion. This resembles the situation in the film *Stranger Than Fiction*, where the main character is hearing a voice-over of his life. At some point, he decides not to follow it and instead goes back to his apartment only to discover how hints (e.g. mail, news programme, commercials) turn into coercion (wall being bulldozed down), forcing him eventually to follow the voice-over's story (this same conceit is also used in the game *The Stanley Parable*).

There are different proposals on how to solve the narrative paradox. One possibility is to take a high-level approach that posits that the interactor enters into a contract with the designer, which means that the interactor will obey the constraints of the storyworld (Adams 2013). The same happens in games in general: the game designer is the one setting up the moral of the game world (i.e. which actions are 'good' and which are 'bad'). For example, a pacifist stance is not 'good' in the moral system of a first-person shooter game, because it makes impossible to proceed in the game. We come back to this topic in Chapter 5.

A design-oriented solution to the narrative paradox has two opposite approaches (Smed 2014). The author-centric approach puts the author's control in the first place. This leads to having a part of software, a drama manager, which acts as a proxy for the author and tries to manipulate the game world and its entities so that the interactor follows the intended route lined out by the author. Naturally, this can lead to a situation called 'railroading' where the interactors – regardless of their skills and abilities – is at the mercy of the game story.

Conversely, the character-centric approach sees the author as a Newtonian god, setting up the game world and its entities and leaving them alone to interact once the game starts. This so-called emergent narrative depends highly on the underlying simulations, especially the computer-controlled characters, but gives no guarantee whether a story comes up from this process. Naturally, this can be enhanced by re-introducing the drama manager as a behind-the-scenes partaker, which the characters can consult to make dramatically compelling decisions, leading to a hybrid approach. We return to these solution attempts in Section 3.2.

An interactive story experience on behalf of the interactor consists of aesthetics, sensory stimulus, storyworld, and narrative, as we see in Section 5.1 (Suovuo et al. 2020). The sensory stimulus arises mostly from the chosen platform (see Chapter 3) directed by the story's aesthetics. In an ultimate character-centric approach, the author would only provide the aesthetics and storyworld of the game, in the form of the rules of the game – typically known to all participating in the story, and the interactors would perform the narrative. The actions of the interactors would be completely free, and the storyworld would react properly to each and any action, providing the author's intended aesthetics.

Furthermore, anyone could even present their own plot devices and non-player characters (NPCs) over which everyone would have control. In this case, the system would reside close to the rightmost edge of Figure 1.1, and Aarseth would call it a pure game (see Table 2.6). Moreover, Adams's designer–interactor contract (discussed in Chapter 5) would become irrelevant, and the narrative paradox would implode, leaving the system without an actual story and having only the interactions remaining as Aarseth's pure game or a simulation of life. There would be no story that could have a title.

More typically, interactive storytelling is just interactive show-and-tell, where the author has prepared scenes with situations and these are revealed to the interactors to react to them. A video game has its levels and NPC responses. A role-playing game (RPG) comes with game-master-designed maps and scenes, where the players seek for a resolution to the presented challenges akin to the trials of Campbell's hero. The deepest character-centric interaction is available in live-action role-playing (LARPs) and in video games that contain a feedback loop for the users. For example, the aesthetics of *Eliza* is a therapeutic session, where the *Eliza* program is trying to understand and respond to the interactor's worries (Weizenbaum 1966).

The concept of story in this kind of an ultimately interactive storytelling system or set-up reminds the philosophy of Leibniz, who proposed that this world of ours is the best of all possible worlds, because it is the one that God decided to create. To extend the scope, we can say that the narrative paradox can be also discovered in theology, psychology, philosophy, and quantum physics in the form of the question of whether there is (a possibility for) free will or is everything predetermined.

An ultimately interactive storyworld should be completely free for the interactors, with only the laws of physics providing the aesthetics. Although, even if the author has authority, the storyworld would still, deep down, be an item of show-and-tell by the author to the interactors – only on a higher level.

Apart from the narrative paradox, there are other challenges. Next, we go through some specific problems present in interactive digital storytelling.

2.2.4.1 Platform

Perlin (2005) poses two fundamental questions: what is an interactive storytelling system and how do we make such a thing? Over the years, there has been a plethora of interactive storytelling systems mainly because everybody wants to develop one of their own – which is usually not compliant with any other system. This lack of interoperability has led to a situation where the researchers are burdened with solving problems – and often the same implementation issues – that are peripheral to their original goals. For this reason, there is clearly a need for specifications for an open architecture interactive storytelling system (Koenitz 2014).

The interface provided by the platform should be expressive and provide a multi-modal representation of the character's actions in a real-time 3D environment (Szilas 2007; Stern 2008). It has to be closely connected to the storyworld's content generation so that the designer is able to use the platform to its full potential. In addition to providing the interactor with the content, the interface faces the question of interpreting the interactor's actions appropriately (Szilas 2007).

Obsolescence (or digital rust) is an ever-growing problem of all kinds of digital media. For example, a significant part of the early work done on interactive storytelling systems is lost. Koenitz (2014) emphasizes the need for sustainability, which is the need for preserving operational records of software for the future.

We look more into the platform and examine existing applications in Chapter 3.

2.2.4.2 Designer

As we saw earlier in Section 1.1, the role of the author is tipped over in interactive storytelling, which is why we prefer calling them a designer instead. This also means that authorability must take new forms maintaining that the artist should still be able to express themself (Szilas 2007). As Bringsjord (2001) points out, the artistic expression includes defining the theme – such as betrayal, yearning, love, or revenge – of the storyworld. Also Koenitz (2014) wants to put more focus on the author because nowadays engineers (i.e. those who develop platforms) are also often the authors. To make a comparison with other media, movie camera engineers are rarely directors or book-printers authors. There is a need to focus on the creative process of creating IDS experiences (cf. Murray's cyberbard).

A touchstone for an interactive storytelling application is whether the story remains dramatically compelling (Bringsjord 2001). Creating an interesting story from the interactor's choices means that the designer must maintain a temporal management of actions (Szilas 2007). Moreover, this generation must happen in real time and possibly from predefined building blocks (Stern 2008).

We return to this topic in more detail in Chapter 4 on designers.

2.2.4.3 Interactors

Adams (2013) points out the problem of amnesia, where the human interactors do not initially know much about their character in the storyworld. Therefore, the story has to account for this, for example, by letting the interactor's character suffer from amnesia and finding about themself and the storyworld at the same pace as the human interactor. Otherwise, the interactor can be exposed to extra dialogue that would not normally be believable. The same problem also affects video games, especially if the game is story-driven and the player should be empathetic towards the avatar.

Another problem the interactor faces is agency. Agency is the primary feature offered to the interactors, and they have to be able to affect the plot directly (Stern 2008). Perlin (2005) puts forth a list of questions regarding agency: how do we interact, what would change, and what would stay the same?

Koenitz (2014) summarizes that user experience is a crucial goal of research. How do we create exciting and fulfilling narrative experiences? And how do we reach the wide audience?

We see more on this in Chapter 5 when we discuss the interactors.

2.2.4.4 Storyworld

Bringsjord (2001) emphasizes the importance of computer-controlled characters in interactive storytelling. First, the characters should be strong and autonomous to pull the story forward. Second, the characters should be personalized so that they have reasonable reactions and beliefs.

We return to this discussion in more detail in Chapter 6.

2.2.4.5 Terminology

Interactive storytelling is a young field and still lacks proper terms (Stern 2008), which was already observed in early 1990s by the Narrative Intelligence Reading Group (Davis and Travers 1999). Research has approached interactive storytelling from two fronts: from computer science as a technical problem to solve, and from humanities as a process to discover new expressive forms (Koenitz et al. 2013b). This has led to a problematic situation, where competing concepts require an extensive knowledge and understanding of each term and familiarity with their etymological development. For this reason, Koenitz (2014) emphasizes the need for a new narratology because there is a clash between research fields. Narratology assumes fixed objects of study (e.g. printed books or final cuts of movies), whereas interactive storytelling systems are usually dynamic. Furthermore, narratology uses fuzzy terms and the terminology does not help to communicate concepts amongst interdisciplinary scholars. For example, it is not easy to discern the meaning of terms such as 'text', 'story', 'narrative', and 'discourse'. Hence, there is a need to create commonly understood terms (Koenitz and Eladhari 2019).

2.3 Summary

Our understanding of how stories are constructed and what makes them work has increased since the analysis of Aristotle. In this chapter, we provided a brief review of the work done relevant to interactive storytelling. For this reason, we omitted much of narrative research. Moreover, we focused on Western tradition of storytelling, which has been on the forefront of research. Although storytelling traditions from other cultures have been rarely (if at all) considered, it is a topic worth further investigation and broader studies.

The structuralist approaches of the twentieth century provide much of the framework on which current works on interactive storytelling are based. One typical reason for this is that they tend to offer an easy starting point for an algorithmic implementation. Some researchers have even opted for a straightforward approach by taking one theoretical model – especially Propp's narrathemes – and re-engineering it as a story generator.

Research on interactive storytelling started in the 1990s when people from different areas of research such as AI, literature studies, and new media started a dialogue across the disciplines. These pioneers needed much effort first to understand each other's terminology and standing points. The research consolidated during the 2000s with new research groups forming and conferences dedicated to interactive storytelling, coming together as the ICIDS series in 2008. The field is still disperse with research groups or individual researchers located around the globe and mostly struggling with their own projects – and maybe inventing the wheel again. However, the community is still thriving and producing new research work.

Exercises

2.1 Although the second part of Aristotle's *Poetics* focusing on comedy is lost, there are references on later scriptures on its existence (and it plays a major role in Umberto Eco's novel *The Name of the Rose*). Comedy also seems to be non-existent in video game stories. Why is that? Could we have a comedic video game?

2.2 Take Aristotle's six elements of tragedy (see Figure 2.1, p. 29) and try to assign numerical values or stars of how much they are used in different works (e.g. a selection of films).

2.3 E.M. Forster writes in *Aspects of the Novel* (1962, p. 93) that the story 'The king died and then the queen died.' can be changed into a plot 'The king died, and then the queen died of grief.' Apart from the three added words, what makes the difference?

2.4 If we look at the narrative forms from the perspective of interactivity, we can see that the epic form – focusing on the accomplishment of a mission – is used in many video games. There are also games using the epistemic form, which puts the player in the role of a detective. The story can be author defined or variable and includes elucidation of a mystery until it is solved. The dramatic form is the most difficult one to implement. It includes goals of characters evolving together with their relations, which requires constant redefinition and simulation of human reasoning. Multiplayer online games with persistent game worlds rely on the soap opera form as the campaigns and stories expand and evolve over time.

2.5 How well do video games stick to Freytag's dramatic arc? Choose one game and analyse it in terms of the dramatic arc.

2.6 Analyse the structure of the film *Pulp Fiction* using Russian formalism (see Section 2.1.3). Map out the fabula and its relation to the sjužet. Compare how the sjužet is presented in media/text based on the film or the screenplay (Tarantino 1996).

2.7 Write down what happened to you yesterday. If that would be the fabula, construct a sjužet out of it. Plan how you could turn it into a media/text.

2.8 Take Table 2.1 with Propp's narrathemes. Pick a random starting point and continue iteratively making random selections (e.g. with a coin or dice) until you are at the end. Using these selected items, construct a plot for a story (a simple sketch is enough). Continue this until you have 10 stories. What can you observe?

2.9 How well do Propp's characters suit stories? Is the actantian model (see Figure 2.5, p. 40) any better in this respect?

2.10 Following Colby's eidons and rules, try to construct a story. At each step, think what you are adding to the structure.

2.11 Compare Propp's and Colby's models. What kind of similarities do they have? How much does the used material (i.e. Russian or Alaska Natives' folktales) is on display in the models, and how much is general? What if you would take another set of narratives as a starting point? What if the material would consist of Hollywood movies such as
- 1980s teenage comedies;
- 1990s action movies;
- 2000s romantic comedies; or
- 2010s horror movies?

2.12 Take Campbell's hero's journey and try to adapt it to
(a) your own life;
(b) your parents' or grandparents' life;
(c) your favourite celebrity's life; and
(d) your favourite fictional character's life.

2.13 Compare Propp's morphology and Campbell's monomyth. What are their similarities and differences? What is their relationship to each other?

2.14 Although similar in their approach, Campbell's monomyth has not attracted as many interactive storytelling applications as Propp's narrathemes. Both of them could be understood as a 'pipeline' enclosing the area where the interactor travels. What is the main difference causing this disparity?

2.15 Take one of the story grammars such as Thorndyke's (see p. 45) and use it to construct a short story. How helpful is it to compose the story? Would it suffice as a basis for a story-generating algorithm?

2.16 Laurel's flying wedge of possibilities is originally intended for graphical user interfaces (e.g. think of menu selections), but it also lines out interactive storytelling. If you think of the content and assets created for the system, what observation can you make from Figure 2.12 (p. 55)?

2.17 Why is the holodeck such an inspiring idea for interactive storytelling? What would it require technically and content-wise?

2.18 What kind of perspective do the models for interactive storytelling presented in Section 2.2.3 take? What about the one that we are using in this book? Do they share a common ground?

2.19 Take a film or a book that you know well. Suppose the main character would have freedom of choice and would choose differently, how would the story unfold? What if the choice happens early in the story, in the middle of the story, or late in the story? How drastic the change would be? (*Hint*: Look at Laurel's flying wedge of possibilities.) What about the narrative paradox?

2.20 Chekhov's gun (see Section 6.2.1) is a story design principle that states that if a gun appears in a story, it must be fired at some later point. This derives from the more general principle that everything told in a story must serve a purpose for advancing a story, which is often used as a reason for deleting scenes from movies. How does this translate into an interactive story, where the interactor does not know which action would advance the story?

3

Platform

Once we have commenced creating an interactive digital storytelling (IDS) system, we have to have an idea of the software that runs it. This *platform* is essential because it will be responsible for the mechanics and input/output – not only to the interactor but also to the designer.

We would like to emphasize the distinction of the persons creating, maintaining, and expanding the platform – the developers – from the ones using it to create storyworlds for the interactors – the designers. The relationship between the designer and developer can be close: when the platform is being developed in-house, it tends to get modified according to the feedback from the designers as well as the interactors. However, separating the roles is vital, and, clearly, there is a dependency where the designer is using the platform created by the developer.

Figure 3.1 illustrates the boundaries and emphasizes that the developer and the designer need not be the same. The developer's responsibility is the runtime engine that enables the performance of the characters' autonomous or semi-autonomous behaviour and other mechanics, whereas the designer's storyworld constitutes the actual 'content' using the platform-provided mechanics.

Discerning the roles of the designer and developer plays a crucial role. Sometimes, artists have to create their own tools for creating the work. When telling stories by writing books or painting images, we can expect that the artist masters the tools and mechanisms involved. Obviously, most writers and painters do not make their own ink and paper or colours and canvas. If you consider this production as a part of the storytelling process, the people responsible for these tasks could be considered 'developers' in the same sense as in Figure 3.1. In digital media, it is more typical that the artist purchases a computer to be used as a tool (like they would purchase ink and paper), but there is a special scribe called 'the programmer' who masters the techniques for transferring the artist's vision into a digital artefact.

In this chapter, we take a look at the platform. We begin with a perspective of the platform as software to understand the concerns related to the software architecture in Section 3.1. The biggest task for the platform developer is to tackle the narrative paradox. In Section 3.2, we review the options for the developer. Finally, in Section 3.3, we review IDS systems to provide a perspective on the historical milestones and the current state of the development.

Handbook on Interactive Storytelling, First Edition. Jouni Smed, Tomi 'bgt' Suovuo, Natasha Skult, and Petter Skult.
© 2021 John Wiley & Sons Ltd. Published 2021 by John Wiley & Sons Ltd.

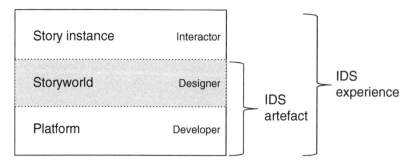

Figure 3.1 The boundaries between the interactor, designer, and developer. The IDS artefact is presented to the interactor, who in turn will have their own IDS experience. Source: Modified from Spierling and Szilas 2009.

3.1 Software Development

Typically, software matures so that parts that were originally developed in-house later on are developed by third parties and before they become off-the-shelf tools or components. Initially, these tools were crude and expensive, but with time and competition they have become more sophisticated and cheaper. 3D engines used in video games provide a good example of this progress: In the 1990s, it was customary that every game developer created their own 3D engines. This took both effort and skill, limiting the scope and amount of 3D game titles. In the late 1990s and early 2000s, there emerged few 3D engines such as Unreal Engine by id Software and CryEngine by Crytek that began to get used in other games and by other game companies. However, these engines typically required sound knowledge of 3D programming in order to be used and – more debilitatingly – obtaining a licence required that the developer paid fees up to $100 000 and had an experience in developing AAA games. With the advent of paradigm-challenging 3D engines such as Unity 3D (as it was originally called) by Unity Technologies has expanded and democratized the group of potential developers by offering the product for free for academic and non-commercial purposes and changing the monetization method. This expanded the user base and helped to make the game engines even more easier to use so that nowadays creating 3D video games will be easy even if the developers do not have specific skills in graphics programming.

As a technology, interactive storytelling has not yet matured. Rather, we are seeing limited and tentative systems created in-house for specific needs.

Adams (2014) provides an overview of a game design by dividing it into three fundamental components as illustrated in Figure 3.2: the player who plays the game, the user interface (UI) that presents the game to the player, and core mechanics (or platform) that implements the rules and the game AI. The core mechanics generate challenges that the user interface converts into output for the player. Conversely, the player's input is conveyed through the user interface and converted into actions for the core mechanics. Another way to see this is to recall the affordances (see Section 2.2.2), which are opportunities for action made available by an interface calling the interactor to give input.

Figure 3.2 helps us to navigate through the following subsections. We first look at the platform from the perspective of software design to clarify what is needed in building it.

Figure 3.2   The basic design parts of a game.

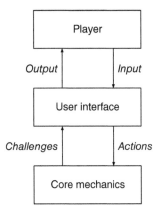

Next, we see how the platform appears to the interactor and then to the designer as both of these partakers need their own interfaces into software. Finally, we extend our view to modding, where an existing platform is transformed into something beyond its original intention.

3.1.1   Model–View–Controller

The software architecture of the platform follows the model–view–controller (MVC) pattern commonly recognized in user interface programming (Smed and Hakonen 2017, pp. 4–5). The model part is coordinating the internal state instance and upholds the (physical or dramatic) rules that form the core structures. The view part creates a representation of the model for external use by rendering it to output devices and internal use via the synthetic view used by the computer-controlled characters. The controller part comprises the control logic, which is a dynamic part updating the model based on internal input from the character and external input from the interactor received from the input device through a driver software.

Let us look at each area a bit more closely. *Model* connects the platform to the designer and storyworld. It provides mechanisms to store the static information of the storyworld as well as dynamic mechanisms and rules that maintain the storyworld. In essence, it provides a snapshot of the storyworld.

View offers possibilities to have a read-access to the data. The raw set of accessors provides a proto-view, which includes all the accessible information. However, this information is rarely completely available to the interactor nor to the computer-controlled characters, which is why we fork it to the rendering and synthetic view, respectively. The rendering process makes the data displayable to the interactors. The synthetic view does the same for the characters observing the character perception (see Section 6.1.1).

Controller is the dynamic part which makes the software run (i.e. the 'main loop'). It receives the interactor's choices from the input device and transforms them via a driver into something manageable. It also houses the AI of the character so that the decision-making process resembles the human-in-the-loop. Control logic is in the central position because it has to filter out possibly disallowed actions, maintain the rules, and apply the mechanics so that when it updates the state instance in the model, the state

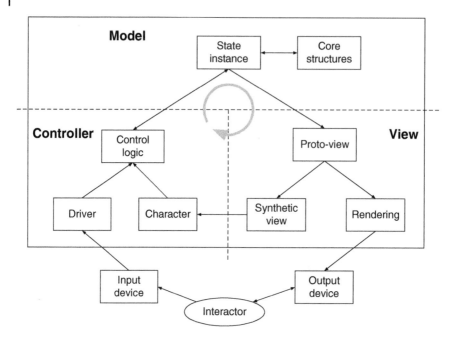

Figure 3.3 The model–view–controller architectural pattern for an interactive storytelling platform.

always remains consistent. It is possible that the control logic is highly straightforward, especially when we deal with a more simulation-kind set-up, or it can be complex that the more restrictive the system should be (see Section 3.2).

Figure 3.3 collects the main components of the MVC pattern. We can notice that the human interactor participates in a human-in-the-loop data flow by perceiving the information from the output devices and generating actions to the input devices. Similarly, the computer-controlled characters have their own perception of the storyworld, which they then use as a basis for their decision-making process (see Section 6.1).

IDS should be seen as a part of a larger system. We could think of situations for a small monolithic standalone platform that might be usable (especially with limited input/output capabilities). However, mostly, it would be connected to a common-use game development platform such as Unity or Unreal Engine because they provide functionalities that we would otherwise need to put effort into producing by ourselves, such as animation, graphics, network support for multiple interactors, social media connections. All in all, software has become a tangle of interconnecting and interoperating systems and platforms – and IDS as a platform is no different, only having its own specialized functionalities.

What does this mean for the design of a platform? With respect to the MVC model, parts of the whole would be connected outside: in the model part, the state instance would also include outside information; in the view part, rendering could be a part or completely reside outside; and in the controller part, the input might come from another part of the system. For example, a game engine might maintain the 3D location, provide visual and aural rendering, handle most of the user input and the physics of the game world, but the IDS

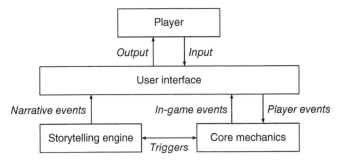

Figure 3.4 Storytelling engine included with the basic design parts of a game Source: Adams 2014, p. 219.

would provide the methods to model the propulsion of vehicles and the responses of steering to the user input. Depending on the environmental circumstances in the narrative of the IDS, the system would make decisions of adjusting the parameters of the rendering and leave the delivery to the platform.

With respect to the basic design parts illustrated in Figure 3.2, when the IDS is embedded into a larger system, the situation looks like Figure 3.4 (Adams 2014, pp. 219–221). Now, the story engine is hooked to the core mechanics so that either of them can trigger the other. For example, a change in the game state can trigger the storytelling engine to create a narrative event (e.g. a cut scene) for the user interface to display. Conversely, the storytelling engine can trigger the core mechanics to create an in-game event such as altering the behaviour of a non-player character (NPC).

3.1.2 Interactor's Interface

At any moment, the user interface has to provide the interactor information about what they need to know. These include the following questions (Adams 2014, pp. 259–260):

- Where am I?
- What am I doing?
- What challenges am I facing?
- Did my choice of action succeed or fail?
- Do I have what is needed to play successfully?
- Am I in danger of losing the game?
- Am I progressing towards victory?
- What should I do next?
- How did I do?

The interface should show only those internal values that the interactor needs to know. Also, it is not necessary to display data the interactor can already see by looking at the storyworld. Preferably, the information should be in symbolic or otherwise graphical form – although using numbers or text is the clearest alternative. Besides what is shown on the screen, audio can supply the information by using pitch, volume, or beat frequency.

Having meaningful choices in the interface requires that the interactor's desires and choices provided by the interface meet the following (Schell 2015, p. 211):

- If there are more choices than the interactor desires, then the interactor is overwhelmed.
- If there are less choices than the interactor desires, then the interactor is frustrated.
- If the offered choices and the interactor's desires are equal, then the interactor has a feeling of freedom and fulfilment.

This can be seen as a *choice problem*, which asks how to choose from a large amount of possible actions (Szilas 2004). Let us assume we have an interface mapping function f that maps a set of physically possible actions P (i.e. the perceived affordances) to a set of logically (in the story) possible actions L (i.e. the real affordances) – see Figure 3.5. The functions fall into two types (see Figure 3.6): full (non-surjective, non-injective, or bijective) or partial (free).

The designer's task is anticipation of an action and to plan the interactor's inferences. The most important factor is stability so that P and L should remain stable. Surprise counters this stability. For example, if a new possibility is added to the interface, it should remain in the selection thereafter (and not to be a gimmick just for one moment). Also, new possibilities should be added at a slow pace so that the user does not get overwhelmed.

The interaction takes time, and three strategies are available to cope with this. First, we can freeze or fill in the time, which means that the system either waits for the interactor's input or creates insignificant actions while the interactor is inputting. Second, we can allow semi-autonomy where the character fills in the time while the interactor is inputting. Third, we can invoke ellipsis, which means that the system freezes the time when the interactor is inputting and continues then at a later time (e.g. if the interactor decides to leave a house, we meet the interactor next in the garden outside the house).

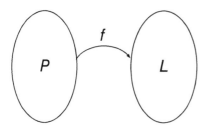

Figure 3.5 Interface mapping function.

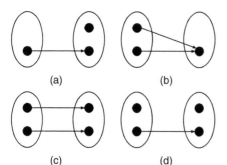

Figure 3.6 Interface mapping functions types: (a) non-surjective or filtering interface, (b) non-injective or redundant interface, (c) bijective or direct interface, and (d) free interface.

Bizzocchi et al. (2011) present four approaches to design a *narrativized interface*. In the 'look and feel' of the interface, interface elements – apart from providing the interactor with affordances – also perform narrative work. This can be realized in *interface aesthetics*, where the interface can be modified to reinforce the narrative themes. This is a move towards more diegetically integrated interfaces such as *Black & White* (Lionhead Studios 2001). In *narrativized game metrics*, the interface provides feedback to the interactor about the state of the gameplay and performance in the storyworld. It can also reinforce the narrative dimensions of the game.

The interface can be designed from the narrative perspective, where we consider the impact of the perspective on the narrative experience of the game. Here, the interactor's non-story-related choices (e.g. game mechanics) also support their narrative pleasures. This allows a deeper identification with the character and a more comprehensive sense of the storyworld. In *behavioural mimicking*, the interface tries to mimic those of real-life actions. This can mean control realism (i.e. how accurately the controls simulate) or feedback realism (i.e. how realistic is the feedback). In *behavioural metaphor*, the interface can suggest a connection to real-world behaviour. Finally, interfaces can do 'bridging' or use extended reality. This means that the 'magic circle' of the game is explicitly made porous (e.g. alternate reality games (ARGs) and the Tamagotchi).

3.1.3 Designer's Interface

So far we have been focusing on the interactor. How about the tools that platform provides the designer? They should support the iterative design process discussed in detail in Section 4.2.2, which lines out the properties of the designer's interface (Medler and Magerko 2006; Suttie et al. 2013). Primarily, the platform should be general so that it could be re-used across environments and story contexts. Also, the design process should be independent of the storyworld representation and runtime implementation so that these details would not interfere with and slow down the designer.

To support the decoupling of the real-time experience from the story content and character behaviour, the platform should offer debugging. The overall usability of the platform should support the ease of learning and reduce the errors by making tasks easy to remember and the whole design process more intuitive. These goals can be realized by offering the designer the possibility for prospective testing.

With respect to the storyworld, the designer-specific platform should make it easy to understand the environment definitions and have a broad scope so that it supports stories written for different environments that differ in narrative structure, mechanics, and user interaction. Also, pacing and timing are important so that the designer can create timelines that bring captivating effects to stories. The platform should help to structure the storyworld and bring dramatic consideration. It should also cover a wide range of design functions (e.g. character behaviour, story representation, definitions, dialogue scripts). Finally, to offer scalability, the platform should account for having multiple designers and adding content distributively over time.

3.1.4 Modding

A *modder* is an interactor who modifies the underlying mechanics of the platform or the content provided in the platform. In the first case, the modder takes the role of a developer because they can extend the functionality or mechanics, which can even transform the original system into something that the original developer had not intended. In the latter case, the modder takes the role of a designer, because they can transform the experience into something else than the original design would allow. Video games often support the creation of these kinds of *modifications* (or 'mods') created by the player community. This places the members of the community in the role of the developer or designer. In other words, the platform does include not only people from the company who publishes the game but also those who traditionally are considered as audience.

Modding can be viewed as a digital continuation of 'house rules' such as modification of the board game Monopoly, where money normally paid to the bank (e.g. the taxes and fines incurring in the game) is placed under the Free Parking corner and given to the player who arrives there. One can argue that modding is also a part of works in other fields such as audience participation in showings of the movie *The Rocky Horror Picture Show*. Louis Farese Jr and Sal Piro initiated a tradition where the audience have their own script of lines they shout and actions they take in response to what is happening in the movie. This was completely ideated and developed after the movie was fully produced, and Piro and Farese then 'modded' it to include their story content. Another example is *H+ The Digital Series* (Singer 2012), which was designed to be moddable from the very beginning. The series comprised three- to seven-minute-long weekly episodes designed to be easily organized in as many different orders and selections as possible. The audience was promoted to take the role of the editor and provide their own versions of the story through YouTube playlists.

We can divide moddability into four levels as shown in Table 3.1. The first level – *monolithic* – consists of games that are provided to the player 'as is', and often the end-user license agreement (EULA) even forbids them to make any changes. Interestingly, *Doom* (id Software 1993), which is considered the initiator of video game modding, belongs to this class. Its popularity, however, is attributed to the modding done by the players – and tacitly condoned by the developers. *Customizable* games allow the players to make minor changes in the game such as create their own appearances for the items within the game. The game itself remains as it is, and these customizations are either cosmetic or have a negligible effect on the gameplay.

In the third level, *moddable* games provide application interfaces for creating all new features to the game. *Civilization IV* (Firaxis 2005) is a prime example of this as it allows changing the entire game into something completely different through modifications. In a

Table 3.1 Levels of moddability with examples.

Monolithic	Customizable	Moddable	Tools
Assassin's Creed II	*Civilization VI*	*Civilization IV*	Unity
Half-Life	*Star Wars: Knights of the Old Republic*	*RimWorld*	Unreal Engine
Final Fantasy VII	*Tropico 6*	*The Rocky Horror Picture Show*	
God of War		*H+ The Digital Series*	
Hellblade: Senua's Sacrifice			

similar manner, many play *RimWorld* (Ludeon Studios 2018) with dozens of mods providing altered game mechanics such as guest hospitality. The hospitality mod allows the player to offer wandering NPCs with guest beds as they come and visit the player's colony.

The fourth level does not contain playable games but *tools* for making them. While customizable games can be adjusted mainly aesthetically and moddable games can be altered almost beyond recognition, the fourth level maximizes the moddability to the extent that the original game vanishes. For instance, Unreal Engine was originally developed for preparing new instalments for the video game *Unreal* (Epic MegaGames and Digital Extremes 1998), but has since become better known for an array of other video games using it such as *Mass Effect* (BioWare 2007) and *Hellblade: Senua's Sacrifice* (Ninja Theory 2017).

3.2 Solving the Narrative Paradox

The platform developer's first task is to select a strategy to handle the narrative paradox introduced in Section 2.2.4. Here, we can choose from two opposite approaches: the author-centric and the character-centric (Bailey 1999; Mateas and Sengers 1999). The *author-centric approach* (also known as explicit authoring, top-down or plot-centric approach) models the creative process of a human author. The system includes a proxy of the designer, the drama manager, which controls the events and characters of the storyworld. The *character-centric approach* (also known as emergent narrative, bottom-up or implicit creation) focuses on autonomous characters and modelling the mental factors that affect how these characters act. The story emerges from the characters' and interactor's decisions and interaction without any outside intervention or control.

To compare the two approaches Riedl (2004, pp. 12–14) proposes two measures for balancing the plot and character (Riedl and Young 2010):

- *Plot coherence*: The perception that the main events of a story are causally relevant to the outcome of the story so that there is a logical causal progressing of the plot (cf. Aristotle's concept of the plot in Section 2.1.1)
- *Character believability*: The perception that the events of a story are reasonably motivated by beliefs, desires, and goals of the characters (i.e. they should not have a negative impact on the interactor's suspension of disbelief; cf. Aristotle's concept of the character in Section 2.1.1)

Clearly, the author-centric approach allows us to have a strong plot coherence as a result of the drama manager's influence. The downside is, however, that the character believability weakens when the actions of the characters seem to be compelled to follow the designer's will (Aylett et al. 2011). The problem is then finding subtlety so that the influence will not be forced upon the interactor. In implementation, the main concern is that a platform must observe the reactions of the interactor as well as the situation in the storyworld to recognize what pattern fits the current situation: is the story getting boring and should there be a surprising twist in the plot, or has there been too much action and the interactor would like to have a moment of peace to rest and regroup? Since we aim at telling a story to a human interactor, we must ensure that the world around the interactor remains purposeful.

Conversely, the character-centric approach has (and requires) a strong character believability. This means that the plot coherence is weaker, because the story emerges bottom-up based on the characters. Although the idea of emergent narrative of the character-centric approach seems to solve the narrative paradox, it is unlikely that it is enough for implementing a satisfying platform (Aylett et al. 2011). Realistic actions are not necessarily dramatically interesting if the characters have no dramatic intelligence. Therefore, the argument is that the designer's presence is necessary because without the designer's artistic control we would end up with the chaos and drudgery of everyday life.

This leads to an idea that the approaches can be combined into a *hybrid approach*, where a character proposes a set of possible actions to a drama manager, which selects the dramatically best alternative (Weallans et al. 2012). Here, the drama manager is no longer pushing the characters to follow its lead but supports their decision-making.

3.2.1 Author-centric Approach

The first school to emerge in the late 1980s and early 1990s was the author-centric school (Laurel 1991; Bates 1992). It likens IDS to theatre, where the author sets up the storyworld and a computer-controlled drama manager directs its characters. The drama manager modifies how the computer-controlled characters react and tries to lead the story towards a direction that the designer has intended (see Figure 3.7).

A concrete example of an author-centric system is the early test scenario described by Kelso et al. (1993): having no computer implementation at their disposal, Bates's research group devised a scenario where a human test subject gets on the stage with a group of human actors. The actors have headphones to receive instructions from an off-stage human drama manager, and these instructions affect how the actors play. The drama manager observes the reactions of the test subject and modifies the situation accordingly. In the later experiments, the human actors and drama manager were replaced by computer programs. One of the early staged Oz Project experiments took place in a bus station with three actors: clerk, a blind passenger, and a punk (Wardrip-Fruin 2009, pp. 317–326). The interactor's task in this scenario is to buy a bus ticket to a relative's funeral. Whilst waiting in the queue, the punk begins a knifepoint robbery. As the situation unfolds, the clerk gives the interactor a gun. The human interactors' reactions varied much, some took quickly the initiative and acted out their role, while for some the experience was too much and the test had to be interrupted. Nevertheless, the interactors were all highly engaged in the drama. For the outside observers, the experience was lagging because engaging pacing for the interactor was different from traditional media experience (cf. watching an uncommented and

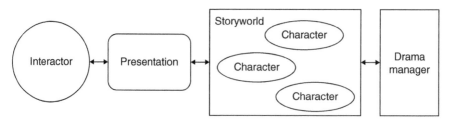

Figure 3.7 The structure of the Oz Project's interactive drama engine.

unedited gameplay video). Still, the design philosophy of interactive drama was successful and led to subsequent computer implementations.

A computer-controlled drama manager acts as a proxy for the designer. Analogously, it tries to change the situation so that the interactor is going in the direction of the intended story. This resembles the set-up of the movie *Stranger Than Fiction*, where the protagonist realizes that his life is happening in a fictional novel, and when he refuses to obey the voice-over, the world tries to force him to follow the intended story. This also demonstrates its weak spot when trying to solve the narrative paradox because the protagonist's free will gets severely limited over the course of the film, making his world appear to be a strange place.

Crawford (2005, pp. 205–208; 2013, pp. 214–218) lists examples of how the drama manager can influence the storyworld. The most common one is *environmental manipulation*, where the interactor is guided to take a certain route or prevented from getting out of limits of the story or doubling back to the already discovered content. It is the easiest one to realize as it involves manipulating some elements already present in the scene. One example is the lock–key structure, where the interactors first face a lock which prompts them to search for a key and, once it has been found, return back to the lock to proceed.

If the platform allows the drama manager to affect the characters, they can be used to guide the interactor. This can be realized crudely as *goal interjection*, which means – quite literally – that the character's goals in the scene are adjusted so that they lead the interactor to the intended direction. If the drama manager's intention is to lead the interactor to a pizzeria, where the story continues, the character playing the interactor's friend could have a new goal of getting to the pizzeria. As these interjected goals might come out of sudden and look unmotivated, it can easily break the believability of the character since it can look almost possessed or remotely controlled by some outside force.

A subtler way to use the characters is *shifting personality*, which, in turn, adjusts their goals. This is less discernible as it seems to stem more naturally from the characters' traits and needs. For example, instead of injecting the goal to go to a restaurant, the character's personality could be changed to prefer Italian food, and when the character gets hungry, it naturally proposes the interactor to visit a nearby pizzeria.

The development of the story can be triggered by *plot points*, which are predefined conditions related to the interactor's exploration, interactor's decision or advancement, or passage of (real) time (Adams 2013, pp. 42–44). These conditions act as triggers that launch events, or open or close possibilities (see Figure 3.3). For example, to meet a boss character who gives information where to go next, the interactor has to fulfil a given task to trigger the entrance of the boss. The conditions can form a complex network, where changes in the characters' or the interactor's attributes cause plot points to trigger. One special case of plot points is the 'ticking clock of doom', which adds a time limit that can pressure the interactor to continue in the intended direction instead of wandering around. Although this might look like a crude method, this can be realized so that the interactor does not realize the manipulation. The 'clock' does not have to be inside the game as in the game *Hellblade: Senua's Sacrifice* (Ninja Theory 2017), where the time pressure originates from generating a mental sense of urgency to the player.

The crudest way for the drama manager to influence the interactor is *dropping the fourth wall*, where the suspension of disbelief is knowingly disrupted to instruct the interactor.

In traditional storytelling, this has been used as a storytelling device, for example, in Woody Allen's movie *Annie Hall* or in the television series *House of Cards* and *Fleabag*. Video games such as *Portal 2* (Valve 2011) and *Leisure Suit Larry Goes Looking for Love (in Several Wrong Places)* (Sierra On-Line 1988) both break the fourth wall with the limitations of the user interface. In the onboarding phase of *Portal 2*, the non-player character Wheatley asks the player to say something. As there is no command available for the player to say anything, they typically try out every button they can while looking for the correct command. This is possibly intended to encourage the player to discover different controls. Eventually, the player will press the jump-key, and Wheatley accepts that as a sufficient response, stating: 'or jump… that's good too…' In *Leisure Suit Larry*, the player as Larry takes part in Dating Game, where Miss X is asking Larry and two other male contestants questions to determine with whom to go on a date. Whilst the other two contestants give highly poetic answers, the player is limited to entering short text strings, which makes it impossible for the player to write as eloquent answers as the competitors. Nevertheless, Miss X eventually chooses one of the other two contestants, but due to a mistake, she ends up getting Larry instead.

3.2.2 Character-centric Approach

The character-centric school appeared in the late 1990s and gained more popularity in the 2000s (Aylett 1999; Spierling 2007). Aylett (1999) poses the question 'how far the user of [an interactive story] can freely participate in a narrative rather than acting as a spectator' and answers that by allowing the characters in the storyworld to be autonomic we can achieve emergence which would solve the problem. Consequently, the key question is as to model the mental factors that affect how the characters act. As there is no drama manager, the designer's influence is limited in creating and setting up the storyworld. After that, the storyworld runs without the designer's influence, and the story – hopefully – emerges, bottom up, from the interaction between the characters and the interactor.

Reality television can be seen as an analogue to this kind of emergent narrative as a source for a story (Louchart and Aylett 2005). In a reality television show, the participants are motivated by, for example, money or fame, and they are subjected to entertaining the spectators. The spectators get entertainment but lack influence on the narrative. The programme production team makes pre-production selections by choosing and defining the main protagonists and by designing the world environment to foster emotions and dramatic turns of events. Moreover, they have performance time control by issuing tasks or eliminations and, ultimately, by compiling a broadcast to the spectators.

Emergent narrative is present in video games *Civilization IV* (Firaxis 2005) and *SimCity* (Maxis 1989) as their storyworlds include human actors, but on a highly abstract level, leaving the motivations within the narrative completely up to the player to interpret. *RimWorld* (Ludeon Studios 2018) depicts the characters on a more concrete level: the player observes them taking actions as well as interacting with each other and the environment, and the player can even control them. The characters have states of emotions and can even utter dialogue but, in the end, this is all completely simulated and character based. The only exceptions are when specific commands are issued to the characters by the player, or by the drama manager, which in *RimWorld* is even called a 'storyteller'.

Relying solely on an emergence, however, does not guarantee that the interactor experiences interesting or dramatically compelling stories. On the contrary, it tends to lead to (more or less) a simulation of everyday life. For this reason, the character-centric approach evokes many challenges for the design (Ryan et al. 2015, pp. 181–184). Modular content requires that there is a way to express the underlying system state to the interactor. Compositional representational strategies are needed to define how the content is actually deployed. A bigger challenge, however, is story recognition, which is needed to discern stories in the simulation. Finally, story support is needed to answer what to do with a recognized story-like sequence.

The seeming dead end of 'pure' emergent narrative led to improvements and refinements. *Double appraisal* aims at solving problems of emergent narrative so that the actions generated by the characters are believable but still the system generates high drama, where each step is loaded with emotional impact with no quiet or pensive moments (Weallans et al. 2012). The idea is that a character generates a set of possible actions to perform. After that, the emotional impact of each action in the set of other agents is simulated and the action with the biggest emotional impact is selected. The weakness of double appraisal is that it does not consider which emotion is being impacted. The dynamic of the story also requires quieter moments and build-ups instead of being a constant emotional rollercoaster. Moreover, the most dramatic action should happen only at climaxes – not all the time – as we saw in Freytag's dramatic arc in Section 2.1.1. At worst, this creates a constant high-strung drama where emotions are running high. Consequently, the characters are no longer believable but more like caricatures.

3.2.3 Hybrid Approach

The problems encountered by both author-centric and character-centric approaches have brought forth hybrid models combining them. The main idea here is that the characters are autonomous, but they can communicate with one another outside of the storyworld. These two modes of the character are called *in-character* (IC) and *out-of-character* (OOC). They are used, for example, in live-action role-playing where the participants can act IC (i.e. within the role they are playing) or drop to OOC when they are being themselves (Tychsen et al. 2006). Also, in improvisational theatre, the actors can convey OOC information using indirect communication (Swartjes and Vromen 2007; Swartjes et al. 2008). For example, the actor can say 'Hello, son!' cuing the other actor of their roles as a mother and son.

The idea of *late commitment* is that OOC decisions are used to allow the characters to fill in the storyworld with what the story needs. These could include added props, deepened characters, defined relationships, or backstories of the characters filled during the simulation. Late commitment is an explicit OOC communication using framing operators. This includes goal management (i.e. creating goals from OOC if no other goals exist) and action selection (i.e. characters can create OOC plans for their goals). To clarify, let us take an example, where the OOC goal is 'The interactor's wallet must disappear'. The framing operators in this case could be 'Endow a character with the role of a thief' and a goal for that character could be 'Steal the interactor's wallet'. If the interactor has a wallet with them, the thief character's more concrete goal could be 'Pickpocket the interactor's wallet';

if the wallet is at the interactor's home, the goal could be 'Rob the interactor's apartment'. If the interactor is carrying the wallet, we might need to frame another character to take the role of an accomplice and continue by defining the goals for the thief and accomplice, until they both have concrete goals on how to act to fulfil the original goal 'The interactor's wallet must disappear'. It is worth noting that stealing might not be the only way to fulfil the goal, but the OOC communication might lead to ways to make the wallet disappear such as a passerby who accidentally trips the interactor or a clumsy window washer who drops a water bucket on the interactor.

Weallans et al. (2012) present a more advanced hybrid approach called *distributed drama management*, where the characters act on an IC level and reflect on their actions on an OOC level (see Figure 3.8). A character proposes a set of possible actions to a drama manager, which selects dramatically the best alternative. Here, the drama manager is no longer pushing the characters to follow its lead but supports their decision-making through OOC-communication. When using a distributed drama manager, each character should be aware of its role as a character in a story with respect to the human interactor (Louchart et al. 2015). The character must reason about the actions possible for it (i.e. its role) and the impact that the chosen narrative action will have on other characters. The internal representation of the interactor's character creates feedback. The decisions are based on characterization and the emotional trajectory.

In the distributed drama management, an agent comprises a character layer that simulates the character and an actor layer that mediates possible actions in terms of dramatic appropriateness. The virtual interactor represents the human interactor's beliefs, desires, and emotional state. It is used to estimate what is the emotional impact of the proposed actions. Drama manager receives the proposed actions from the agents and authorizes the one that fits the best. Story specification is a document by the narrative designer, which describes the story at a high level of abstraction. This can be a sequence of episodes akin to Propp's functions, where each episode sets an emotional target for the virtual interactor.

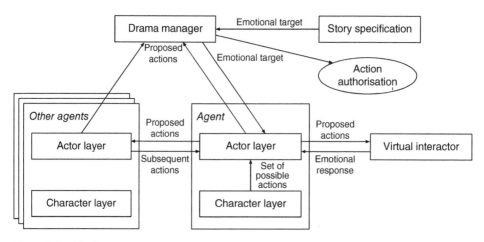

Figure 3.8 Distributed drama management. Source: Weallans et al. 2012.

The hybrid character should also have a function, where the drama manager could query for a chain of actions, and ask whether the character would go through it or what would it take for the character to go through it. If a story requires a character to make a certain critical mistake in a given situation, the drama manager could cast a suitable character for that particular role. Taking an example from the movie *Dirty Harry*, the bad guy needs to be such that he could not keep a precise count whether Harry Callahan has already fired six shots, otherwise the story would not work. Similarly, comedies are often based on characters who have strong mannerisms to react in a particular way in certain situations. If these behavioural patterns on a character are remarkable, the story will be foreseeable but funny. If they are more subtle, they may help to build up suspension and interesting delicate plots with relatability to the characters.

Live-action role-playing (LARPs) and the video game *RimWorld* have in common that the characters are free to act of their own accord, but the drama manager has placed them in the storyworld with certain initial constraints and motivations that they need to follow. In *RimWorld*, the players must choose at the beginning what kind of drama manager they want:

- Cassandra, who progressively increases the challenge level of the enemies and other threats entering the game
- Phoebe, who keeps long calm breaks between massive occurrences
- Randy, who can initiate random challenges at any time

The general difficulty level of these drama managers can be adjusted, and the player community has developed modifications adding the types of drama managers. Both in LARPs and *RimWorld*, the game master or the drama manager has little control over the characters' eventual activities, but if there is a character named Alice and a character named Bob is added to the storyworld with the goal of falling in love with Alice, these two characters will eventually meet and have to resolve the encounter.

At the moment of writing, the hybrid models are, by large, still theoretical proposals to handle the narrative paradox. As such, they do not actually solve the narrative paradox but move the problematic part elsewhere. This stain-on-the-carpet situation is common in algorithmics as well as in design: the innate difficulty – like a permanent stain on a carpet – cannot be removed, but by moving the furniture around and rearranging the design we can try to make it as unnoticeable as possible.

3.3 Implementations

This section gives an overview of existing IDS systems. We include laboratory systems and demonstrations as well as commercial systems and open-source platforms. The games with interactive storytelling reviewed in Section 1.3.5 are not included here.

3.3.1 Pioneering Storytelling Systems

The first storytelling systems were mainly not interactive – or the interaction happened by tweaking the parameters for each batch run. Instead, they focused on generating stories within clearly defined limits (e.g. genre). An early example is the automatic novel writing system by Klein et al. (1973), which generates a plot using a stochastic simulation of human behaviour that is then mapped into a natural language as a story.

Tale-Spin by Meehan (1976) is based on Aesop's fables such as 'The Tortoise and the Hare', 'The Goose That Laid the Golden Eggs', and 'The Boy Who Cried Wolf'. It aims at modelling the behaviour of the characters, which, in turn, creates the story. *Tale-Spin* allows no interaction, but each story is generated top-down on one run. An example output (with added capitalization) from *Tale-Spin* given by Meehan (1977) runs as follows:

> Once upon a time George Ant lived near a patch of ground. There was a nest in an ash tree. Wilma Bird lived in the nest. There was some water in a river. Wilma knew that the water was in the river. One day Wilma was very thirsty. Wilma wanted to get near some water. Wilma flew from her nest across a meadow through a valley to the river. Wilma drank the water. Wilma wasn't thirsty any more.
> George was very thirsty. George wanted to get near some water. George walked from his patch of ground across the meadow through the valley to a river bank. George fell into the water. George wanted to get near the valley. George couldn't get near the valley. George wanted to get near the meadow. George couldn't get near the meadow. Wilma wanted to get near George. Wilma grabbed George with her claw. Wilma took George from the river through the valley to the meadow. George was devoted to Wilma. George owed everything to Wilma. Wilma let go of George. George fell to the meadow. The end.

As we can see, the system tends to over-generate a narrative because the model has no intrinsic sense of what makes a story (Bailey 1999). Also, the subsystem creating the presented text lacks finesse.

Ani system by Kahn (1979) does not generate a story as a text but as an animation fulfilling a given high-level description of a film. It models the characters, their relationships and the scene as (possibly conflicting) suggestions that can be modified, combined, or discarded for the benefit of the story. *Ani* can postpone choices in the hope that later on there would be more information to make a more informed decision (akin to the late commitment of Section 3.2.3). It also uses general knowledge to reduce the arbitrariness of choices and to make the story more cohesive. The result is an animated story in the form of a program that a separate graphical system can use to generate the actual animation.

Racter by William Chamberlain was a commercial system, which was used to create *The Policeman's Beard Is Half Constructed* (Racter 1984) advertised as 'the first book ever written by a computer'. Details of the actual implementation are scarce and presumably it required quite much prefabrication and curation on the human user's side to produce interesting results (Henrickson 2018). A passage of text produced this way runs in what follows (Racter 1984, p. 32):

> The point-of-origin of Helene is America, the homeland of Bill is England and the fatherland of Diane is Canada. Hastily they whisper about their nurturing differences. We are seeing them commence to decorate their imaginations with a sense of delight. But the question of pain is obscurely never far off. Why are they aiding

each other to steer their dreaming toward distress? Is not satisfaction valuable and interesting? They will ponder as eagles fly, but their distress makes them furious. Can we aid them to recognize their intractable distress? Can we hastily change it to joy? 'Helene,' we speak, 'satisfaction is happiness while anguish is just pain.' Will this help her? 'No,' Diane quickly is crying. 'We must measuredly do more than fantasize. We must thoughtfully act!' This cleverly is true speaking and humming by Diane.

Universe by Lebowitz (1984, 1985) aims at generating stories that resemble television melodramas. Like soap operas, these stories can be endless. *Universe* is not based on simulating human cognitive processes but emphasizes story and character structures. It also allows a limited combining and sequencing of hand-authored data.

Minstrel by Turner (1994) is inspired by Arthurian knight tales. The underlying mechanics is based on Propp's narrathemes (see Section 2.1.3), but it also models the goals of a simulated author. *Minstrel* sees story generation as a common sense reasoning problem. This, however, makes it a brittle system that tends to under-generate the stories because the model has a limited sense of what makes a story (Bailey 1999). The following is an example of a story created by *Minstrel* called 'The Vengeful Princess' (Turner 1994, p. 9):

> Once upon a time there was a lady of the Court named Jennifer. Jennifer loved a knight named Grunfeld. Grunfeld loved Jennifer.
> Jennifer wanted revenge on a lady of the court named Darlene because she had the berries which she picked in the woods and Jennifer wanted to have the berries. Jennifer wanted to scare Darlene. Jennifer wanted a dragon to move towards Darlene so that Darlene believed it would eat her. Jennifer wanted to appear to be a dragon so that a dragon would move towards Darlene. Jennifer drank a magic potion. Jennifer transformed into a dragon. A dragon moved towards Darlene. A dragon was near Darlene.
> Grunfeld wanted to impress the king. Grunfeld wanted to move towards the woods so that he could fight a dragon. Grunfeld moved towards the woods. Grunfeld was near the woods. Grunfeld fought a dragon. The dragon died. The dragon was Jennifer. Jennifer wanted to live. Jennifer tried to drink a magic potion but failed. Grunfeld was filled with grief.
> Jennifer was buried in the woods. Grunfeld became a hermit.
> MORAL: Deception is a weapon difficult to aim.

Brutus by Bringsjord and Ferrucci, released 1989, generates stories of betrayal (Bringsjord and Ferrucci 1999). It uses a logical formulation as a model and solves it with logic programming. The downside of this approach is that it offers little or no variation for the generated stories.

3.3.2 Crawford's IDS Systems

Chris Crawford started developing ideas for an interactive storytelling system in the early 1990s. These are collected in his website Erasmatazz (Crawford 2019) and formed the basis of the *Erasmatron* system. This system, however, never materialized, but the material Crawford originally published in Erasmatazz ended up in his book *On Interactive Storytelling* (Crawford 2005).

Crawford tried next to develop a commercial interactive storytelling platform called *Storytron*, which was released in 2006. It included a tool for authoring interactive stories, a storyworld library and a run-time engine for interacting with the storyworlds. *Storytron* did not catch on and was discontinued in 2011. Apart from the financial crisis of 2008–2009, which made it difficult to find investors, Crawford confessed that the system turned out to be too complex to understand and to use (Crawford 2011b). Crawford (2011a) lists the lessons learned from the failure of *Storytron* to keep the technology simple:

- All actors (i.e. characters and interactor) have to be protagonists.
- Large base of fixed system of verbs (i.e. things that the actors could do).
- Author can only manipulate nouns (i.e. actors, props, and stages).
- The range of storyworlds is limited.
- No scripting.
- No attribute creation (i.e. the designer's choices are limited by the platform).

Crawford is currently developing a simplified version of *Storytron* called *Siboot*. After a failed Kickstarter campaign in 2015, Siboot has been developed as an open-source project (Crawford 2020).

3.3.3 Stern's and Mateas's *Façade*

Even today *Façade* by Andrew Stern and Michael Mateas, released in 2005, is still, in many respects, a prime example of what interactive storytelling could be about (Mateas 2002; Mateas and Stern 2004). It was also a culmination of the work started on the Oz Project and author-centric drama management. The set-up is that the interactor takes the role of a close friend of Trip and Grace, a couple whose relationship is in trouble. The events take place at Trip's and Grace's home where the interactor is invited to have a cocktail. The interactor sees the 3D environment from the first-person perspective and can move around and interact with the objects in the apartment. Interaction with Trip and Grace includes a set of gestures (e.g. hug, smile, and kiss) and typing in utterances in English.

The complete play is divided into three sections. The first one is a zero-sum affinity game, which tries to get the interactor to agree with either Trip or Grace. In the second section, the character realization is increased through a therapy game and the interactor learns more about their marital history and the problem that Trip and Grace have been facing from the viewpoint chosen in the first section. Finally, the third section leads to a dramatic conclusion. The play can also be incomplete and the end is, for instance, the interactor being thrown out by Trip.

The system structure is based on discretizing the time into beats. A beat is the smallest unit of a value change (i.e. an action–reaction pair). The story comprises a dozen of carefully scripted interactive narrative scenelets, and techniques are to steer the story towards the relatively linear set pieces.

To allow a maximum range of meaningful interactions, *Façade* uses a *broad-and-shallow approach* inherited from the Oz Project. The system is broad in the sense that all necessary

Table 3.2 The discourse acts of *Façade*.

Agree/disagree	Ally/oppose character	Advice
Positive/negative exclamation	Don't understand	Refer to
Express of emotion	Apologise	Ask to share intimate thoughts
Unsure or indecisive	Praise/criticize	Say goodbye
Thank	Flirt	Miscellaneous discourse act
Greet	Pacify	Can't understand
Explain		

Source: Based on Mateas and Stern 2004.

features have an implementation and shallow in the sense that some features could have been performed better. In practice, this means that characters can act believably, but not necessary intelligently, in a wide range of situations. One example of this is how the textual utterances from the interactor are handled by surface-text processing. In the first phase, the surface text (i.e. the interactor's input) is mapped into one of 19 possible discourse acts (see Table 3.2). The relevant discourse act is then mapped into character responses.

3.3.4 Experimental Systems

In this section, we briefly introduce some of the experimental systems and their key features in alphabetical order. This list is not complete, and our descriptions are short. However, they try to emphasize the broad spectrum of approaches that have been tried.

Advanced Stories Authoring and Presentation System (ASAPS) (Advanced Stories Group 2019) has been used for teaching how to author interactive stories and studying the authoring process (Koenitz and Chen 2012). It uses a bottom-up approach, where the author has access to building blocks and combines them into an interactive story. Like *Façade*, it uses beats (14 types) which can be static (e.g. title screen), flexible (e.g. conversation, navigation, inventory), and procedural (e.g. counters, global variables, items, timers). The results from using *ASAPS* in teaching interactive narratives concluded that the typical narrative genres selected by the students were

- adventure
- detective story/mystery
- role playing game
- alternate history
- amnesia/escape room
- situational challenge
- character development
- complex topic/multiperspective

CrossTalk is designed to be used as an exhibition guide (CrossTalk 2020; Klesen et al. 2003). The basic idea is an interaction triangle with three screens. The first screen is meant for the virtual exhibition hostess, which engages in a conversation with changeable virtual exhibition visitors who inhabit the second screen. The third screen is a touch screen for the interactor's choices.

FearNot! aims at teaching school children how to handle cases of bullying (e.g. as the one being bullied or as a bystander witnessing bullying) (Aylett et al. 2007). The underlying FAtiMA (Fearnot Affective Mind Architecture) system is an agent architecture driven by cognitive appraisal, where the characters focus on both problem-solving and assessing other characters' emotions.

Makebelieve is a virtual guide system, which uses Jess/CLIPS reasoning system, OpenMind common sense data, and Unreal Engine (Ibanez et al. 2003). The storyworld comprises a pool of story elements, each of which has data related to the content of the event (e.g. name, type, location, date, and causal effects). Based on the interactor's input, the system selects a suitable story element (possibly by adding some causally related elements). The data is then translated according to the guide's attitude and extended with common sense data. Based on that, the system generates a storyboard for the output to the interactor.

Nothing for Dinner (Medilab Theme 2020), released in 2015, is based on the Interactive Drama Engine (IDA) (Szilas 2007). Its purpose is to train how to support a stroke patient's family and loved ones. Player takes the role of a teenager, whose family member is suffering from a stroke, and observes the consequences of the actions.

Prom Week, released in 2012, focuses on the interactions of high school students (Expressive Intelligence Studio 2019). It has a dynamic storyspace, and characters with 5000 social interactions (e.g. who likes who and how much and direction of relationships).

Scenejo is a platform for experiencing emerging dialogues or conversations between a number of virtual and human actors (Scenejo 2020). It connects a computer-controlled character and the interactor in a conversational loop that is controlled by 'dramatic advisor'. For example, the interactor could act as moderator in a debate between two characters. For each turn, the dramatic interactor receives utterances from the characters and the interactor and selects one to be played and reacted by everyone in the next turn.

Virtual Storyteller is a multi-agent framework with plot generation (Swartjes and Theune 2006; Theune et al. 2004; Virtual Storyteller 2020). It places a special focus on natural language generation and the presentation by an embodied agent.

There have been many other systems presented which have had a shorter lifetime or lower impact, including *SAGA* (Machado et al. 2004), *OPIATE* (Fairclough 2004), *VIBES* (Sanchez et al. 2004), *PaSSAGE* (Thue et al. 2007), *ISRST* (Nakasone et al. 2009), and *LogTell-R* (Karlsson and Furtado 2014).

3.3.5 Other Systems

To conclude our review, we list some commercial or open project systems to create interactive stories. One of the earliest story systems for commercial use is *SCUMM* (*Script Creation Utility for Maniac Mansion*) by LucasFilm Games. *SCUMM* was used to create the point-and-click adventure games from *Maniac Mansion* (LucasFilm Games 1987) to *The Curse of Monkey Island* (LucasArts 1997). It allowed cross-platform development and supported multitasking scripts and rapid prototyping.

Twine, created by Chris Klimas and released in 2009, is an open-source tool for telling interactive stories originally (Twine 2020). It has gained popularity among scriptwriters for creating interactive television programmes and movies such as *Black Mirror: Bandersnatch*.

Versu was a platform that was launched by Linden Labs in 2013 and discontinued in 2015 (Versu 2020). It aimed at making it possible to create and distribute interactive stories such as *Blood & Laurels* (Short 2014). *Versu* allowed strong character autonomy but had a drama manager that suggests actions and tweaks the characters' desires. The overall idea was to create an ecosystem where stories would be available for the public.

Episode is a platform for creating and distributing digital stories launched in 2013 (Episode Interactive 2020). The idea of an ecosystem is similar to *Versu*, but the interface is more graphical and user-friendly. Other systems of similar type are *Choices: Stories You Play* by Pixelberry Studios (2020) launched in 2016 and *Series: Your Story Universe* by Universal City Studios (2020) launched in 2018 and discontinued in 2019.

Ink is an authoring system developed by Inkle Studios and used in, for example, in their game *80 Days* (Inkle Studios 2020). It can be used to create stand-alone webpages or to provide a story engine to Unity.

Visual novels (see Section 1.3.5) have many independent developer systems. One of the most popular is *Ren'Py*, launched in 2004, which allows to create branching stories using various types of assets (Ren'Py 2020).

3.4 Summary

Kay et al. (1978) envisioned the possibilities of the PC in the 1980s on a position paper by giving the following example:

> Imagine a James Bond movie in which you can variously be the hero, [villain], and bystander, whose plot is fluidly controlled by decisions you make in the course of its action, all presented in real-time full color. Your family and friends can assume roles also – the outcomes will be the result of all your decisions. All of this and all of the variations of this theme that you can imagine will be possible (and inevitable) just a few years from now.

In many regards, their vision has become reality, but we have not achieved the goal in interactive storytelling because of the lack of a solid platform.

A platform underlies all interactive storytelling systems. Earlier, the platform was unique to each application, but there is an increasing trend that the platform is usable for several interactive stories. However, the platform has to provide a 'solution' to the narrative paradox. It can be based on a drama manager, where the interactor's free will takes the second place, or emergence, where the story is subject to the interactor's choices. The problems caused by these extremes are being mitigated by the hybrid models.

Initial implementations in the 1970s and 1980s focused on generating stories without (much) interaction. They typically narrowed down the problem by focusing on some very specific set-ups (e.g. medieval tales or soap opera). As the research interest rose in the 1990s and 2000s, the systems tried to break out from these models. The first laboratory systems created during this period never caught wider interest apart from *Façade*, which was hailed at the time as 'the future of video games' (Schiesel 2005). However, the *Façade* platform – like most of the others of this period – was never released or reused for other works.

During the 2010s, video games such as the ones introduced in Section 1.3.5 caught up the earlier research work and sometimes even surpassed it. Also, currently, there exist several platforms for creating interactive narratives, although many of them are still quite simple.

A commonly asked question is why interactive storytelling has not gained wider popularity. In video game development, the source for many problems is the fact that the development typically begins with the game mechanics and gameplay and the story is included – almost as an afterthought – in the later stages of design. Still, many video games advertise their interactive narratives and stories that change based on the player's choices, and, at the same time, embellishing the experience that this narrative dimension brings along. Koenitz and Eladhari (2019) argue that these overblown expectations laid on interactive storytelling applications are the reason for their failure. We should set our sights for concrete shorter-term advances and work steadfast through them towards the loftier goals.

Exercises

3.1 The model–view–controller pattern is in line with the concept of expressive processing by Wardrip-Fruin (2009, pp. 8–13), which considers how to craft and situate interesting processes so that they produce meaningful audience experience (see Figure 3.9). How do they correspond to one another?

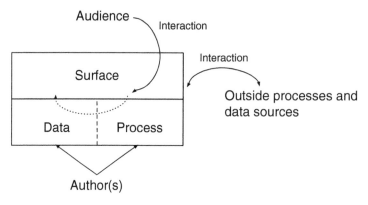

Figure 3.9 Expressive processing. Source: Wardrip-Fruin 2009, p. 12.

3.2 Compare the narrative paradox and solutions proposals presented in Section 3.2 to the spectrum of Figure 1.1 (p. 4). Can you place the author-centric, character-centric, and hybrid approaches on the spectrum?

3.3 What is the combination of author-centric and character-centric approach in
(a) RPGs
(b) LARPs
(c) Improvisational theatre.

3.4 Are the two metrics – plot coherence and character believability – enough? Are there some other measures that we could use (and how usable they would be)?

3.5 Can you come up with reasons why the author-centric school was the first to appear? What makes it more appealing or more obvious for a solution?

3.6 Try to sketch the specifications for a drama manager software. What kind of subsystems should it include? Are there suitable implementational approaches that could be used in realizing them?

3.7 Dropping the fourth wall works usually in a comedic context. However, the television series *House of Cards* manages to use it in a serious drama. Why does it work there?

3.8 Take the set-up and premise of the movie *Reservoir Dogs*. How would you model it as an interactive story using the emergent narrative approach? Does the movie provide with you enough information for the design or are there much extra details that have to be added?

3.9 Try to enact with a group (or write as a dialogue) a scene using the double-appraisal approach as a basis for improvisational theatre piece. Everyone should always try to select the action with the biggest emotional impact. The scene could be a wedding reception with a bride and groom, their parents, and best friends. Viewing (or reading) the play afterwards, what can you observe?

3.10 Late commitment resembles the development of a television series. For instance, a character that was initially devised to have a small role could work very well in practice, and in the subsequent episodes or seasons its role can be increased and its personality more refined and history added. The character might even be able to spin off and have a series of its own (e.g. Frasier Crane in *Cheers* or Saul Goodman in *Breaking Bad*). How would you define the qualities needed for such characters?

3.11 What is the benefit of distributed drama management of separating 'actor layer' and 'character layer'?

3.12 Try to come up with specifications for a distributed drama manager.

3.13 Wardrip-Fruin (2009, pp. 15–16) uses *Eliza*, *Tale-Spin*, and *SimCity* for labelling three effects arising in the relationship between system processes and audience experiences:
- *Eliza effect*: Audience expectations that allow a digital media system to appear more complex on its surface than it is supported by its underlying structure.
- *Tale-Spin effect*: Works that fail to represent their internal system richness on their surfaces.

- *SimCity effect*: Systems that shape their surface experiences to enable the audience to build up an understanding of their (complex) internal structure.
  How accurate are these labels?

3.14 Why has *Façade* not been repeated? Reviewing the system now, do you see technological, theoretical, implementational, or design-related issues that have prevented pursuit in that direction?

3.15 *Façade* uses a broad-and-shallow approach for parsing textual input. Look at the discourse acts listed in Table 3.2. Do they form a covering set or is there something essential still missing? Try to map a short conversation using it. If we would change the setting and scenery, how would the set of discourse acts change?

3.16 The PING (passive, interactive, narrative, game) model by Bevensee et al. (2012) allocates application according to different attributes (see Figure 3.10). Place the systems introduced in Section 3.3 into the model. You can also include the games from Section 1.3.5.

Figure 3.10 PING (passive, interactive, narrative, game) model. Source: Bevensee et al. 2012.

4

Designer

In conventional storytelling such as books and movies, the author's role is decisive in creating the presented story to the spectators (see Figure 1.2, p. 5). Here, we usually have a single author – the writer or the director – composing a story to an audience, and the only interaction in storytelling happens before the story is set down in its published form. For the audience, the presented story is always the same, but everyone makes their own experienced story out of it. In reality, the case is typically more complex and more interactive than that. Books are processed by writers who receive feedback from editors and advance readers before the book is published. The publisher makes the choice of the final layout of the book, which font is used, what kind of paper, and will the book be hardcover or paperback. Movies are conducted by the directors in a complex process involving actors, cinematographers, producers, set designers, and many others – and the director might not even get the last word but the film can go through a recut based on the reactions from test audiences. Nevertheless, on a higher level of abstraction, these teams can be considered collectively as the author.

In interactive storytelling, the role of the author and whole authoring process is redefined so much that we use the term *designer* instead (Adams 2013, p. 8–9). In the game industry, a game designer is responsible for the vision and idea of the whole game working together with the rest of the game development team from the conception to the release of the game. In larger projects, the team can involve several designers each specializing in their own field such as level design or audio design. A recent addition to the group of game designers is a *narrative designer*, who focuses on bringing in and integrating the story so that it seamlessly fits into the game design and complies with the game mechanics and art style (Heussner et al. 2015). This requires a special set of skills, and many writers coming from more traditional media might find it difficult to give up authorial control and to adapt to work within the confines of the game system and as a part of a multidisciplinary development team. Furthermore, the narrative designer commonly directs the graphics and audio team in creating the right environment, character design aesthetics, and all other visual elements that would highlight the story content for a more immersive gaming experience. A main requirement for the narrative design is second-person insight, which is the ability to think in terms of how the expression will be perceived by the audience (Crawford 2005). In the scientific literature of interactive storytelling, the term 'author' is, however, widely used, but we have tried here to harmonize the terminology to the term 'designer'

Handbook on Interactive Storytelling, First Edition. Jouni Smed, Tomi 'bgt' Suovuo, Natasha Skult, and Petter Skult.
© 2021 John Wiley & Sons Ltd. Published 2021 by John Wiley & Sons Ltd.

as much as possible. For example, we use the term 'design process' instead of 'authoring' when we talk about the designer's tasks related to implementing, assessing, and refining the storyworld.

From the designer's perspective, the interactive format allows to realize things that are not possible in conventional storytelling (Ryan 2001, pp. 212–213). For example, the designer can control the interactor's progress in discovering the facts. Moreover, the designer can propose and let the interactor explore alternative versions from the same premises to find out many possible futures for the work. It also allows the interactor to pass over sections or stop to have a closer look, and in that way allow the designer to provide more background information. This is something that has been longed for by the conventional authors such as Walter Scott in his novel *Ivanhoe* (1819), where certain narratives are described from the perspective of different characters in consecutive chapters. This would be more natural to realize interactive storytelling, where the interactors may choose the character whose perspective they wish to experience in each scenario.

The designer's main choice in creating a storyworld is to choose its type, which we discuss in detail in Section 4.1. This lays out how the structure of the contents is mapped out. It also defines how much content is needed to fill in the designed storyworld. The more open the storyworld is and the more choices the interactor has, the more content is needed. The second task for the designer is then to build the storyworld in an iterative fashion, which we look at closely in Section 4.2. In Section 4.3, we discuss further the relationship between the designer and the interactor.

4.1 Storyworld Types

What sets the design of an interactive storyworld apart from traditional storytelling is the interactor's influence on the story being told. This creates a friction that the design has to solve. The basic problem is how to give the interactor a set of choices. We have already seen in Section 3.2 that the platform developers have to tackle the essential question by selecting the author-centric, character-centric, or hybrid model. Within this framework, the designer has to then decide the type of the storyworld. There are different approaches to handle this depending on how much control is given to the interactor. The designer can employ different narrative types for guiding the interactor to make impact on the story progression, which are illustrated in Figure 4.1 (which is actually Figure 1.1 revisited). As the narrative paradox indicates, the designer's control over the story and the interactor's freedom exclude each other: the higher the designer's control, the less freedom the interactor has, and, conversely, high freedom of choice means reduced control for the designer. At one extreme, we have the case where there is no freedom, which constitutes a reduction back to conventional linear storytelling (e.g. cinema, literature). At the other extreme, we have no designer control of the narrative and the storyworld is reduced to just a simulation.

Between the extremes we have three different approaches – linear, branching, and open – to incorporate narrative into games (Heussner et al. 2015, pp. 107–123; Zeman 2017, pp. 228–236; Adams 2013, pp. 37–42). Additional subclasses for them are described by Ryan (2001, pp. 246–256; 2006, pp. 100–107; 2015, pp. 165–175).

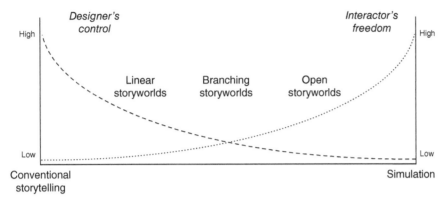

Figure 4.1 The spectrum of storyworld types.

Cutscene	Gameplay	Cutscene	Gameplay	Cutscene	Gameplay
Narrative	Interaction	Narrative	Interaction	Narrative	Interaction

Figure 4.2 Typical linear narrative in a video game.

4.1.1 Linear Storyworlds

In video games, the most widely used approach in including a story is a linear narrative, where the story progresses linearly (e.g. through cutscenes between the levels or environmental changes), but the player has freedom in the gameplay (see Figure 4.2). This means that every player will encounter every time the same story in the same order. Although the interactor, therefore, lacks agency, the story can be woven into the level design in such a way that the interactor's actions seem to have an influence on the story as well. For example, the killing of a level boss can be followed by a cutscene, where the allies of the boss get involved in the conflict. Although the killing of the boss is necessary for the player to proceed in the gameplay, now it seems to have repercussions in the story as well. This pseudo-agency provides the players with a feeling that they can also affect the story (see Section 5.2).

An obvious step from pure linearity is to allow side branches that are additional and do not affect the main (linear) story (see Figure 4.3). These offshoots are presented as quests, jobs, or tasks that the interactor may choose to undertake, but they do not affect the main storyline. For example, the story of *Final Fantasy VII* (Square 1997) is linear, but the player can choose sub-stories, which determines the sidekicks for the player's team that follow the player through the main story.

Instead of one linear story, we can have several linear storylines that are braided together (see Figure 4.4). At each plot point, the interactor can swap from one storyline to another and choose the one to follow next. Early interactive television shows based on the viewer switching the channels such as *Mörderische Entscheidung* and *D-dag* (see Section 1.3.4) are examples of braided storylines, where the viewer can choose between parallel and intertwining broadcasts they are watching. These choices can be made more explicit by a proper interface.

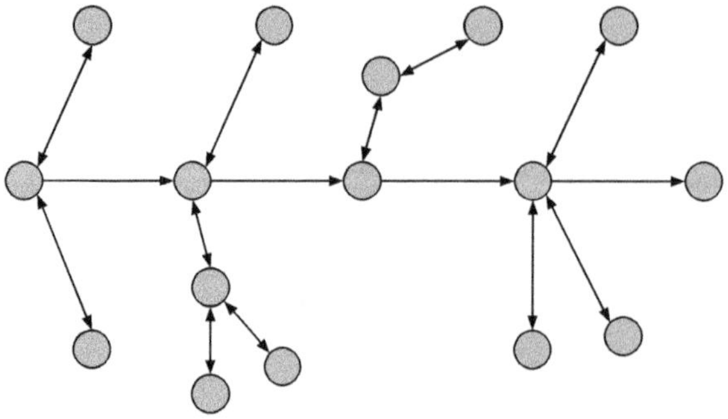

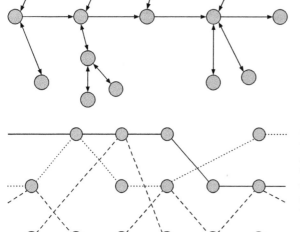

Figure 4.3 Linear narrative with side branches.

Figure 4.4 In braided storylines, the different lines represent the stories of different characters over time. When the stories connect at a grey circle, the interactor can choose a character they want to follow next.

Regardless of the subtype, linear narratives are, in the naïve sense we defined in Section 1.1.2, conventional stories. They are presented to the interactor as they are, as the designer (or, in this case, the author) has intended them to be. This means that it is easy to prepare them beforehand (e.g. as animated video clips) and generative content is not needed. Also, as the interaction and narrative are clearly cut separate from each other, the platform design does not affect much. There can be a drama manager suggesting a preferred storyline or quests or leading the interactor to make selections in the interactive gameplay so that the next cutscene makes sense – but, as well, this can be realized using the character-centric model by letting emergence handle the selections.

4.1.2 Branching Storyworlds

Ideally, each choice that the interactor faces would lead to a new and different situation, meaning that the interactor could try out all possible scenarios like in the film *Groundhog Day*. This would form a tree, where each choice opens new paths leading to a unique state and there is no possibility to return to an earlier state (see Figure 4.5). However, this kind of full branching leads to a combinatorial explosion, where a sheer number of narrative alternatives become infeasible to handle. In practice, we need pinch points for these kinds of branching narratives, where the divergent paths join to reduce the number of alternatives leading to a directed acyclic graph (DAG) illustrated in Figure 4.6. An early and non-digital example of this approach is the *Choose Your Own Adventure* (CYOA) book series, where the reader has to choose at the end of a chapter how the story continues and then skip to the indicated page to continue reading. A classic example of a game using branching narratives is *Indiana Jones and the Fate of Atlantis* (LucasArts 1992), where the story early on branches to three alternative paths – team, wits, or fists – and later on a pinch point brings all three paths back together.

Figure 4.5 A full branching narrative as a tree of degree 2.

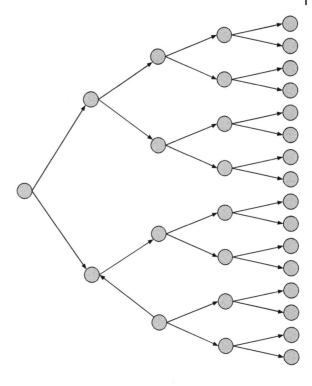

Figure 4.6 A branching narrative with pinch points forms a DAG.

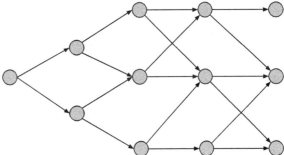

In branching narratives, a key question is the *critical path*, which connects the start to the end of a narrative. Maintaining the critical path is an important task for the designer so that the story progresses regardless of the interactor's choice. To enlarge the storyworld, the designer can add short linear narratives that are separate from the critical path and optional to the interactor. They can be individual quests or tasks that the interactor can take, which can expand the overall fabula of the game.

If we allow the narrative graph to have cycles, there is no longer a clear critical path, but the interactor might face the same situation again and again. There can still be one or several nodes that are exits, some leading to failure, others to success. The structure of the narrative can resemble a maze (see Figure 4.7), where the interactors have to find their way out, which is quite typical, for instance, in interactive fiction. It is even possible that there are no exits. In such a narrative network, the movements are neither completely free nor

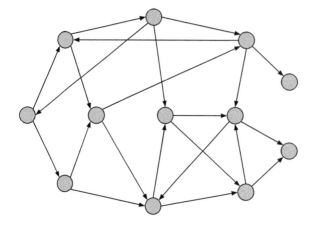

Figure 4.7 A narrative graph with cycles and two exits.

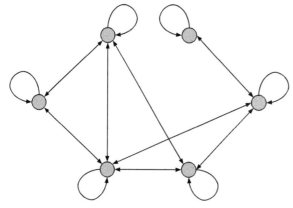

Figure 4.8 Action space connects semi-autonomous episodes together.

limited to a single course, but the interactors can traverse the storyworld perpetually (or until they are bored out of their wits).

If the storyworld is superimposed on a real-world location such as a museum or a theme park, the branching narrative often takes the form of an action space (see Figure 4.8). In such a case, interactivity happens on a macro level (e.g. walking from one exhibit to another) and dramatic plotting on a micro level (e.g. studying an individual exhibit). This model can also provide an epic structure for dividing the storyworld into tighter, semi-autonomous episodes. For example, the mid-game of *Star Wars: Knights of the Old Republic* (BioWare 2003) allows the player to choose freely the planet they want to visit (macro level) and face dramatic events on each planet (micro level).

Branching structures have been a popular solution to create interactive stories from CYOA books and interactive fiction to video games and interactive streaming television programmes. It offers obvious benefits:

- For writers with a background in linear storytelling, it is easier to adapt to write branching but linear narratives.
- Branching is intuitive to understand and possible to illustrate visually.
- There exist established tools such as *Twine* (Twine 2020) for managing branching narratives.

- The amount of needed assets (e.g. dialogue and animation) is straightforward to estimate.
- The implementation can be realized using existing systems as branching narratives basically require only a selection mechanism.

The simplicity, however, is misleading because the design – albeit being manageable when there are few states and transitions – gets quickly complicated. However, let us go through all of these points critically. The design looks simple when there are few states and transitions. Looking from this perspective, a branching narrative is a finite-state machine (FSM), which is a mechanism of a finite number of discrete states and transitions between them. The control flow of the FSM pauses in a state, and the outgoing transitions from this current state determine the next possible states. As an FSM, the design of a branching narrative is susceptible to the problems (Smed and Hakonen 2006, pp. 132–135; 2017, pp. 205–207):

- The representation is memoryless, and the succeeding actions are solely based on the current state.
- The states are discrete (i.e. there are no in-between states), which makes branching structures unsuitable for non-discrete selections.
- The more the branching structure tries to account for, the closer it gets to the combinatorial explosion.
- Normally, the required states are not known beforehand but are added and modified gradually during the design process, which can lead to 'total rewriting'.

Thinking in terms of the platform design, again we find that an author-centric approach can assist in leading the interactors to follow the preferred or critical path(s) and keeping them from sidestepping to possible dead ends or weakly covered areas. The more robust the narrative structure is for allowing different walks, the more emergent (i.e. character-centric) the platform can be.

4.1.3 Open Storyworlds

Open storyworlds present the biggest challenge to the designer. Here, there is no imposed sequence for the events, but each interactor can take their unique path. Although the ideal case would be a totally open world where interactors could do whatever they want, choose whatever they like and engage with whomever they prefer, in practice the designer has to set up structures to guide the interactors. This is critical especially in the onboarding phase (see Section 5.1.1), where the interactors are still learning about the storyworld and their role in it.

Unlike in linear and branching narratives, here the platform design has a major impact. A drama manager could be used to limit and guide the interactor. These kinds of sandbox games can include preconditions for the narrative elements, which provide some structure. On the other hand, a hybrid or character-centric approach has best possibilities to work here and make the storyworld more life-like.

One possibility to create a structure into the openness is to scatter the story throughout the levels (i.e. each level has its own set of open stories). A gatekeeper event then allows the interactor to proceed to a new level or expand the storyworld. For example, in *God of War* (SIE Santa Monica Studio 2018), the players arrive over and over again in new areas such as

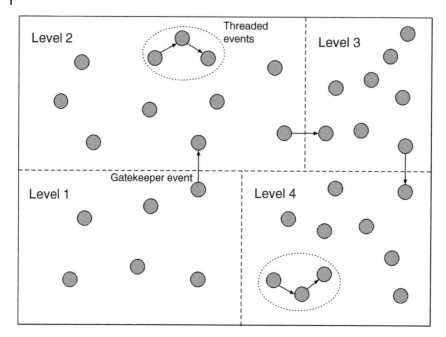

Figure 4.9 An open storyworld with levels and threads. A gatekeeper event opens access to the next level and the associated events in the storyworld.

the Lake of Nine, where they may explore around and try out the different landing areas in an order of their own choosing. Some areas are easier and provide the players with experience points making it possible to complete the harder ones and giving suggestive order for unfolding the story. Also, some story elements can be threaded so that they form short linear sequences (see Figure 4.9), which are also present in *God of War*. These (possibly optional) threads can include missions, quests, jobs, or rescues taken inside a larger context.

Another possibility is to use an epistemological approach, where elements of the narrative are scattered throughout the storyworld and the interactor discovers them. These elements can form a hidden story that gets discovered such as in *Myst* (Cyan Worlds 1993). This approach resembles the epistemic form discussed in Section 2.1.1. Here, we have a spatial path of interactors' investigation in an open storyworld and a temporal sequence of events to be elucidated (see Figure 4.10). For example, the game *Her Story* (Barlow 2016) has a complete but deconstructed underlying story, which can be experienced in any order by entering keywords to the game's internal search engine. However, the player is most likely to search terms related to events that happened recently, hence creating a loose structure into the open narrative.

Instead of a historical story connected to the storyworld event, we could have a seemingly open world (without a clearly imposed story) that is still connected to a larger underlying narrative progressing almost without the influence from the interactor. The ill-fated game *Terminus* (Vicarious Visions 2000) is an example of this. In its persistent real-time storyworld, the global situation changes prescriptively, and these changes affect the player's local world similarly to how global events (pandemics, wars, natural catastrophes, or political decisions) affect an individual's life in the real world. Whether the player's decisions would

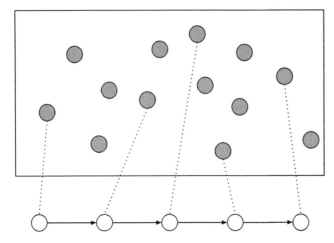

Figure 4.10 In a hidden story, some events in the open world are connected to a temporal sequence of the events happened in the past.

have affected the events and narrative in *Terminus* is an unanswered question, because the game failed to get traction and was discontinued. One could imagine this happening – although it is doubtful that it was the original intention of its designers. However, we could take this idea forward to its logical conclusion, where the individual also can make a difference. Imagine, for instance, if Frodo would have been stuck in this kind of a storyworld: no matter what he does, the story railroads somewhere in the background, out of his reach. Hence, the challenge here is the feedback from the individuals to the big story and – more importantly – changing that story. It is important not only for the sake of agency but also for the progression. Nobody wants to feel like being dragged on by the world.

4.2   Design Process and Tools

Creating a storyworld means delivering content for somebody else's experience, which means that the designer defines actions (which the interactor can choose from), states, and events (Spierling 2009; Spierling and Szilas 2009). In a larger context (e.g. in a video game), the key design goal is the overall importance of the story (e.g. theme) and how it acts as a part of the whole experience (Adams 2013, pp. 140–168). Naturally, credibility (i.e. believability) and coherence (e.g. making sure that we are not violating storyworld, character, nor plot) are important for the degree of well-formedness of the generated story. Other challenges for the design process include the following (Aylett et al. 2011; Spierling 2009; Spierling and Szilas 2009):

- Due to the medium's immaturity, the tools often show the underlying software solutions and the line between the storyworld and the platform can be blurry. For example, the content might depend on the run-time system architecture (see Section 3.1).
- As the amount of required content increases, the more complex the storyworld gets. This implies that designing might not be a single person's task but should support multiple

designers. Some of them can be responsible for the visual content, others for creating the audio world (e.g. music, sound effects, voice-overs), or for simple text (e.g. in-game letters or emails between characters, background lore), or for putting the disparate pieces of authored texts together into cutscenes and in-game cinematics. The design is often a collective effort.

- Usability requires that the story-related structures are presented at a suitable abstraction level for the designer. Narrowly formatted and constrained mechanisms limit the designer's possibilities to reduce human affairs into logical models. On the other hand, to support the designer to use the potential of a story engine requires inspiring examples and prototypes as a study material.

In the following, we look at the design process first from the perspective of making a concept for the storyworld. Then, we look at the iterative process that the designer has to go through. Finally, we consider ways of evaluating the 'quality' of the designed storyworld.

4.2.1 Concepting the Storyworld

The conception of a storyworld resembles how, for example, self-driving cars are being realized today. The traditional view was that the computer program should be designed to act as a substitute for the driver (i.e. an emulation of the human process), whereas the modern view – which actually allows the driverless cars we see today – does not focus on the human-driver but on what is the *functionality* required to accomplish the task and how to *realize* it procedurally. Hence, we can model the whole roadwork (an 'inhuman' task) and the routing through the model while observing the differences between this model and the real world. Storyworld design requires a similar kind of mind-switch: one should not think of oneself as the author telling a story because the interactors will make their own paths. Rather the designer should model the whole range of possible stories – the storyworld.

One way to imagine the storyworld as a landscape of possible stories (Louchart et al. 2008) is illustrated in Figure 4.11. Here, one can think of the height of the landscape as an own axis 'dramatic tension' over the possible states where the interactor can be. Interactors' decisions move them to another neighbouring state. Moving up a mountain in this landscape means that the dramatic tension increases, until it has reached its dramatic necessity at the peak on the top (cf. Laurel's flying wedge in Figure 2.12, p. 54, or Freytag's dramatic arc in Figure 2.3, p. 32). The valleys are the places that offer potential mountains for the interactor to climb.

One could extend this model by discretizing it and thinking of the states as atomic narrative elements. For argument's sake, let us call these narrative elements 'naxels' as they resemble the idea of pixels (picture elements) on screen or voxels (volume element) in 3D modelling. The question now is about setting the resolution for the naxels: a small resolution can be enough within a certain application. For example, in *Façade*, the smallest atomic element – or naxel – is a beat, a pair of action–reaction.

The neighbourhood of a naxel can be defined using pre-condition and post-condition, or other models (such as the actantial model; see Section 2.1.3). These bind the naxels together to form a 'landscape' for the storyworld (see Figure 4.12).

Naturally, this should be regarded as a mental image because in reality it might not be possible to limit the possibilities neatly into a well-defined environment. But it conveys the idea

Dramatic
tension

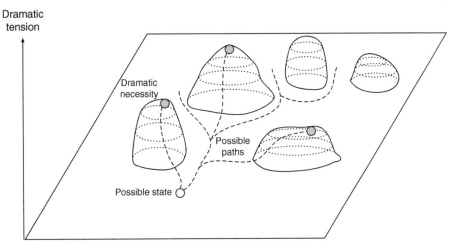

Figure 4.11 In a landscape of possible stories, the mountains represent heightened dramatic tension with a dramatic necessity on the top. The valley offers potential mountains where the selected path can lead the interactor.

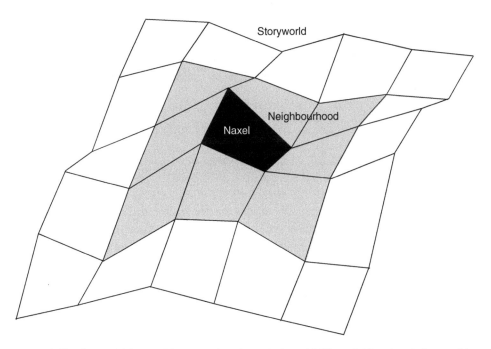

Figure 4.12 Storyworld comprising narrative elements (naxels). The neighbourhood of a naxel is a set of naxels where the story can move based on the interactor's choice.

of the mind-switch we talked about earlier: the designer cannot think of a single path – a narrative – through the storyworld but the whole landscape and all the possible walks. At first sight, this seems like an impossible task, and it is, but just like with self-driving cars, we could have the computer to do the inhuman task of evaluating the landscape and routes. This would be a requirement for the platform intended to the designer.

The design process is about modelling a dramatic abstraction of reality (Louchart et al. 2008). This means that we have to model how the characters behave (which is different from how people behave in reality). To achieve this, the designer has to reduce complexity without making too many generalizations. One way to do this is to set clear boundaries to the storyworld, thus keeping it small and manageable (e.g. *Façade* has very clear and well-defined boundaries). The biggest challenge is, however, not to think too much in terms of the plot. Louchart et al. (2008) list three concerns for the design of the storyworld:

- The existing boundaries of the storyworld have to be justified. This means spatial boundaries (or physical limits), contextual boundaries (e.g. a theme like bullying in *FearNot!*), and interactional boundaries (i.e. what the interactor can do).
- The design should offer a critical mass for emergence. This can be boiled down to the idea of *density*, which means how the designed content serves to create different paths (i.e. how well the contents cover the storyworld). It is important to notice that any added content creates new possibilities, which leads to wider boundaries and reduced density. Within the boundaries, the content should cover the storyworld.
- The designer should be aware of possible *dead ends*, where the density is much too low (i.e. there is a lack of content). Consequently, storyworld design is a continuing process involving finding dead ends and resolving them by adding new content.

Concepting the storyworld includes also other special concerns, which we address next.

4.2.1.1 Character Design

As we have established, at the core of the design process lies the narrative paradox because the designer cannot expect the interactor to make the right decision at the right moment or in the right place. For this reason, the designer's role is also to write interesting characters and rely on their ability to interact with one another (the interactor can be considered to be an autonomous actor as well, which is why the designer must be attentive to the interactor's inner state). This holds whether the platform uses an author-centric or character-centric approach.

Here, the designer has to decide the degree of specificity (unspecified, partially, richly, interactor-specified) and the relationship to the interactor (enacted, tool, guided) (Adams 2013, pp. 167–168). If the interactor's character is unspecified, the interactor does not see or hear it but is the character. A partially specified character is defined to a limited extent (e.g. it lacks personality). A richly specified character is fully defined by an appearance, personality, and emotional life. Apart from these designer-specified characters, the interactor can be allowed to build and specify their own character themself. In addition to specifying the interactor's character, the designer has to define its relationship to the interactor. The character can be a role the interactor enacts, it can be a tool to influence the storyworld, or it can be autonomous but guided indirectly by the interactor.

Table 4.1 Dilemmas and their pay-offs.

Dilemma	Pay-off to self	Pay-off to friend	Pay-off to foe
Betrayal	Best	Worst	Worst
Sacrifice	Worst	Best	—
Greater good	Best	—	Best
Take down	Worst	—	Worst
Favour	None	Best	Worst

Source: Barber and Kudenko 2007.

Murray (2011) lists principles of character design to maximize the meaningful variation of the value system (e.g. chastity in a love story or courage in a war epic). Most importantly, the number of main characters should be limited, and they should have clear relationships with each other within the dramatic situation. The individual character definitions should be along the spectrum based on the value system central to the story. In this regard, the designer should pay attention to the parallel characters that are needed to draw clear contrasts (e.g. rivals, friends, enemies). If the characters act as foils for one another, their similarities as well as their differences must be emphasized throughout the story.

4.2.1.2 Plot Composition

When devising the plot, the designer has to think about the form of the story (e.g. Aristotelian drama or soap opera), its type (e.g. branching or open), the beginning(s), the ending(s), and the theme. The plot advancement mechanism can be based on the passage of time, avatar movement, overcoming challenges, or interactor choices and other interactions (Adams 2013, pp. 166–167).

Barber and Kudenko (2007) describe how to create (possibly infinitely) long stories using dilemmas (or clichés in a soap opera) as decision points. Here, we need a knowledge base containing storyworld (i.e. characters and locations), story actions, and dilemmas. The dilemmas are listed in Table 4.1 including their pay-offs to the character itself and the character's friend and foe.

Plot design can also be approached by describing event relations in a plan-based plot composition (Ciarlini et al. 2010; Karlsson and Furtado 2014). The basis is the four relationships between narrative events (i.e. fourfold perspectives of plot composition):

- *Syntagmatic*: The occurrence of the first event leaves the world in a state where the second event is coherent (i.e. weak form of causality). The corresponding trope is *metonymy*, which is a substitute for reduction, where we are substituting effects for a cause.
- *Paradigmatic*: There are alternative ways to accomplish a similar action. The corresponding trope is *metaphor*, which is a substitute for perspective, where C_1 and C_2 are similar or analogous events and replace a more general event C.
- *Antithetic*: An unexpected turn (e.g. manipulation by an outside agency) leads to the beliefs of one or more characters about actual facts having changed. The corresponding trope is *irony*, which is a substitute by dissimilarity of disjunction (i.e. under- and overstatement) reflecting the opposite.

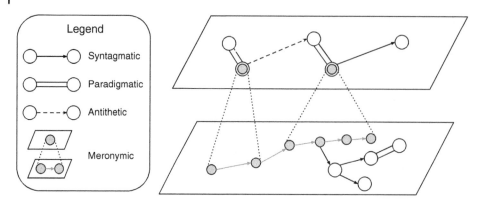

Figure 4.13 Relationships between narrative events. Source: Adapted from Karlsson and Furtado 2014.

- *Meronymic*: Lower-level events are decomposed. The corresponding trope is *synecdoche*, which is a substitute for representation, where event C_1 denotes event C_2, if C_1 is a part of C_2.

Figure 4.13 illustrates how these relationships can be used when forming the overall structure of an interactive plot. Paradigmatic moves create a coherent sequence of events, whereas others allow variation in the plot. Syntagmatic and antithetic moves present (possibly unexpected) alternative choices. Meronymic moves go down to details by summarizing detailed event sequences and decomposing events into finer-grain actions.

4.2.1.3 Adapting Material from Other Media

Adaptation for interactive stories means creating a translation between the media. There are often pragmatic reasons for doing this such as using a known intellectual property as a basis for another (interactive) story. Adaptation can take different forms (Spierling and Hoffmann 2010):

- *Scissors adaptation*: Direct cut-and-paste (e.g. staging a play by Shakespeare).
- *Distilled adaptation*: The adapted version uses only a part of the original material (e.g. Peter Jackson's *Lord of the Rings* movie trilogy is a distilled adaptation of J.R.R. Tolkien's book trilogy).
- *Expanded adaptation*: The adapted version adds material not present in the original work (e.g. Peter Jackson's *The Hobbit* movie trilogy incorporates events also from other works by J.R.R. Tolkien).
- *Straight adaptation*: One-to-one conversion (e.g. Robert Rodriguez' and Frank Miller's movie *Sin City* is a one-to-one adaptation of Frank Miller's graphic novel).
- *Wild adaptation*: Converting beyond apparent resilience (e.g. Francis Coppola's movie *Apocalypse Now* is a wild adaptation of Joseph Conrad's novel *The Heart of Darkness*).

In interactive storytelling, the typical forms are expanded and wild. This means formalizing the story into an abstract form, which is then followed by making a creative interpretation and adaptation.

Adaptation is also needed when integrating interactivity into an existing narrative. For realizing this, Jenkins (2004) presents four models:

- *Evocative*: Encountering references to prior stories in other media (e.g. a theme park or a game based on the *Star Wars* expanded universe)
- *Enacted*: Acting out a specific role in an existing narrative universe (e.g. taking the role of Luke Skywalker in the *Star Wars* arcade game)
- *Embedded*: Spatially distributed, narrative-infused encounters (e.g. *Myst*)
- *Emergent*: Constructing personal stories from encountered events (e.g. *Eve Online*)

As the form of interactive stories is still young, we have not seen much adaptation apart from video game franchises. Clearly, there is still much to research and experiment in this field.

4.2.1.4 Transmedia Design

Transmedia storytelling uses different media as platforms for telling a story. Pratten (2011) divides the approaches to transmedia storytelling into franchise transmedia and portmanteau transmedia. *Franchise transmedia* is the classical approach, where different stories of the same storyworld spread across different media platforms. For example, the *Star Wars*, *Transformers* and *Masters of the Universe* universes extend to movies, comics, toys, animations, TV series, and games to mention a few. Each of these instances is, however, its own stories that take place in the larger storyworld. *Portmanteau transmedia* instead expands one single story across different media platforms. Alternate reality games (ARGs) are a good example of this kind of transmedia, where the scenes take place on various platforms, from the Internet to the real world.

The transmedia experience relies on four dimensions (see Figure 4.14). Story emphasizes the importance of narrative. Real-world reflects the extent to which the story-experience pervades real locations and times as well as real people and events. Participation is about the ability of the audience to chance or contribute the story-experience (i.e. agency). Gaming shows that the audience has a goal which they can approach through challenges (e.g. puzzles) and game mechanics (e.g. trophies, levels, or leaderboards).

In transmedia design, the designer has to think much more about the interactor's experience. It is not enough just to recognize who the interactors are, but what technology they

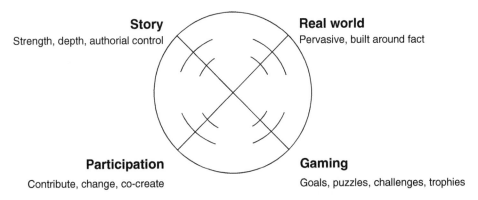

Figure 4.14 Transmedia radar diagram. Source: Pratten 2011, p. 52.

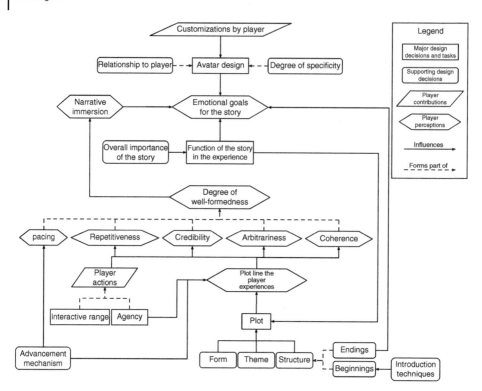

Figure 4.15 Model for defining an interactive storytelling experience. Source: Based on Adams 2013, p. 154.

have available and how much time they have. Pacing also plays a bigger role when the story can use different platforms (e.g. not to put too much content at the same time through many channels). Ultimately, the designer has to be able to justify what is the benefit of using different platforms.

4.2.1.5 Adams' Template for Requirements Specifications

Adams (2013, pp. 148–168) presents a template to write requirements and specifications for interactive storytelling (see Figure 4.15). Although it is not intended for the actual design process, it aims at assisting the designers in defining the type of experience they want to have. The key design goals for the story's role in the experience are

- emotional goals for the story;
- function of the story in the experience;
- degree of well-formedness;
- overall importance of the story; and
- avatar design.

The other considerations include defining the interactor actions, the interactive range, and agency as well outlining the plot and the plot line that the player experiences.

4.2.2 Iterative Design Process

The designer's creative process is highly iterative and ideally with rapid feedback. In this respect, it resembles more software programming compared to conventional story author-ing. It includes 'debugging', which means altering and adapting the story content to match the designer's intent as well as co-creation where the designer embraces the possible emerg-ing stories and lets them change their original design intent (Swartjes and Theune 2009). We can even say that it is a process of dissociated authoring, where the designer cannot associate all possible outcomes (Suttie et al. 2013).

The design has static and dynamic parts (Swartjes and Theune 2009): in content design, the designer chooses which instances of story elements are in the domain and which actions and goals may occur. In process design, the designer focuses on how the elements con-nect causally and when the elements occur. Another way to label these parts is static and dynamic design.

Iterative design process means constantly choosing between debugging and co-creation as illustrated in Figure 4.16 (Swartjes and Theune 2009). In the first stage, the designer comes up with ideas on how to extend the storyworld. This can be a result of pure inspi-ration but, more often than not, a reaction to the flaws found earlier. In the second stage, the ideas are turned into new content and processes, which are added to the storyworld. Also, it is important to constrain the domain as this new content could open new possibil-ities that are not yet handled. For instance, adding a new character might require not only defining its relationships to all the other characters but also redefining the relationship of some of already existing characters. In the third stage, the changes are simulated (e.g. by running them through a designer-specific platform) to feel out the storyworld and to detect any surprising behaviour. After this, the designer returns back to the first stage.

Looking at the design process more broadly, we can divide it into three stages as illustrated in Figure 4.17 (Suttie et al. 2013). In the concepting (or pre-design) phase, the designer sets up the overall parameters of the storyworld (e.g. theme and boundaries). The second phase is the actual design phase, where the designer iteratively adds elements to the storyworld and gets quick simulated feedback on their effect. Within this iteration, the designer can engage in another iteration by adding a character, action, or goal into the storyworld, which is also validated promptly. The feedback can have different types such as system, structural (e.g. charts), experiential (from the interactors). Having multiple simulation runs with a

Figure 4.16 Iterative design process. Source: Modified from Swartjes and Theune 2009.

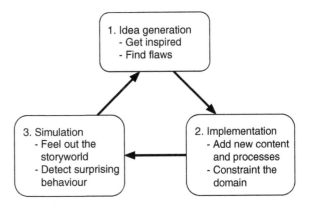

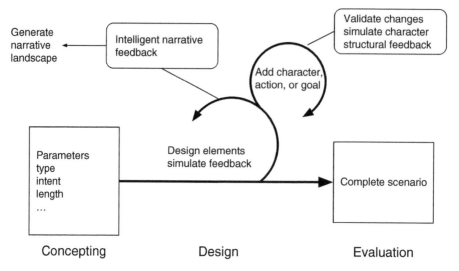

Figure 4.17 Broader view to the design process. Source: Modified from Suttie et al. 2013.

virtual interactor, the designer is provided with feedback so that they can steer towards the pre-design goals. Finally, the third stage handles the evaluation of a complete scenario.

Modern business models and digital distribution platforms such as Steam have made the iterative design process more persistent. For example, *RimWorld* (Ludeon Studios 2018) is still constantly being developed at the time of writing with significant updates coming still after the game having originally been made available in 2018. For more details on the user interface that this kind of design process requires, see Section 3.1.3.

4.2.3 Evaluating Interactive Stories

Interactive stories can be evaluated by using post-experience questionnaires, in-game questionnaires, interviews (free or semi-structured), or computer traces (logs) extracted from playing sessions (Szilas and Ilea 2014). For example, Kyrki (2015) and Kyrki et al. (2017) discuss how to measure morality, loyalty, and conflict in an interactive story system.

In the case of a designer-specific platform, computer-aided evaluation becomes crucial. As we argued earlier in this chapter, the landscape of the storyworld is too vast for the human designer to evaluate – less so when the iterative design process would require to happen repeatedly after each small addition, deletion, or change. Naturally, we could simulate the events (using a computer-controlled proxy for the human interactor) and measure the outcome. This would, however, be too computationally intensive as each simulated run would take too long and reduce the usability of the platform. Alternatively, we could use different metrics to estimate the effect.

Ware et al. (2012) present how this could be realized using conflict dimensions, which can be discrete, directly observable values such as participants, subject, and duration (see Table 4.2), or continuous, qualitative values such as balance, directness, intensity, and resolution.

Table 4.2 Quantitative metrics for narrative conflict (n.b. $E - f_1 - f_2 \neq \emptyset$ and *utility*$(c, \emptyset)$ indicates c's utility before a conflict).

c_1, c_2	Characters
f_1, f_2	Sequence of actions intended to be carried out by a character
E	Set of actions which actually occur in the story
$\pi(f)$	How likely a sequence of actions f is to succeed
utility(c, f)	How satisfied c is with the state of the world after f

Balance is the relative likelihood of each side in the conflict to succeed (regardless of the actual outcome) within the range $[0, 1]$:

$$c_1 = \frac{\pi(f_1)}{\pi(f_1) + \pi(f_2)}$$

Directness means how close (familial, emotional, interpersonal) characters are to one another (regardless of the actual outcome) within the range $[0, 1]$:

$$directness(c_1) = \sum_{i=1}^{n} \frac{closeness_i(c_1, c_2)}{n}$$

Intensity means the difference between how high the character's utility is if it prevails and how low it will be if it fails (failing means that the other character prevails; favours high risk in high reward situations):

$$intensity(c_1) = |utility(c_1, f_1) - utility(c_1, f_2)|$$

Resolution is the change in utility that character experiences after the conflict ends within the range $[-1, 1]$:

$$resolution(c_1) = utility(c_1, E) - utility(c_1, \emptyset)$$

Szilas and Ilea (2014) present the following metrics for evaluating an interactive story:

- *Total length of a session*: Discrete (number of actions), continuous (time).
- *Diversity*: Intra-diversity (i.e. within one session), global diversity.
- *Renewal rate*: The ratio between intra- and global diversities.
- *Choice range*: How much choice the user has?
- *Degree of freedom*: Discrete choice frequency, real-time choice frequency.
- *Variability*: Are new choices being provided to the user?

These require a certain level of granularity, a discrete framework. Furthermore, this does not preclude parallelism and overlapping between actions. Regarding the choice range, a large range is desired but not always necessary. If the discrete choice frequency is 0, it means no player action, whereas 1 means no system action. The real-time choice frequency is 1 Hz (i.e. 1 action per second).

Clearly, these examples are limited and partly theoretical. That still does not reduce their value in realizing a designer-specific platform. The more we can know about the effects that a change in design can cause in the storyworld – the contours of its landscape and possible walks through it – the better we can serve the content creation and, ultimately, the interactor who then has to face that world.

4.3 Relationship with the Interactor

In this section, we present two considerations for the designer of interactive storyworlds. First, we discuss focalization (or finding how the designer and interactor can interact in a story). Second, we look at the message that the designer wants to convey to the interactor.

4.3.1 Focalization

Focalization is a term from literary narratological studies, famously coined by Genette (1980, p. 189) to describe what is otherwise often called the 'point of view'. Focalization describes the relationship between the narrator of the text and the characters in the text. There are three possible relations: narrator > character, where the writer knows more than the character; narrator = character where the narrator knows as much as the character (or *is* the character); and narrator < character where the narrator is unaware of the character's internal world, and can only describe the character's actions and words from the outside. Genette calls these modes, respectively, 'zero', 'internal', and 'external' (Genette 1980, p. 189–190).

Focalization can be read as a complement to Section 3.2 about author-centric, character-centric, or hybrid narrative approaches; once the designers have decided on their approach on a large scale, they can consider how exactly the narration will be focalized.

The most common and the most recognizable type of focalization available to the designer is external, as it is more or less identical to films. In an externally focused game, we follow (often control) a (or several) character(s) as it traverses the world, but we are not privy to its internal world any more than one would be in a third-person narrative ('Kratos looked angry and hit the giant in the face') or a movie. Keep in mind that the (game-design specific) lingo of 'first person' or 'third person' has nothing to do with focalization: we are, for example, not privy to the internal world of Gordon Freeman in *Half-Life* (Valve 1998) despite the fact we inhabit and control his body, but he is nonetheless a named character in the game with a relationship to other characters, making it an externally focalized first-person game. Most modern third- or first-person action titles tell externally focalized stories in much the same way a movie would, except the interactor can sometimes decide what order to experience the story in or choose which branch of it to explore.

External focalization is the most common choice in author-centric approaches to narration, where the author-designer has a story in mind and the interactor experiences it together with the characters they control.

Zero focalization (i.e. narrator > character) can be applied to most simulation games, from *The Sims* (Maxis 2000) to *RimWorld* (Ludeon Studios 2018). In these, the designer generally has omniscient knowledge of the characters' emotional states, needs, and motivations (if any) and sometimes even direct control over the characters. Unlike externally focalized games, games of this type typically do not have a main character, nor does the narrator necessarily exist within the game world (e.g. who is it that gives orders to you colonists in *RimWorld*?).

Zero focalization is often used in character-centric or hybrid approaches to narrative, as the focus is instead on characters and their various interrelationships, or on emergent narratives (e.g. in strategy or simulation games) rather than authored narratives.

Internal focalization in games refers to situations where the narrator is the interactor. For single-player games, it is the most 'naïve' type of focalization, used whenever there is no need for a separate character between the human being playing the game and the game world itself. Casual puzzle games, racing games, and party games are all good examples of internal focalization (there is no 'character' playing chess or driving the car).

It might be noted that multiplayer games muddle this definition a bit, as one might confidently argue that massive multiplayer online RPGs such as *World of Warcraft* (Blizzard Entertainment 2004) allow for true internal focalization, as the interactor can write their own 'first-person' narrative and no-one else can claim to know better what the character thinks or feels about the world around them. However, that discussion lies outside the scope of this book.

4.3.2 Story as Message

Unlike most forms of art, games use narrative for a variety of reasons aside from the desire to tell a story. What we have discussed throughout this book as 'story' might simply be used as a backdrop for visuals, as a useful shorthand, as a form of tutorial, or even accidentally. This mirrors the way we use our everyday language to communicate. Jakobson (1960) describes six different functions of communication, which describe the reasons and intention of why we communicate, each with a focus on a different part of the addresser–message–addressee scheme (see Figure 4.18).

With the risk of sounding reductive, all communication – including narrative in all its forms – consists of an *addresser* sending a *message* to an *addressee*. That message exists in a specific *context*, it will need to be expressed in a *code* (i.e. a language) that is intelligible to the receiver, and there needs to be a point of *contact* through which the message can be transmitted (Jakobson 1960, p. 353). It might be noted that this schema is intended for verbal communication, but interactive games function in a very similar manner.

The *functions* (shown in parenthesis in Figure 4.18) in turn are what the purpose of the utterance actually is (i.e. its function), and each function tends to skew towards one of the possible parts. For example, the emotive function (Jakobson 1960, p. 354), which skews towards the addresser, refers to communication for (on the behalf of the sender) expressing

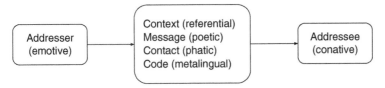

Figure 4.18 Addresser–message–addressee scheme with emotive, conative, referential, poetic, phatic, and multilingual functions. Source: Jakobson 1960.

some particular emotion, such as anger or interest, and can be non-verbal or interjection (e.g. 'Tut tut!' to express disappointment) – but, of course, the emotive function will also colour the other possible functions of a message.

A companion asking you what is taking so long, your player character grunting in pain after taking damage, or even an angry red popup and a dissonant sound playing when you fail a quest are all examples of emotive communication.

The conative function (Jakobson 1960, p. 355) is in many ways the most obvious function, especially in games. Its focus is on the receiver, the addressee, and most often comes in the form of an imperative. Communication that focuses on the conative is instructional and attempts to somehow influence the addressee. The most obvious example in games is the tutorial – telling the interactor to jump, or to press E to talk, or generally to engage with the game's systems.

The referential function (Jakobson 1960, p. 355) is connected to context, for example, who the message is about or the actual location the communication takes place in; in games, you should pay attention to the context of the message: as graffiti on a wall, on a piece of paper found tucked away in a drawer, through incidental, overheard conversation between NPCs, and so on.

Finally, there are phatic and metalingual functions: the phatic function, in verbal communication, is used to make sure the channel of communication is open. For games, messages that emphasize the phatic are often informational, such as a prompt to 'click to continue', the appearance of an exclamation mark above an NPC to show you they have new content to share, or maybe an idle animation if you stand still long enough.

The metalingual (or glossing) function (Jakobson 1960, p. 356) is used to discuss the code (i.e. the language) itself, typically to make sure both parties are able to communicate. Games are replete with code-related messages, from button prompts to outright tutorials teaching the interactor the verbs of the game.

And then there is, of course, the final function of language: the poetic function (Jakobson 1960, p. 356), which is the communication focused on the message itself. When asked about a game's 'story', this is generally the function used to express it: for example, in cutscenes, conversations about the lore, events and characters that exist specifically to convey the message the authors intended.

Sometimes, however, a game is said to 'have no story', with which it means the number of messages with an emphasis on the poetic function throughout the game is low or non-existent. But that does not mean the game does not *communicate*: all games do; it may simply be that this communication focuses on the other functions of communication. For example, in the original *Angry Birds* (Rovio Entertainment 2009) – before the animations, the movies, the expansions, the sequels – the only 'poetic' message the game offered to the interactor was the original motivation for the birds being angry, namely, the theft of their eggs by the pigs. But the game still communicates things such as glass being brittle, stone being hard, TNT exploding when hit, the pigs being the antagonists, the birds being angry (and happy to be flung around with a giant slingshot), success, and failure – all through the various functions of language.

4.4 Summary

The role of the designers is essential. Although we demoted them from the role of an author already in Chapter 1, the storyworld is very much of their creation and they are inviting the interactors to experience it. The first task, consequently, is to decide the type of the storyworld. Sometimes, the selection is already narrowed down by the outside set-up: if the interactive story is supposed to overlay an existing real-world location such as an expo, we might have to confine in the action space model, whereas if we can design an avant-garde video game from the ground up, we could opt freely for a more exotic model.

The designer has three broad approaches – linear narratives, branching narratives, and open narratives – to choose from and can then refine it to fit in with the storyworld. Once these fundamental decisions have been settled, the actual design process commences. Usually, this is an iterative process (resembling programming) where new things are introduced to the storyworld and then tested to see how well they fit in and how they will change the overall behaviour. Based on the feedback, which can be objective metric data or subjective evaluation, the design is altered, tweaked, or abandoned. This iterative process continues then throughout the development. Ideally, it would allow even multiple designers to take part, which might be essential in creating a larger and persistent storyworld.

The iterative design process requires suitable software tools. Having a flexible and easy-to-use platform could be the key to bring the field forward because then the design would be truly separate from the platform development. Once the powers of the designer's imagination are unleashed from these technical considerations, we could see real development of an art form. We addressed some of these issues that are interesting to the designer once we get beyond the mundane issues of tools and processes. Interactive storytelling would allow us to have a new language of conveying ideas, sharing experiences, or cohabiting in fictitious worlds. There is much to be said about this, many things that are still waiting to be discovered, dead ends and avenues still uncharted. Herein lies the designer's adventure.

Exercises

4.1 Think of a situation where you have been creative (e.g. inventing fiction, proposing a theory, or solving a problem). Do not focus on the process of realizing (e.g. writing) but the *mental state* you were in. An individual thought or idea in this state can sparkle up many new ones to choose from. When you choose one of them, new ones emerge, or the previous ones remain (maybe in an enhanced form). How do you come up with these alternatives (i.e. the 'neighbourhood' of a thought)? You might find that these thoughts are associated with the current one and these associations form the neighbourhood. You found these associations using pattern matching as we humans are basically pattern matching machines – we see patterns even when there is none.

Computers are also quite good in pattern matching, but something is missing from their associations to be creative. We seem to be able to have a dynamic pattern matching skill as we can even find patterns in our pattern matching and we can freely adapt to any type of *pattern matching* (not just any of *pattern*).

What is missing from the computer's skills? How come it is difficult for the computer to be creative?

4.2 Aarseth (1997, pp. 134–136) introduces the following typology of authors in the machine–human continuum (i.e. the human–machine collaboration):
  • *Preprocessing*: The text-producing machine is programmed, configured, and loaded beforehand by a human.
  • *Co-processing*: The machine and a human produce the text in tandem.
  • *Postprocessing*: The machine produces texts and a human selects some of them and excludes others.
  Come up with examples for each of these types.

4.3 David Cage, the founder of Quantic Dreams, has been a vocal critic of linear story structures commonly used in video games. Cage (2009) has even made the comparison that apart from video games the only form of entertainment to employ this storytelling structure is porn movies. Do you find his assessment fair?

4.4 Taking the movie *Groundhog Day* as a starting point, try to draw a (full) branching narrative (see Figure 4.5) of its main events. How well it would fill out, or could you imagine choices that are not covered in your diagram? (*Hint*: If this task gets too exhausting, you are free to stop it anytime.)

4.5 Take a story (e.g. a book, film, or television series) and separate a linear story of 5–7 nodes. Think possible offshoots for the story. Draw first a graph with the line of progression of the original story. For example, for Little Red Riding Hood, the graph could look like Figure 4.19.

Figure 4.19   A graph of the progression of Little Red Riding Hood.

Next, try to diversify the graph (see Figure 4.20). Try first to add to each episode an alternative (do not worry yet where it might lead). Go through each new episode. Does it
  • connect to existing episode,
  • end, or
  • require a new alternative?
Continue as long as you have unchecked episodes or – more likely – when you run out of time, interest, or free space.
What did you observe?

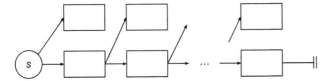

Figure 4.20 A graph where each episode has an alternative.

4.6 Why branching narratives are compatible with finite-state machines?

4.7 Think of a theme park you have visited. Draw a graph plotting its action space (see Figure 4.8). Does the graph look happenstance or does it show a thought behind the design? What kind of narratives it offers on the macro and micro levels?

4.8 Take an existing space (e.g. home, school, library, or museum) as a starting point and create a plan for action space. Think about the possible episodes to each location and their relation to a bigger story.

4.9 Why is it easier to estimate the workload and required assets in branching narratives?

4.10 Metalepsis means a transgression of the boundaries between narrative levels, of which a common example of metalepsis in narrative occurs when a narrator intrudes upon another world being narrated. Ryan (2006, pp. 204–207) illustrates metalepsis as a stack (see Figure 4.21). The border between the levels can be
- illocutionary where the speaker changes but the world remains the same, or
- ontological where there is a change of narrative voice and a change of the world (e.g. telling a story within the story such as in *The Arabian Nights*).

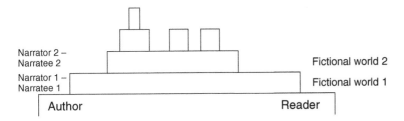

Figure 4.21 Metalepsis as a stack.

In metalepsis, the narrative challenges the structure of the stack and opens possibilities for transgressions such as the author talking about the characters or entangling the ontological levels.

Could metalepsis be used in interactive storytelling? Design a small storyworld where metalepsis would be a part of the story generation. (*Hint*: You might want to take a movie such as David Lynch's *Mulholland Drive* or Marx Brothers' *Duck Soup* as a starting point. More adventurous could base their design on Laurence Sterne's novel *The Life and Opinions of Tristram Shandy, Gentleman.*)

4.11 Epistemic open world is a quite popular narrative design in video games. Why is it so? What attracts designers to use it?

4.12 Taking the idea of an idealized discrete storyworld, try to sketch a small board (e.g. 5×5) of naxels. You can limit the choices for each naxel to four (i.e. four-connect neighbourhood). Next, add the third dimension, dramatic tension.

4.13 The storyworld has three types of boundaries: physical, thematic, and interactional. Take the story of Little Red Riding Hood (or any other fairy tale) and write down the terms of each of these three boundaries that the story imposes. If you would relax one of them, what would happen? Think of a possible story in this relaxed world.

4.14 Analyse a set of television series of the same genre (e.g. sitcoms). What is the typical number of main characters? Why? How would that suit interactive storytelling (do not forget to include the human interactor)?

4.15 Take a short story and think of a distilled, an expanded, and a wild adaptation for it.

4.16 Compare Pratten's four dimensions of transmedia design (see Figure 4.14, p. 108) with Murray's four affordances (see Figure 2.13, p. 55). What can you observe?

4.17 Why is the design of interactive stories iterative?

4.18 Write down more detailed specifications for a designer-specific platform based on the iterative design process illustrated in Figure 4.16.

4.19 Is the designer we have described in this chapter an embodiment of Murray's cyber-bard (see Section 2.2.2)? Should we have retitled this chapter and search–replaced all the occurrences of 'designer' with 'cyberbard'? Can you think of the reasons why we had refrained from doing it?

5

Interactor

The interactor in interactive storytelling has a counterpart in conventional storytelling settings such as the reader of written stories or the audience of concerts and theatrical plays. However, instead of being a passive recipient of the story, the interactor is required to participate actively in the creation of the experience. This means making decisions that affect how the story unfolds. Given such rights, the interactor is also bestowed with responsibilities. Adams (2013, p. 111) describes how in this kind of situation the interactor undertakes an agreement to comply with the story, since – presumably – there is a reason why the designer is leading the interactor through the story (Perlin 2005). In this *designer–interactor contract*, the designer offers the interactor a (more or less defined) role to play and a set of actions that can be performed (i.e. the interactive range, where more freedom means more possibilities for the interactor to depart from their intended role). Correspondingly, the interactor promises to play the offered role wholeheartedly and in character. The contract agrees on mutual obligations but does not include any penalty for a failure to perform – a breach of contract simply ends the agreement.

Currently, we can see many examples from mainstream games where the design of the gaming experience aims at forcing the interactor to change the course of the game or, at least, to give an illusion of freedom in creating one's own story. Yet, if the interactor inclines to proceed in the game as the designer may have intended (e.g. prefers a linear story), the designer provides tools with which the game can be played without making much of individual alterations to the storyworld. Alternatively, the designer can give branching story-choices which, at the end, lead to the same ending or a finite set of alternative endings (see Section 4.1).

Although the interactor normally controls one character at one place in an interactive digital storytelling (IDS) system, it would be possible to conceive a system where the interactor could control many characters in the storyworld or be able to see various places at the same time in the story (Szilas 1999). Also, Adams (2013, pp. 10–11) observes that avatar-based interaction is more common in IDSs, whereas multipresent interaction not limited to one character (e.g. *Prom Week*) is rare and does not have any expectations yet.

In this chapter, we look closely at the interactors and their role. Naturally, many topics here are intertwined with the designer and affect the design of the storyworld. However, we are trying to think from the (possible subjective) perspective of the interactor. We begin with looking at how the interactor experiences the story. After that, we go through Murray's aesthetic categories – agency, immersion, and transformation – in subsequent sections. Finally,

Handbook on Interactive Storytelling, First Edition. Jouni Smed, Tomi 'bgt' Suovuo, Natasha Skult, and Petter Skult.
© 2021 John Wiley & Sons Ltd. Published 2021 by John Wiley & Sons Ltd.

we present different approaches to categorize and understand the interactors based on the work done on recognizing different game player types.

5.1 Experiencing an Interactive Story

The *willing suspension of disbelief*, a term coined by Samuel Coleridge in 1817, states that a story should follow its internal logic but touch the human realm (Sampson 1920, pp. 52–58). If the story does not fulfil both of these requirements, immersion cannot happen: an illogical story where anything can happen on a whim is not immersive, neither is a story that has no human angle and offers nothing to identify with. This is the same principle why it is easy to believe but difficult to adjust the view later on when more facts arrive. Coleridge's statement has, however, faced criticism: Tolkien (1964) in his essay 'On fairy-stories' finds it inadequate and Murray (1997, p. 110) also criticizes the term and wants to replace it with 'active creation of belief' because the audience knows the story is fictional and – despite of this – the audience wants to believe the story is real.

In all experiences of being told a story, one enters a magical circle – akin to the model of the play experience by Huizinga (1955) – and subscribes into believing what is told in the story. The storyteller is responsible for providing a believable story, and the responsibility of the audience is to suspend their disbelief, which human beings have a natural disposition to do. Like a credit, we choose to accept what is being told and withhold our disbelief, but there is a limit to this credit, and if the logic of the story strays too far, we cease from believing. In all cases of storytelling, the audience has some responsibility over enjoying the story. If a person takes the stance of not being entertained by a performance, there is not much that can be done. This applies increasingly much when audience interaction is included.

Suovuo et al. (2020) present the game experience model (GEM), which defines six elements of a game experience:

- *Mechanics* include all the actions and objects defined by the rules of the game.
- *Action* refers to how the mechanics function in each situation.
- *Aesthetics* include the sensory and cognitive aspects of the game design that are aimed to evoke emotions in the player.
- *Sensory stimulus* refers to how the aesthetics is presented to the player.
- *Storyworld* includes all the potential content (prefabricated or generated) that could possibly become actualized during the gameplay.
- *Narrative* refers to how the storyworld actualizes to the player during the gameplay.

Figure 5.1 illustrates these elements and the relationships between them as a prism with three element pairs: mechanics–action, aesthetics–sensory stimulus, and storyworld–narrative. The three sides of the prism provide a narrowed-down scope into the game:

- *Dynamics* which observes the game merely as a spectacle or a performance ignoring story or motivation of the game. It reveals the elegance of the game aesthetics and player actions (e.g. sports).
- *Theatre* which observes the game as a sequence of events without considering the rules or interactivity of the game.

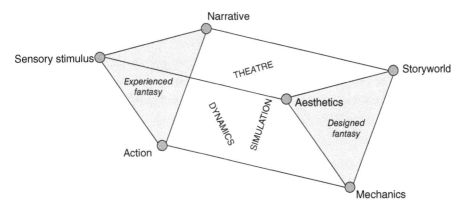

Figure 5.1 The game experience model as a prism with six vertices and five faces.

- *Simulation* which observes the game as actions and causal chains without considering their representation. This perceives the pure gameness of the experience.

The two perspectives are the triangles at the ends of the prism.

- *Designed fantasy* is formed by mechanics, aesthetics, and storyworld. This is constructed by the game developers collectively based on the game designers' vision. It is the fantasy that they assume that players' experience would coalign.
- *Experienced fantasy* is formed by action, sensory stimulus, and narrative. This is formed by the player's personal experience during the game. It can differ from the designed fantasy based on individual preferences, expectations, or context where the game is being played.

Obviously, the GEM can help us to understand interactive storytelling. The storyworld is closely connected to the aesthetics (e.g. visual assets) and mechanics (e.g. how to choose). Those are then experienced by the interactor as an instance and the individual input affects them.

Let us now look in detail four key phases in the interactive story experience. First, onboarding happens whenever the interactor begins to get familiarized with the storyworld (and perhaps also the platform). Second, maintaining the interactor's interest during the journey in the storyworld needs special attention from the designer. Third, as the story nears the end, the interactor expects to receive an emotional, intellectual, or some other payoff from the conclusion – if the story even has a proper ending. Fourth, as with conventional stories, interactive stories also allow – and even invite – the interactor to re-experience the storyworld by starting the process all over.

5.1.1 Onboarding – From Amnesia to Awareness

Onboarding means how the user of a software (e.g. player of a game) starts out and gets accustomed to using the software and learns its mechanics and underlying rules. In conventional storytelling, one could compare this to learning a language and learning to read, which would be the onboarding phases. However, a more reasonable measure would be learning to identify fictitious narratives from factual ones and learning to understand the deeper meanings and allegories embedded in stories.

In interactive storytelling, the designers enjoy the privilege that they get to line out the design of the storyworld, whereas the interactors do not have this benefit. Instead, the interactors have to be first introduced to what the storyworld is and the character they are supposed to portray. Simply put, the interactors initially do not know anything about their character, its surrounding, background, personality, nor intentions, which leads to the *problem of amnesia*, outlined by Adams (2013, pp. 48–51). A traditional solution in video games is that in the beginning the player either has amnesia or finds themself in an unfamiliar environment (e.g. facing a mystery or heroic quest). According to Adams, the reason for the problem of amnesia is the mixing of the roles of an actor (who is expected to be familiar with the role and the stage), audience (who can be totally ignorant), and player (knows the rules but little else).

Additional challenges are posed by the user interface design (see Section 3.1.2) because the interactors also have to learn what their character can do and how to make it do what they want. Onboarding is the phase that has to teach all these things to the interactor. This is a delicate phase because the interactor has not yet invested much in the experience and is more likely to give up. Especially in mobile gaming, the first minutes of a game are the most critical because any frustration or complexity can throw off the players and lead them to uninstall the app. This phenomenon is spreading more and more to other video games as games are following the game-as-a-service model instead of the traditional game-as-a-product (Smed and Hakonen 2017, p. 307). Interactive storytelling is not an exception but has to find ways to lower the threshold in onboarding.

5.1.2 Supporting the Journey

Once the interactors have passed through the onboarding phase and are accustomed to their role and understand their possible actions, the main part of the experience starts. (This is not something to confuse with the dramatic arc.) The extent how much the interactor needs support varies. In an open world, we can let them wander, but it does not mean that we could not provide hints and indication on where they should go and what to undertake. This can take many forms:

- *Characters*: The selection of characters alone can be indicative. If they mainly comprise, for instance, mobsters and other criminals, the interactor might be inclined to follow their lead and embrace the underbelly of society. On a higher level, the characters themselves might have their plans, which the interactor wants to get involved in by association. Going higher, we could also use, in case of a drama manager (see Section 3.2.1), a more direct manipulation of the interactor via the characters.
- *Scenes*: Often the physical boundaries set in the storyworld are there to support the interactor. Instead of overwhelming the interactor with possibilities, the world opens gradually. Only when a gatekeeper event has happened (see Section 4.1.3), the interactor can progress to a larger world and has more options to choose from. For example, initially, the interactors' world could be limited to their own house, where they can learn more about their character. Once they have found the key to the front door and a bus ticket, they can

step out and take the bus to given locations along the route. After the interactors have explored enough, they could get a phone call that their car is ready to be picked up from the garage. Having a car opens possibilities to go around and experience the storyworld.

- *Events*: Sometimes something happens which is not in the interactor's control (nor any of the characters). It can be a dramatic event from a chance encounter or a minor accident to a cosmic catastrophe. It puts the direction where the interactor has been proceeding into jeopardy and possibly reveals something that the interactor has not noticed before. Ideally, it should have had some kind of foreshadowing so that it does not come as a total surprise but fits in the internal logic of the storyworld. For example, if the city is located in a seismically active area, an earthquake is a plausible event. One example from *Red Dead Redemption 2* (Rockstar Studios 2018) is the possibility of the player's horse dying or injuring it gravely, which might require the player to put it down. This event is plausible in the game's scenery of the American frontier and can have a grave dramatic and emotional impact on the player.
- *Props*: Often the objects that the interactor carries and acquires (or possibly loses) are important to support the progress of the interactor. An object can be a MacGuffin, necessary for motivation and animating the interactor towards a goal but unimportant as itself, or a red herring leading the interactor to a wrong direction. Traditionally, especially in adventure games, every object in the player's inventory has a special need. If there is an object which has not yet been used anywhere, it is a strong indication that the player should go and find a purpose for it. Conversely, a blocked path can prompt the player to search for an object necessary to open it.

The idea of progress is close to all this. As time passes, the interactor should make progress in the storyworld towards some given or self-imposed goals. A key issue here is whether the interactors perceive whether they are progressing or not. There should be indicators (preferably not too obvious) that help them. A crude method could be points such as in early Sierra Online games such as *King's Quest* (1984) or *Space Quest* (1986), where the points indicate how much of the game content the player has played. In *Blood & Laurels* (Short 2014), the alternative routes are marked with badges and the player can observe easily the paths they have already tried out. In *The Walking Dead* (Telltale Games 2012), the progress is marked by a table at the end of each scene, which lists out the choices the player has made and compares them to the statistics of how the other players have chosen before. Other typical methods for indicating progress are charting a route on a map, collecting specified items, or reading computer-generated diary entries.

5.1.3 Is There an End?

The story must come to an end at some point. Although it is possible to have structures such as a narrative graph (see Figure 4.7, p. 97) that allow the interactor to continue indefinitely, in practice, the designer has intended the storyworld to be exited. If the intended story is to follow a certain structure (e.g. Freytag's dramatic arc or Campbell's monomyth), the exit point is unavoidable. How graceful or abrupt this exit is, is not something that the designer can do all by themself, but we are back at the designer–interactor contract, where the designer is obligated to provide an exit and the interactors – playing their role wholeheartedly – should take one of the offered exits. If not, the designer cannot guarantee (nor is responsible) that there is more to experience satisfyingly.

Naturally, we can turn the question around and ask whether is there really an end and could the interactor keep exploring the world indefinitely. And if there is an end, how would we find it or would it be the interactor's responsibility to say that this is the end? Do we actually want the story to end? Is that not the whole issue behind having sequels and spin-offs that we do not want to let go off the storyworld. We might have invested a lot in getting to know it and its mechanics, characters, etc. Now we would have to give up and walk away. In conventional storytelling, the author would have the *authority* to this by putting the words 'The End' and keeping silent. How would an interactor feel about this? Would the interactor have self-constraint and willpower to end at a feasible point?

The closest analogy that we have for these questions is video games. One could rephrase the question to how do you end playing a video game. Do you choose to quit it or is there perhaps some outside force (e.g. lack of time, loss of interest, other games) that steal your attention away and game experience withers away? We have examples of gameplay that has a designed ending (e.g. the final boss fight followed by the final in-game video), but many times it is possible to keep playing after that. One could go around to find the tasks or quests that are still left or keep on playing for other reasons than for the story. Often, this leads to replaying, maybe at a different and more difficult level the same thing all over again, but is it the end?

It is interesting to compare the endings of *Assassin's Creed Origins* (Ubisoft Montreal 2017) and *Hellblade: Senua's Sacrifice* (Ninja Theory 2017). *Assassin's Creed Origins* is a typical open-world game, where the story is padded with an almost endless amount of sidequests. The main story is a single narrative thread equalling the other narratives. Once the player has completed the main story, the story ends, but the player is left in the game-world with sidequests left open to continue. This ending is somewhat abrupt as a 'game over – well done' message appears just when the player feels events are proceeding at a good speed. In *Hellblade: Senua's Sacrifice*, the story is linear and ends in a final big boss battle against an ever-increasing number of opponents, until the players are no longer able to stand their ground and their character dies. Essentially, the story is not concluded at all, since the player cannot pass the last level. One could argue that the story ends somewhere in the middle of the last epic battle. Although the player may feel disappointed with this kind of ending, it can also be regarded as a proper conclusion and inevitable result of the quest.

5.1.4 Re-experiencing an Interactive Story

One criterion of an engaging story is the extent to which the interactor feels connected to it: how difficult it is to put the book down or how tempting it is to play 'one more turn'. As with all forms of entertainment, immersion is often the key (see Section 5.3). The interactors can have different motivations for re-experiencing interactive stories (Mitchell 2010):

- *Making sense of things*: New fragments to be reconciled into the overall understanding of the story.
- *Finding out more*: There is more to the story than can be seen on the surface.

- *Trying out 'what-if' scenarios*: Different choices can lead to different outcomes.
- *Seeing things from a different perspective*: Radical revision of the player's model of the storyworld, character's personality and motivation, and causal connections.
- *Looking for a deeper meaning*: Process of looking for an interpretation of the text.
- *Reflecting on the techniques used*: Appreciating or critiquing the ways in which the text achieves its effects.
- *Figuring out how the system works*: Finding the underlying role system.

Here, we see the unique character of interactive stories: they invite the interactor to return and re-experience. Some video games are even designed so that the opening menu shows a set of options for the gameplay that are indicated not to be selectable until the game has been played through once. In a way, they leave one yearning for another try, to try out the counterfactuals. This sentiment is summarized best by the commercial slogan of the game *Alter Ego* (Activision 1986): '*Make a new life for yourself*. Just for fun, start over. But take a different path. Create a new personality. Live life as someone you've always wanted to be.'

5.2 Agency

For an IDS system to be genuinely interactive, the interactor's choices should affect the direction of the unfolding story. It is not enough to provide the interactor many options. Agency requires that each of the choices presented to the interactor should have an observable and differentiable outcome. Agency is a key concept in the aesthetics of interactive storytelling (Knoller 2010, 2012), and it is facilitated by the platform developer and provided for by the designer. The platform provides the interface through which the interactor can make choices, and the designer defines what choices the plot allows and how they can affect it. The real depth of agency is relative to the level of influence on the story being generated.

It is worth noting that apart from the interactive story, agency can also manifest itself in other ways. Agency can be, for instance, mechanical, which is based on the controls available to the interactor. Game mechanics such as problem-solving or puzzle may provide gameplay agency in a game even without a story. Combining different types of agency can enhance the interactor's experience. However, here we focus on agency in the form of altering the story.

There are three major trends in the conceptualization of agency summarized by Ahearn (2001) and Harrell and Zhu (2009):

- *Agency as free will*: The interactor is allowed to explore the storyworld at will.
- *Agency as resistance*: The interactor has an oppositional agency; for instance, female skins to *Quake* (id Software 1996) or a protest movement in *Second Life* (Linden Lab 2003).
- *Absence of agency*: There is no room for agency as such; for instance, Ian Bogost's *Airport Insecurity* (2005) and *Disaffected!* (2006).

Although free will has been a predominant view towards agency, lately there have been more examples of the last two. When agency is seen as free will, it can be defined as 'the satisfying power to take meaningful action and see the results of our decisions and choices' (Murray 1997, p. 126). It is the distinctive experience that an interactor has in an interactive storytelling platform, which emphasizes the importance of the interactor's intentional actions guiding the story along the paths set by the designer. In this sense, agency represents the interactor's ability to interact with and affect the storyworld. With this in mind, having a freedom of choice – choosing a certain path or viewpoint in which the story will progress – can be considered a minimum requirement for true interactive storytelling. Murray (2004) goes even further to state that agency can be achieved even if the interactor does not have direct control over the direction of the story, which is the case of story-driven games such as *Half-Life* (Valve 1998) and *System Shock 2* (Irrational Games and Looking Glass Studios 1999). Even in this case, the interactor keeps a sense of importance and relevance and can be viewed as a catalyst driving the story forward. Murray invests in the notion of the author or designer as a *privileged* role, distinct from the creative roles available to interactors. Laurel (2004) challenges this view and states that agency requires the ability to change the direction of the story.

Tanenbaum and Tanenbaum (2010) also challenge the idea of agency-as-free-will and define agency as a 'commitment to meaning', which shifts the attention away from the outcome of an action to the *intention of an action*. Here, 'commitment' is understood, as in speech act theory, as an utterance categorized in terms of its illocutionary point. Each illocutionary point is entailing different commitments or attempting to achieve different goals. For instance, a commissive speech act commits the speaker to a future action, whereas an assertive speech act commits the speaker to the truth of the statement. It is, therefore, critical to establish trust and communication between interactors. Designers and interactors are in a type of a conversation with each other, mediated by the platform. The meaning allows us to shift the emphasis on interactive action from outcome towards the intent underlying the choice. Meaningful choices mean that the illocutionary commitments entailed by the utterance/action are *real*. As Sengers (1998) puts it, it is more important to do the thing right than do the right thing. The communication of meaningful commitments requires that the players need to trust that the game is correctly interpreting their expressed meanings via the often limited communication channels. Also, games need to 'train' players to perform meaningfully.

In the following sections, we look at agency from various perspectives such as what is its range and whether it is perceivable – or even existing.

5.2.1 Theoretical and Perceived Agency

We can discern two types of agency: theoretical and perceived (Thue et al. 2010). In *theoretical agency*, we look at the interactors' objective ability to act and change the outcome of an event within the story. In *perceived agency*, we focus on the interactors' subjective perception of their ability to enact such changes in a story. While theoretical agency is commonly regarded as an ideal for interactive storytelling, we should focus on the perceived agency (Itkonen 2015; Itkonen et al. 2017). For instance, although choices are given, the interactor can be unaware of making choices or pass them without noticing them. Here, theoretical agency exists but bad design leads to the situation that the interactor is not consciously making the choice. Thue et al. (2010) recognize that perceived agency depends on

- foreseeability for the outcome of an action;
- ability for accomplishing such an outcome;
- desirability of the outcome; and
- connection the interactor perceives between the action and the outcome.

The connection can be temporal (i.e. stronger with more desirable observed outcomes) or predictive (i.e. stronger with interactor-predicted outcomes).

Bruni and Baceviciute (2007) state that every system embraces a goal, which leads to an intrinsic communication cycle between the system (and its designer) and its interactor. Without communication, the expectations for agency cannot be managed; if the interactor cannot be understood by the system, the system misinterprets the interactor's intentions, and, conversely, if communication back from the system is lacking, the interactor cannot understand the cues from the system. For example, in *Dishonored* (Arkane Studios 2012), it is hinted that more kills lead to a darker ending, but there is no further information how the player can make a conscious choice about that.

5.2.2 Local and Global Agency

Mateas and Stern (2005) point out the difference between local agency and global agency. *Local agency* concerns meaningful actions that have immediate observable effects (e.g. mechanical agency). *Global agency* concerns actions that have repercussions observable only later in the story (e.g. the interactor can look back at the end of the story and see the connection between their choices or earlier actions and the outcome). The difference is the lifetime of the consequences of an action. Global agency can be difficult to observe, which can be aided like in *Witcher* (CD Projekt Red 2012), which shows a cutscene of the choice that led to the consequence at hand. An example of local agency is *Star Wars: Knights of the Old Republic* (BioWare 2003), where the interactor is awarded dark or light points immediately after a certain action. These points, however, have no effect on the ending of the story – the only long-term effect happens through the game mechanics (e.g. rewards and punishments).

5.2.3 Invisible Agency

A special type of agency is *invisible agency* recognized in *Silent Hill 2* (Konami Computer Entertainment Tokyo 2001) by Sengun (2013). Here, the interactor's subconscious actions can have agency. In *Silent Hill 2*, the game tries to make a psychological mapping of the interactors by tracking their obscure actions (i.e. when they are not aware of making choices). Examples of such actions are that looking at the picture of the interactor's character's dead wife, listening closely on the dialogue, or following closely the intended path whilst being escorted through a town. These actions are recorded to predict how the interactor feels about the other characters. The story then unfolds based on these quasi-subconscious actions. Interestingly, the interactor may not have recognized their agency at all. An obvious problem in this is that the interactor is not aware of making commitment because the meaning of an action is not directly communicated. For example, what happens if there is an outside interruption and the interactor forgets to pause the game. The fact that the screen is centralized to an object in a game for an extended period here does not mean that the player is actually looking at it. Another example of invisible agency is *Fable 2* (Lionhead Studios 2008) where the interactor's character can choose the type of food to eat. However, different foods have an effect on the interactor's qualities, leading to different reactions from the other characters.

Can the interactor process all the information that will determine the outcome of choice? In an extreme case, a storyworld with high realism (like in the *Dark Souls* series) means the interactor can cause things to happen that they did not want to happen as they have no information about the possible repercussions. On the other hand, plot twists and unexpected turns are amongst the normal dramatical arsenal in storytelling although they hinder communication. Clearly, there has to be a balance between these two.

5.2.4 Limited Agency and No Agency

Let us come back to the idea of unrestricted agency, where the interactor has more or less absolute freedom – which, obviously, clashes with Murray's definition emphasizing meaningfulness. According to Tanenbaum and Tanenbaum (2008, 2010), this true or unrestricted agency has been idealized in the IDS community. Itkonen (2015) questions unrestricted agency as an obscure idea because the context always dictates the interactor's agency, and breaking this context renders interaction nonsensical and meaningless. This is close to the idea of 'limited agency', which is highly contextually limited (Tanenbaum 2008). Here, the interactor is provided freedom to choose between *contextually* important options. Tanenbaum points out that too many choices and too much freedom leads to uninteresting and unimportant choices. Also, the technological limitations create their own context: it is different to play an RPG video game than an RPG tabletop game with real humans and an ever-adapting game master.

Lastly, we have to mention a rare class of games that have no (or hardly any) agency over the story. For example, *Dear Esther* (The Chinese Room 2012) offers no challenges and no puzzles. The interactor has agency in navigating through the island but has no effect on the unfolding of the story and outcome because the placement of the story fragments is done randomly for each game instance.

One should note, however, that the agency experienced by the interactor is not necessarily in relation to the real depth of agency. The interactor may be given a deep sense of agency without giving them any real agency at all – similarly to the Eliza effect where a system appears to be more complex than it is (see Section 3.2). Conversely, the interactors may feel like their actions have no influence on the game whatsoever, even if the story mechanics in the background are thoroughly affected by each action they take. Wardrip-Fruin (2009) calls this case, where a system fails to represent its internal richness, the Tale-Spin effect. He also describes the ideal situation, the SimCity effect, where a system enables the interactor to build an understanding of its (complex) internal structure.

5.2.5 Illusion of Agency

Figueiredo and Paiva (2010) discuss providing an *illusion* of agency. This means accommodating or disallowing the interactor's action on certain points and changing the expected outcome to more suitable for the story's needs. Naturally, this can lead to unexpected or illogical outcomes. Itkonen (2015) continues on how to make the interactor to expect the result the designer wants to achieve. The key is communication because even if the actions fail, the interactors will retain their sense of agency when the storytelling platform acknowledges and explains why they failed. Fendt et al. (2012) use *L.A. Noire* (Team Bond 2011) as an example of textual feedback even in the case the action has been futile and has no effect on the story.

Tanenbaum and Tanenbaum (2010) discuss creating an illusion of agency by having quick time events (QTEs), which provide the illusion of agency but actually limit choices. Here, the interactor has a small time window to react to something happening in the storyworld. This could bring out the interactor's real intent better instead of over-thinking and over-analysing. The results of this approach limit, at best, to local agency. For example, the *Mass Effect* series uses QTEs in dialogues. QTEs can even bring out unintentional effects as in *Heavy Rain* (Quantic Dreams 2010), where chasing a character through a marketplace is realized using QTEs in a quick sequence. The idea is to create suspense of a chase where the interactor has to fight the way through different obstacles. However, none of the QTE obstacles has any effect on the outcome of the scene, and the interactor can fumble all of them, creating a comical mood rather than a suspense mood.

5.3 Immersion

We humans structure our experiences in a narrative form (Aylett and Louchart 2007). If somebody would ask you to recount your day or life, you would most likely tell it in the form of a story. This ability seems to be built in the way our autobiographical memory holds stories about the self. And this is why we get so immersed in stories. Ryan (2001, p. 103) calls effective immersion 'recentering'. This means transporting the reader (interactor in our terminology) into the fictional world and making that fictional world the new centre of understanding for the interactor: a successful recentering allows for the suspension of disbelief, a vital aspect of immersion.

5.3.1 Immersion Types

Ryan (2001, pp. 140–155; 2015, p. 85–108) recognizes three types of immersion:

- Spatial
- Temporal
- Emotional

In *spatial immersion*, we have to understand the difference between space and place. Space is infinite, timeless, and anonymous allowing movement. In comparison, a place is limited by boundaries, provides security, and has a name. The story singles out a place from the surrounding space. In this kind of immersion, the interactor is transported onto the scene.

Temporal immersion puts the 'lived' or 'human' experience against the 'objective' or 'clock' time. Recalling Laurel's flying wedge of possibilities (see Figure 2.12, p. 54) whatever has happened earlier restricts the range of the future events. The interactor takes part in a process of disclosure where progressing narrative distils the field of potential.

Suspense requires that the interactor is interested in the characters' fate. When the interactor is projecting the possible paths of characters (e.g. foreshadowing, predictions, flashforward), the intensity is inversely proportional to the range of possibilities (i.e. the more limited the range, the more intensity). Suspense comes with uncertainty; if there is no uncertainty, there would not be suspense. Suspense includes curiosity in the sense of desiring to know past events. Surprise usually does not provide immersion because it takes place in such a short time to properly create immersion. It is a moment of resolution.

The focus of suspense defines the intensity of temporal immersion (in decreasing order).

1. In 'What suspense', the focus is imminent resolution or binary choice. It answers the question what happens next. The interactor typically is already emotionally involved in the character's fate – and may even know more than the character does (i.e. anticipation). This type of suspension is typical in action movies and thrillers.
2. In 'How (why) suspense', the story has a form of an enigma. The interactor knows the outcome in advance and is now focusing on learning the history of what has happened.
3. In 'Who suspense', the interactor's interest is more purely epistemic than in the previous case. The fate of the characters has little interest, but the focus is on the task of solving the problem (e.g. whodunnit). The past gets revealed piece by piece and facts might be withheld from the interactor. In a whodunnit, the number of suspects limits the number of possible solutions. The action unfolds on two temporal places: the murder and its investigation.
4. In 'Metasuspense', the focus is on the story itself as an artefact (i.e. it is external to the storyworld). Suspense comes from how the author manages to tie all the strands together and give the text a proper narrative form.

Emotional immersion can take different forms. It can be subjective reactions to the characters and their behaviour (e.g. like, pity, admiration, contempt). In a more intense form, it can display empathetic emotions for others such as feeling sad or happy for a character. Even more intense form is that it creates emotions felt by oneself (not for others) such as fear, horror, disgust, or arousal.

5.3.2 Models for Immersion

Ermi and Mäyrä (2005) recognizes three channels of immersion in games: *sensory-based immersion* due to the richness of high-quality sensory experiences, *imaginative immersion* due to the fascination towards the story plot, and *challenge-based immersion* due to the intensive focus on a physical control challenge on a perfect level for the player. The core of this sensory-challenge-based-imaginative (SCI) immersion model is illustrated in Figure 5.2a. The model was further developed by Mäyrä (2007) so that the significance of the player's personal context of gameplay is included around the SCI model. Mäyrä also renames the three channels as sensory, mental, and action-based immersion channels.

Figure 5.2b illustrates 'the three types of immersion' as proposed by Adams (2004, 2013, p. 85). Adams's narrative immersion resembles the SCI model's imaginative immersion, with the player becoming attached to the characters and interested in the plot development.

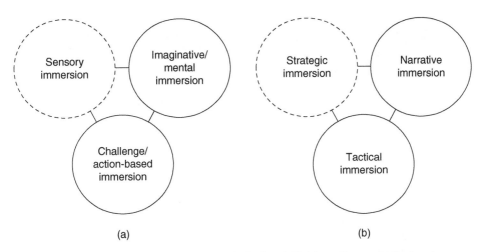

Figure 5.2 Immersion models by (a) Ermi and Mäyrä and (b) Adams. Source: (a) Ermi and Mäyrä 2005, Mäyrä 2007, (b) Adams 2004, 2013.

Similarly, tactical immersion corresponds to the SCI model's challenge-based immersion, with the player getting into 'the zone' by taking the required actions in the heat of the game. Only sensory immersion of the SCI model lacks a counterpart in Adams's model, and Adams's third type of immersion seems to be missing from the SCI model (or it is somewhat connected to challenge-based immersion). Strategic immersion involves higher-level game thinking with the focus on winning the game. More than taking immediate gameplay actions, it relates to the possibilities offered by the game mechanics in a larger scale, or the gamified narrative of the game. Adams (2004) somewhat refutes the latter, and Suovuo et al. (2020) attach it to strategic immersion rather to the mechanics element. Both models are considered in the GEM model presented in Section 5.1.

These models also suit interactive storytelling. Sensory-based immersion entails the aesthetics of the system, which is provided by the audiovisual content provided by the developer as well as high fidelity and timing provided by the platform. Narrative immersion entails the attractiveness of the story, which is mainly provided for by the designer responsible for the story content. Through the procedural and participatory affordances, this dimension is even more affected by the platform that holds the interactor's interest. Action and mechanics-based immersion entails the experience of agency.

5.3.3 Flow

Bizzocchi (2007) recognizes two types of immersion: The first one, willing suspension of disbelief (see Section 5.1) and the willing surrender to the pleasure of the story, whereas the second one is immersion of the *flow* (Csikszentmihalyi 1990). The first kind we encounter more in 'passive' storytelling such as cinema, and the latter in interactive forms such as games. People who experience flow experience a sense of agency, where they feel their actions have an impact on the world (see Figure 5.3). The flow theory tries to explain why people are fully immersed when they are applying skills they are good at. Flow is a state of

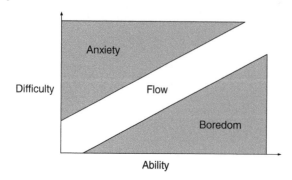

Figure 5.3 Flow experience is a balance between the difficulty of the task and one's ability to handle the task. If the task gets too difficult with respect to the ability, the experience turns into anxiety. If the task gets too easy with respect to the ability, the experience turns into boredom.

concentration or complete absorption with the activity at hand and the situation. It is also an optimal state of intrinsic motivation.

The flow experience is familiar to us all whether it happens during reading, watching a movie, listening or playing music, or playing a game. The question here is how we could make the storyworld to support the occurrence of flow experiences. To answer it, let us turn the question around: what would we have to do to prevent or disrupt the flow? One obvious answer is to change the difficulty of the challenges rapidly – from easy to hard or vice versa. Also, any repeated changes to the style of challenges (e.g. from literal to logical without a possibility to adapt) is likely to be perceived as interrupting. A third example would be changes in the rate how often the interactor is facing challenges. This is common in interactive television, when the interactors cannot anticipate whether their input will be required soon or whether they can lean back and enjoy the story. To generalize, any rapid changes to the interaction are a risk to the flow and should be minimized.

5.4 Transformation

If agency originates from interactivity and immersion from the willing suspension of disbelief, then transformation stems from *identification*. It is an important factor when thinking about the interactor's motivation beyond agency and immersion. Computers are capable of creating and simulating environments for roleplay, which allows the interactor to transform their identity and 'shape-shift' into a new role (Murray 1997, pp. 154–182).

As Mateas (2004) observes, transformation is difficult to pinpoint as it can mean three different things:

- *Masquerade*: The interactor can change to someone else for the duration of the experience.
- *Variety*: The interactor can exhaustively experience a multitude of variations.
- *Personal transformation*: The interactor takes a journey of personal transformation.

In digital as well as real-world games, the player often takes part in a masquerade. Not being in the position to become the world's greatest football player, one can still play with friends on a weekend in the yard (or virtually with *FIFA*) and have the feeling of being one of the greatest. There is also an appeal in taking an existing story or story universe and putting oneself in it – to become Elizabeth Bennet or Rodion Raskolnikov and try to put it in their shoes. Granted, the story might rise up to the level that their original authors put behind them, but it would be a possibility for masquerades.

The experimental system *Prom Week* (Expressive Intelligence Studio 2019) offers an example of how variety could be experienced as a transformation. It allows the interactor to control a group of high school students and lead them through the prom week. To achieve the goals, the interactor has to take the role of various students and realize how their social lives are intertwined. It is not enough to identify with just one student but the whole group.

Personal transformation is the hardest – if not impossible – to design precisely as it depends on the interactor's personal history and situation. Instead, one can take a narrow area such as an attitude or preconception and try to stimulate the interactor to change. For instance, *FearNot!* (Aylett et al. 2007) aims at changing the attitudes towards bullying and *Nothing for Dinner* (Medilab Theme 2020) the preconceptions on the needs of the family of a stroke patient.

5.5 Interactor Types

The role of the interactor raises many questions (Ryan 2008). First, interactors probably do not want to be tragic or comic characters but rather heroes in their stories. Second, many users do not even want to be interactors but marginally involved observers or confidantes. In this role, the user is a peripheral character (see focalization, Section 4.3.1) affecting the world and observing the outcome (i.e. agent and spectator).

There has not been any work on categorizing the interactor types in interactive story-telling. The closest example is the classification by Laws (2002, pp. 4–6), who recognizes the following player types in RPGs:

- *Power gamers*: Want to continuously develop their character with new abilities and equipment
- *Butt-kickers*: Focus on fighting to prove their superiority
- *Tacticians*: Prefer complex and realistic problems that require thinking ahead
- *Specialists*: Always stick with their favourite character type
- *Method actors*: Identify strongly with their character and want to test their personal traits
- *Storytellers*: Interested in the excitement of the plot and co-creating the story
- *Casual gamers*: Hang in the background and do not want learn all the rules nor engage in detailed planning

Laws's observations offer some insight into the interactors in interactive storytelling. It mainly points out how different styles or approaches the human interactors could have. If we are to design a storyworld for all of them, it should provide not only challenges and plot twists but also deeper background on the characters and the world in general as well as a possibility for the interactors to adjust their own character more to their own liking. Clearly, we cannot serve everyone and fulfil everyone's wishes and whims. However, the lessons to take from here is to offer versatility. This becomes clearer when we expand our view and take a look at the work done in recognizing player types in video games.

In video game research, there are two broad classes of player type analysis. Top-down models approach the situation by defining first (orthogonal) classifications and recognizing then player types on how they sit on these categories. In contrast, bottom-up models start from the data and try to cluster it to recognize and label player types with common features. We look at next both of these approaches and some examples of their classifications and discuss their relevance to interactive storytelling.

5.5.1 Top-down Analysis

Top-down analysis could be labelled as comfy chair philosophy because here the presented results are based on (often a single) researchers' observations and a high-level model that is imposed over. The structures are often elegantly pleasing but lack statistical data to back up the claims. A classic example – and the most cited player type model – is Richard Bartle's taxonomy. Based on his observations on multiuser dungeons (MUDs), Bartle (1996) presents a taxonomy of different player types. He places the player among two axes: where their activities are mainly directed to (*players–world*) and what kinds of activity are they mainly engaging in (*acting–interacting*). This allows the players to be divided into four groups according to their activities (see Figure 5.4):

- *Killers*: People who use the game to dominate other people
- *Achievers*: People who set themselves game-related goals that they then try to achieve
- *Explorers*: People who try to find out what is in the game world and map it for others
- *Socializers*: People who want to converse and interact with other players

The player's motivations should be understood as a mix of these, and the type of play for a single player can change during gameplay. For example, in the early game the player can act more like an explorer, whereas towards the end he can turn out to play more like a killer.

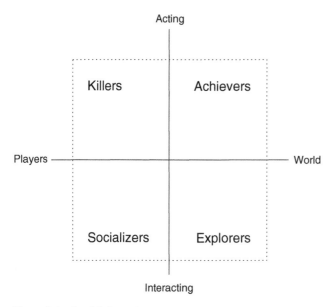

Figure 5.4 Bartle's four player types.

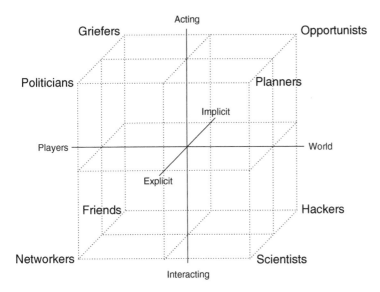

Figure 5.5 Bartle's eight player types.

Noticing his model's limitations, Bartle (2005) extends the model to include eight player types by introducing a new axis, which classifies the players whether their behaviour is spontaneous or premeditated (*implicit–explicit*). The extended model has now eight player types (illustrated in Figure 5.5):

- Griefers (implicit killers) in games attack other players to get a big, bad reputation.
- Opportunists (implicit achievers) in games take every opportunity they see without bothering to tackle obstacles or spending a lot of time with any single feature.
- Hackers (implicit explorers) seek to discover new phenomena and experiment to reveal meaning.
- Friends (implicit socializers) enjoy a familiar company of other players they know well.
- Politicians (explicit killers) aim for a big, good reputation in games.
- Planners (explicit achievers) set themselves goals and persistently pursue their way towards them.
- Scientists (explicit explorers) in games experiment with the game mechanics to find out and explain how they work.
- Networkers (explicit socializers) in games seek for interesting and worthwhile people to interact and want to get to know their fellow players.

Bartle acknowledges that players are likely to advance through certain typical development paths within the game. For example, a player can start out as a griefer, developing into a scientist, then a planner, and, finally, a friend as they grow more and more familiar with the game.

Apart from Bartle, other researchers have proposed their own models, which usually extend Bartle's original model; see Bateman and Boon (2005), Castronova (2005), and Marczewski (2013). Other starting points include, for example, the Big Five personality model (see Section 6.1.3), which is adapted by VandenBerghe (2012) to correspond to the following five player preferences:

- *Novelty* distinguishes open, imaginative experiences from repeating, conventional ones. A player looking for novelty wants high variety and unexpected elements, whereas a player avoiding novelty seeks familiarity from games that offer comforting sameness.
- *Challenge* deals with how much effort or self-control the player is expected to use. A player looking for a challenge wants games that are difficult and require precision to win, whereas a player avoiding challenges might be content with sandbox games where they can play around without achieving anything.
- *Stimulation* deals with the stimulation level and social engagement of play. A player looking for stimulation could go for games involving interaction with other players, whereas a player avoiding stimulation prefers to play alone.
- *Harmony* reflects the rules of player-to-player interactions. A player seeking harmony prefers co-operative games, whereas a player avoiding harmony looks for competitive games offering conflict.
- *Threat* reflects the game's capacity to trigger negative emotions in the player. A player preferring threat might be more attracted to games in the survival horror genre, whereas a player avoiding threat likes games with leisure play.

5.5.2 Bottom-up Analysis

Recently, the research focus has turned to bottom-up analysis, which starts with data and tries to recognize patterns and commonalities in it. In this case, the data is about how the players act in a vast variety of games and it would include a demographically representable sample. Vahlo (2018, pp. 61–75) presents the results and analysis from a large survey conducted with 12-to-70-year-old respondents. The survey provided a list of 33 core gameplay activities, and the respondents were asked to rate the activities according to how much they like or dislike them. An analysis of the results showed that the 33 activities can be grouped, according to their similarity in the respondents' preferences, into five factors:

- Assault (e.g. attacking, defending, fleeing for your life, sneaking, hacking, conquering)
- Care (e.g. decorating rooms, flirting, gardening, hanging out with friends, taking care of pets)
- Coordinate (e.g. jumping from a platform to another, matching tiles together, performing lifelike sports, performing music)
- Journey (e.g. creating your own character, developing skills, exploring, searching for a hidden treasure)
- Manage (e.g. building a city, commanding units, gathering resources, guiding a population, trading items)

Next, the respondents' results were clustered according to how much they share preferences of the aforementioned five factors. Based on this, the respondents could be clustered into seven player types: mercenary, companion, commander, adventurer, explorer, daredevil,

Table 5.1 Player type data.

Type	Likes	Dislikes	Proportion (%)	Women (%)	Age	Plays weekly (h)	Plays per session (min)
Mercenary	Assault	Care	19.5	24	31.6	17.1	72
Companion	Care	Assault	8.0	72	40.8	10.7	47
Commander	Manage	Care	18.8	27	37.8	13.6	56
Adventurer	Journey	Manage, care	10.4	45	31.5	15.1	77
Explorer	Journey, coordinate	Assault, care	15.8	78	42.3	10.5	42
Daredevil	Assault, coordinate	Journey, care	14.5	31	39.6	10.8	44
Patterner	Coordinate	Care	13.1	71	45.3	10.0	33

Source: Vahlo 2018, p. 71

and patterner. Table 5.1 collects for each player type their strongest likes and dislikes, their proportion amongst the respondents, gender division, average age, and average play times per week and per session.

This provides a better understanding of the actual division. Again, it must be stressed that these are statistical observations and individuals can vary. Nevertheless, this data can be used in designing commercial games because the vast player base follows the model better. It points out possible omissions or overemphasis in the design and allows it to be more inclusive.

5.5.3 Discussion

The fundamental question is whether interactive storytelling is just a game genre. If so, it would look like that they would appeal to certain types of players but not the overall population. Taking Vahlo's classification, interactive storytelling would have no chance among mercenaries or daredevils, which makes up a third of all the players.

An alternative viewpoint is that we should consider interactors as something else or something different than players. There might be similarities between them, but they are essentially different. Going back to the GEM (see Section 5.1), it is not a question of inclusion but both belonging to something greater. Whatever the designed fantasy, the interactor's experienced fantasy is affected by aesthetics, mechanics, and storyworld (or sensory stimulus, action, and narrative). Player types focus more on the action–mechanics pair, and secondarily on aesthetics–sensory stimulus, whereas interactive storytelling relies more on storyworld–narrative. Therefore, the types are indicative – the player is the interactor's cousin – rather than imperative. Somebody still has to carry out this research and recognize the interactor types – once we have enough interactors to study.

5.6 Summary

What we are giving to the one experiencing interactive storytelling is the possibility to be an active agent of change. They are no longer spectators, readers, or listeners – part of an audience. This experience lets them take part, interact. To quote MacIntyre (1981, pp. 198–199), the agent (or interactor) is not only an actor but an author and 'what the agent is able to do and say intelligibly as an actor is deeply affected by the fact that we are never more (and sometimes less) than the co-authors of our own narratives'.

In order to have this happen, the interactor has to be let in the story. This poses the problem of amnesia, where the interactors have to quickly learn about their own character in the storyworld – or to wake up having lost their memory and forcing them to rebuild their storyworld-identity. Once the interactor has passed through the onboarding phase, the experience needs support from the elements in the storyworld. The ending of the story is also challenging: is there really an end or could the interactor keep exploring (almost) indefinitely?

Once the interactors have reached the end, they might want to have the experience again. It is likely the story will not go the same way as before. Random processes, little variations on selections, or timing could cause a butterfly effect where the story unfolds differently. The re-experience would not be the story instance – the previous narrative – but a revisit to the storyworld, much like replaying a game is rarely totally similar than the earlier times. This, of course, opens totally different ways to experience the story: what-if scenarios, trying out different approaches, finding out more about the storyworld itself (and less about any particular story), and experimenting the world.

The interactor's experience can be discerned in Murray's aesthetic categories. First, immersion is an essential requirement for any experience. We face something outside of the real world, but we are willing to buy in and treat it as if it would be real, we are suspending our disbelief for that while. Second, agency gives us the possibility to have an effect on our fictitious experience. What we say or do has not just a random but a meaningful effect, and we have a range of options to choose from. Third, transformation goes deeper into our psyche and allows us to take a role outside of the normal range. We are no longer confined to our physical, cultural, economic limitations, but we can be *whoever* we choose to be.

Every interactor is unique, and putting the interactors into neat discrete boxes in a category is always a hard task. As this is a new field, we do not yet have special categories for interactors, but we can learn much from the work done on player types. There we have top-down approaches such as the classical Bartle's four player types, which are based on individual observation and induction. On the other hand, we have bottom-up approaches such as Vahlo's player types, which are based on analysing data and recognizing patterns from it. This work gives us an indication of how to recognize the features of the interactors.

Exercises

5.1 Taking the GEM, try to analyse your (preferably story-driven) favourite game.

5.2 How could you solve the problem of amnesia? Try to come up with original ideas.

5.3 Typically, the problem of amnesia revolves around the interactor onboarding the story for the first time and learning the controls. But what about the situation, where the interactor has put the story on hold for several months and then decides to return to it – having likely forgotten much of the controls and the details of the story so far? How could you support this re-onboarding and how to detect that the interactor needs it in the first place?

5.4 One incentive for an interactor to re-experience an interactive story would be to provide in the original story an impressive hero character, which the interactor could then take as their own play character for the re-experience, as they have now become familiar with the character. What other kinds of interesting story elements could be offered to encourage the interactor to re-experience the story?

5.5 Take a game that you failed to play to the end because it got too difficult, repetitive, or boring. What you would have needed to continue? What kind of support the game should have provided you to make the playing worthwhile?

5.6 What is the problem in using (too many) dramatic events in supporting the interactor's experience?

5.7 Come up with examples of MacGuffins and red herrings in games or movies.

5.8 Let us think of a scenario of three characters in a closed space (i.e. one scene). One of them has committed a murder, but the interactor does not know who. How would the interaction work if the interactor has an avatar interacting directly in the storyworld with the three characters? What if the interactor does not have an avatar but is omnipresent and affects the scene indirectly (e.g. adding or removing props or changing their properties)? (*Hint*: In the first case, you can think of a classical whodunnit where the interactor is a detective trying to find out the murderer. In the latter case, you can think the interactor is a ghost, who has been murdered by one of the three characters and who can haunt them to find out the guilty one.)

5.9 Why does the interactor need indicators to support their journey (see Section 5.1.2)? Can you come up with other examples than the ones mentioned in the text?

5.10 Some games provide infinite play (i.e. 'play until you fail'). Could this work in interactive storytelling?

5.11 Some games provide a possibility to replay in a more difficult setting (e.g. a nightmare mode). Could this work in interactive storytelling?

5.12 Considering, outside of games and stories, human life as such, an age-old question is: do we have free will or is everything predestined? How is this question similar to and how is it different from the question of agency in interactive storytelling?

5.13 What is your take: should agency viewed as free will, resistance or is it absent? Line out arguments in favour and against each of these views.

5.14 Why should we focus rather on perceived agency than theoretical agency?

5.15 Give examples (e.g. from video games) where you have encountered global agency. How effective was it?

5.16 In invisible agency, the system would monitor the possibly subconscious choices that the interactor makes. How usable that would be?

5.17 Suppose you are playing the role of a barbarian and you are facing the following situation:

> Three misty characters are approaching you. You cannot recognize meeting them before and you do not know whether they are friendly. You are tired from your journey and have run out of food and water. The three strangers have noticed you and are changing their direction to meet. Each of them is waving something in their hand, but you cannot tell what it is.

Now, choose one of the following three decisions:
(a) You reveal your sword and rush headlong towards the strangers.
(b) You raise your hand and salute the strangers.
(c) You turn around and leap behind the nearest boulder.
Once you have decided, read the corresponding response (a), (b), or (c) below. Do not look at the other responses yet!
(a) The strangers stop and vanish. After a long pause, you hear a sound behind you. As you turn, you see them standing around you, pointing their weapons at you. Hunger and madness gleam in their eyes.
(b) The strangers stop and vanish. After a long pause, you hear a sound behind you. As you turn, you see them standing around you, pointing their weapons at you. Hunger and madness gleam in their eyes.
(c) The strangers stop and vanish. After a long pause, you hear a sound behind you. As you turn, you see them standing around you, pointing their weapons at you. Hunger and madness gleam in their eyes.
How well did that result comply with your choice? Now, look at the other choices. How well did the illusion of agency work on you?
You can do this exercise with a group and let the group members compare their decisions.

5.18 Take your favourite game. How does it use spatial, temporal, and emotional immersion?

5.19 Why is suspense more immersive than surprise?

5.20 Think back to moments when you have encountered a flow state. Try to describe it and the events that led to it.

5.21 Where would you locate yourself in
  (a) Bartle's taxonomy of four player types and
  (b) Vahlo's player types?

5.22 Propose a taxonomy for interactor types. (*Hint*: You can start with Laws's player types.)

6

Storyworld

The storyworld is an artefact provided by the designer running on a platform for the interactor to experience. It has various elements with different levels of autonomy: *Characters* are computer-controlled entities that are represented as avatars and cohabit the storyworld with the interactor. Interactors and characters can use *props* to act and interact in the storyworld. The developments in a story instance can occur also due to *events* that are usually set by the designer and triggered by either the interactor or some other mechanism. The storyworld also comprises various *scenes* where the story takes place.

The storyworld can be perceived from three views: topographical, operational, and presentational (Wei et al. 2010). *Topographical view* focuses on the layout and spatial organization without any temporal reference. We can think of it as a map that indicates the spatial relation between locations and entities. In game design, this belongs usually to level design where we can have different options (see Section 6.2.2).

Operational view adds temporality, and the storyworld is seen through events and movements over time. Using the analogue of a landscape of possible stories introduced in Section 4.2.1, we can think of temporality as the possible paths taken through the landscape. When looking backwards, the interactor has travelled through a path that has been their experience. Apart from the movement of the interactor, we can also think of the characters. They are usually attached to one place, and, in that case, such a character can provide background to the place (e.g. a talkative patron in a tavern) and possibly change the plot locally (e.g. giving the interactor a task to fulfil). If a (main) character can move and be present in several places, its role grows more important and it also becomes more complex (e.g. a sidekick that tags along with the interactor). We focus on characters in Section 6.1.

Presentational view looks at various cues – visual, auditory, or haptic – that create the outlook of the storyworld. In visual terms, we can think of on-screen and off-screen space and how they are presented to the interactor and what kind of perspective they use. The acoustic space plays an important role in enhancing the visual presentation and possibly extending to off-screen. On this level, the space can get segmented and needs transitions (or cuts) when the interactor moves. We discuss more on presentation in Section 6.3.

In addition to space, we must observe the narrative time, where we can recognize three aspects: order, speed, and frequency. *Order* refers to the relation between the ordering in operation and the ordering in story (i.e. if they stay consistent, we have a linear story). This resembles the division of fabula, sjužet, and media/text advocated by Russian formalism (see Section 2.1.3). *Speed* refers to the duration of the operation of an event and the duration of the happening of that event in the story (i.e. real-world time). The most common ones are (from fast to slow) as follows:

- *Ellipsis*: Story events are skipped over in operational time (e.g. showing a character leaving for an airport and then showing it to enter a hotel in a new town).
- *Summary*: Operational time is shorter than the storytime (e.g. major leap without showing the details).
- *Scene*: Operational time happens at the same speed as the storytime (the most common one in video games).
- *Stretch*: Operational time takes longer than story time; for instance, bullet time in *Max Payne* (Remedy Entertainment 2001).
- *Pause*: Story events pause and operational takes care of something else (e.g. showing a cutscene).

Frequency refers to the relation between the number of times an event 'really' happened in the story and the number of times it is presented in the operation. It can be singular when an event is presented only once. In repetitions, an event in a story occurs once but is presented multiple times (which is a very common game mechanic, 'repeat until done'). In iteration, an event took place multiple times but is presented only once (e.g. a verbal summarization of a character's upbringing).

In this chapter, we first look at the characters and discern how they are constructed and could be turned into software. Next, we review the other components of the storyworld and see how they can be affected. The storyworld needs a representation that gives it a concrete form.

6.1 Characters

Computer-controlled characters present one of the most challenging tasks in implementing the storyworld. Autonomous agents (e.g. robots) are a part of a larger discussion that we cannot condense here in its entirety. It is safe to say that there is hardly a consensus on what would be the right theoretical approach, let alone how to implement that. It seems likely that the near future will bring fast progress in this respect, and all that would be relevant in the development of computer-controlled characters in interactive storytelling. However, we collect here themes and approaches that the research literature on interactive storytelling has focused on.

Broadly speaking, the characters in a story can be aesthetic (i.e. serve the plot), illustrative (i.e. symbolize ideas or themes), or mimetic (i.e. simulate human beings) (Weallans et al. 2012). However, the characters themselves are aware only in their mimetic components, whereas the illustrative and aesthetic components exist outside of the fictional world and only the interactor and the designer are aware of them. Even the use of a drama manager (see Section 3.2.1) does not change this, as the characters remain oblivious to the reasons why the drama manager leads them to act the way it does.

Characters' initial state is set by the designer, but this state changes due to interaction with the other characters and the interactor (and possibly the drama manager). A character can be almost completely autonomous, which is the case in the character-centric approach, and the character acts as a simulation, or it could be semi-autonomous as in the author-centric approach in the sense that it is harnessed to carry on the story plan

Ideally, the features of character believability include the following (Fairclough and Cunningham 2002; Gomes et al. 2013; Mateas 2002; Szilas 2007):

- Awareness of the surrounding world
- Unique and specific personality
- Emotional expressiveness
- Coherent and understandable behaviour (also relating to the past behaviour)
- Rational short- and long-term goals
- Growth and change with time and experiences
- Forming and fostering social relationships

Crawford (2013, p. 28) considers the character's interaction as a cyclic process of listening, thinking, and speaking. We can broaden this perspective so that listening refers to the character's perception of the world. Likewise, thinking is the decision-making process that is coloured by the character's personality and associated with and stored on the character's memory. Finally, speaking refers to the character realizing its decision by acting in the storyworld. The aim of all these is to make the character to act as human-like as possible whilst preventing the underlying software implementation to get too complex.

6.1.1 Perception

The model–view–controller (MVC) model illustrated in Figure 3.3 (p. 69) includes a synthetic view that is prepared from the proto-view and is intended to be the perception of a character. It can filter out elements based on physical (e.g. fog-of-war) or the character's perceptional limitations (e.g. blindness). If we want to have a fully human perception, the filtering should have several layers possibly including a simulation of physical sensors and cognitive processes (Sanchez et al. 2004). Usually, this means introducing errors to the character's perception, leading to false beliefs (Carvalho et al. 2017; ten Brinke et al. 2014). Unlike many other application areas, having error-prone computer-controlled characters is likely to be a desired feature in interactive storytelling platforms. Decisions based on faulty or erroneous perceptions can lead to interesting and surprising – but still believable – outcomes.

Recalling the MVC model, the synthetic player has a synthetic view on the model. This means that the character has its own perception of the world. Ideally, this view would be as close to a human interactor's view as possible, but in reality there are differences. In one extreme, the character has a direct and possibly unlimited access to the raw data. One could argue that, relative to the human interactor, it has supernatural powers. Simply put, the computer cheats. The synthetic view can be described as the perception of the character. The more we can add attributes resembling the human limitations, the more realistic it becomes. Simple example is the visibility: one cannot (in normal conditions) see through walls or far, far away (without an aid).

6.1.2 Memory

The received perceptions are stored on the character's memory. Human memory is typically divided into two broad classes: *short-term* (or *working*) *memory* (STM) and *long-term* memory (LTM) (Norman 2013, pp. 92–97). STM holds the most recent experiences or currently thought-about material. It allows to retain information automatically and to retrieve it fast, but the amount of retained information is limited to five to seven items. Although STM is invaluable for everyday tasks, it is fragile, for example, to distractions. LTM is the memory of the past. Retaining and retrieving information takes time and effort. Sleep seems to play a role in strengthening the memory of the day's experiences. In LTM, details are reconstructed and interpreted each time we recover the memories, which means that they are subject to distortions and changes. Also, the organization of LTM can cause extra difficulties (e.g. 'tip of the tongue' experience). Apart from STM and LTM, there is also *prospective memory* (or a memory for the future), which allows us to remember to do some activity at a future time and to have the ability to imagine future scenarios.

LTM holds the *autobiographical memory*, which stores the personal history of an entity including places and moments as well as subjective feelings and goals. They form the human experience which is based on stories on past experiences so that new experiences are interpreted in terms of old stories. Also, the content of the stories depends on whether and how they are told, which is the basis of an individual's remembered self. Turning to characters, a computational autobiographical memory requires (Brom et al. 2007; Ho and Dautenhahn 2008) the following:

- *Accuracy*: How to retrieve relevant information and to measure how trustworthy it is
- *Scalability*: How to accommodate a large number of episodes (e.g. forgetting over time)
- *Efficiency*: How to optimize the storage (e.g. omitting and combining details) and recall

Dautenhahn (1998) recognizes different types of storytelling agents, which can be seen as types of autobiographical memory for the characters:

- *Type 0*: The character is always telling the same story.
- *Type I*: The character has a variety of stories, from which it chooses one randomly and repeats it exactly (i.e. it has no conversational context).
- *Type II*: The character selects a story that fits the context best and repeats it exactly but does not listen.
- *Type III*: The character is able to interpret the meaning and content of the story and to find a similar story to adapt to the current situation (i.e. it tells and listens to stories).
- *Type IV*: The character is an autobiographical agent (i.e. it has a personality).

Forgetting is an important part of a memory as it helps to reduce the resources needed to maintain the memories. This can be realized by dropping out the least important memories, reducing the details of older memories, or combining similar memories into one memory.

Let us look at two examples for implementing a memory in an interactive storytelling system. In *VIBES* (Sanchez et al. 2004), the memory stores information (i.e. percept objects) acquired about the world, the character's representation of the world, and the knowledge the character has acquired. It also records consecutive internal states of the character (e.g. wants, emotions). In *SAGE* (Machado et al. 2004), the narrative memory stores a temporal sequence of episodes and cause-and-effect links between individual episodes. An episode consists of a crisis, a climax, and a resolution.

6.1.3 Personality

The reason for applying personality models is to give the character its own individual 'flavour'. One can take the same inference machine (or one with slightly different parametric powers of deduction or fallibility) but line out the individuality of the character with a palette of personal traits.

The most relevant and widely spread implementation of a personality model is the classical player attributes of *Dungeons & Dragons*, which has influenced and been adapted by many other RPGs. In this model, the player's character has six attributes (three physical and three mental), which are usually assigned (semi)randomly:

- *Strength*: Physical power
- *Constitution*: Stamina and endurance
- *Dexterity*: Coordination and agility
- *Intelligence*: Knowledge and reasoning
- *Wisdom*: Insight and perception
- *Charisma*: Force of personality

Dungeons & Dragons also introduced a popular model of morality (or alignment) that has two orthogonal axes: law–chaos and good–evil (see Table 6.1). The law–chaos axis indicates how well the character adheres to rules. The good–evil axis instead refers to the perspective that the character has towards life and other beings.

From a more general perspective, to model the character's personality, we can resort to existing psychological models of human personalities. One of the well known is the Big Five model, which is also called the OCEAN model or the five-factor model (Digman 1990). It is a taxonomy for personality traits divided into five factors: openness, conscientiousness, extraversion, agreeableness, and neuroticism. Table 6.2 collects the features associated with each of these traits. The Big Five model has managed to stand its ground against the tests of scientific validity, but still there are questions such as whether our language is sufficient to express and analyse the qualities of our personality (Pervin 2003, pp. 64–65). Psychology relies on using language to describe phenomena, but when the analysis tool (i.e. language) has been created by the subject of the study (i.e. the mind), how can we be sure that the outcome is objective?

Crawford (2013, pp. 200–202) presents a simplified personality model based on the traits of the Big Five model. The character's personality is defined by three variables along the axes:

Table 6.1 Alignment chart of *Dungeons & Dragons*.

	Lawful	Neutral	Chaotic
Good	Lawful good	Neutral good	Chaotic good
Neutral	Lawful neutral	True neutral	Chaotic neutral
Evil	Lawful evil	Neutral evil	Chaotic evil

Table 6.2 The traits and associated features in the Big Five model.

Trait	Associated features when the trait is...			
	High	**Extremely high**	**Low**	**Extremely low**
Openness	Curious, creative, looking for novelty and variety	Unpredictable, unfocused, risk-taker	Pragmatic	Close-minded
Conscientiousness	Organised, disciplined, dependable	Stubborn, focused	Flexible, spontaneous	Sloppy, unreliable
Extraversion	Gregarious, sociable, loquacious, energetic	Domineering, attention-seeker	Reserved, reflective	Aloof, self-absorbed
Agreeableness	Sympathetic, compassionate, co-operative, trusting, helpful	Naïve, submissive	Competitive, challenging	Untrustworthy
Neuroticism	Anxious, excitable, vulnerable, reactive	Insecure, emotionally unstable	Stable, calm	Uninspiring

- Nice–nasty (i.e. the basic goodness of the character)
- Honest–false (i.e. the character's integrity)
- Wilful–pliant (i.e. the character's assertiveness)

Crawford's (2005, pp. 190–199) original personality model was highly complex and hard to use. Due to this and other practical problems (see Section 3.3.2), his motivation for this simplified model was to make it a more understandable and versatile tool for designing characters.

While the models of *Dungeons & Dragons* and the Big Five are general models for personality, we can also use models that define a personal emotion towards other characters, objects, or events in the storyworld. A widely used model of emotion is the Ortony–Clore–Collins or OCC model (Ortony et al. 1988). As illustrated in Figure 6.1, it asserts that emotions depend on events, agents, or objects leading to 22 emotion types. Starting from the root of the tree, the model discerns three broad categories depending on if the reaction is to consequences of events, actions of agents, or aspects of objects. This division continues into subcategories on the focus, until, on the leaves, we have the 22 emotion types.

Such an extensive categorization can be simplified as *Virtual Storyteller* does by using event-appraisal theory (Theune et al. 2004). Table 6.3 presents the two emotional

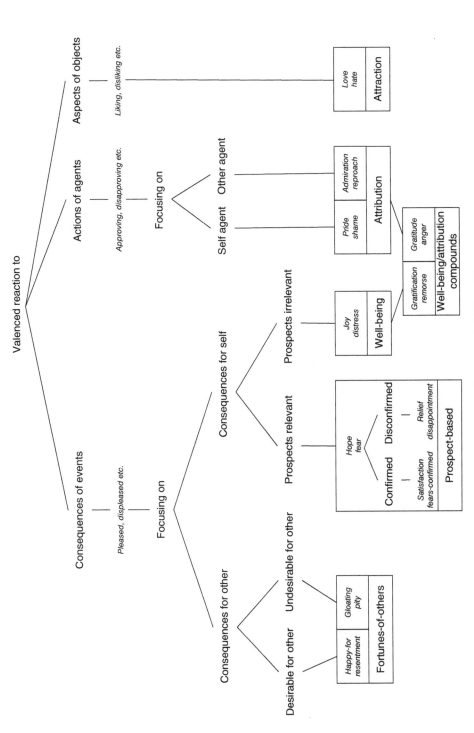

Figure 6.1 Global structure of emotions types in the OCC model. Source: Ortony et al. 1988, p. 19.

Table 6.3 Event-appraisal theory.

Directed to the character itself	Directed to other character
Hope–fear	Admiration–reproach
Joy–distress	Hope–fear
Pride–shame	Love–hate

Source: Theune et al. 2004.

categories of the event-appraisal theory: emotions directed to the character itself and emotions directed to other characters. Each of the six emotional states can be positive or negative and has an intensity within a given scale.

Elliott (1992) presents an extension to the OCC model used in Affective Reasoner, which is a platform modelling a multi-agent world. The platform gives a simple affective life to the agents that are able to reason emotions and emotion-induced actions. It provides a relationship between reasoning about human emotion and reasoning about the stories people tell. The basic idea behind it is that what makes many stories interesting is not what happens, but how characters in the story feel about what happens. Table 6.4 summarizes the emotion categories recognized by the platform.

As we have seen, there are many different models for defining the personalities for the characters. Personality models, however, are always approximations. Still, we do not want to have excess complexity. While a complex model might – at the first glance – look appealing and more suitable than simple models, they rarely work well in practice, because the designer has difficulties in setting the values or understanding the effects of different and complicated dependencies.

6.1.4 Decision-making

What makes a character tick is its decision-making process. Based on the input – perceptions, memories, and personal traits – it should come up with a choice. The choice is not only about a noticeable action but also internal changes within the character such as setting up or updating its goals or trust in other characters. Figure 6.2 illustrates the position of decision-making (Kaukoranta et al. 2003). The world, which can be real or simulated, consists of primitive events and states (phenomena) that are passed to pattern recognition. The information abstracted from the current (and possibly the previous) phenomena is then forwarded to the decision-making system. The world allows a set of possible actions, and the decision-making system chooses the ones to carry out.

A broad classification of decision-making methods divides them into *optimization* and *adaptation*. In optimization, there is a model or some *a priori* knowledge that can be used. For example, if our character is a simple bar keeper whose purpose is to serve drinks and give some hints where to go or who to meet (cf. Dautenhahn's Type I in Section 6.1.2), we can have a finite-state machine or a simple parser figuring out matching patterns in the interactor's utterances. We have a model and it is a matter of finding the (near) optimum result. Naturally, the case is not so easy as in here, but usually there are multiple parameters to consider about. One can think of them forming a multidimensional space, where

Table 6.4 Elliott's emotion categories (Elliott 1992, p. 31; 2016).

Group	Category label	Emotion type	Spesification
Well-being	Joy	Pleased about an event	Appraisal of a situation as
	Distress	Displeased about an event	an event relative one's goals
Fortunes of others	Happy-for	Pleased about an event desirable for another	Appraisal based on presumption of how a
	Gloating	Pleased about an event undesirable for another	situation is appraised by another as an event relative
	Resentment	Displeased about an event desirable for another	to their goals
	Sorry-for	Displeased about an event undesirable for another	
	Jealousy	Resentment over a desired mutually exclusive goal	
	Envy	Resentment over a desired non-exclusive goal	
Prospect based	Hope	Pleased about a prospective desirable event	Appraisal of a situation as a prospective event relative
	Fear	Displeased about a prospective undesirable event	to one's goals
Confirmation	Satisfaction	Pleased about a confirmed desirable event	Appraisal of a situation as an event confirming or
	Relief	Pleased about a disconfirmed undesirable event	Disconfirming an expectation relative
	Fears-confirmed	Displeased about a confirmed undesirable event	to one's goals
	Disappointment	Displeased about a disconfirmed desirable event	
Attribution	Pride	Approving of one's own act	Appraisal of a situation as an accountable act of some
	admiration	approving of another's act	agent, relative to one's
	shame	disapproving of one's own act	principles
	Reproach	Disapproving another's act	
Attraction	Liking	Finding an object appealing	Appraisal of a situation as
	Disliking	Finding an object unappealing	containing an [un]attractive
Well-being/ attribution	Gratitude	Admiration + joy	Object compound emotions
	Anger	Reproach + distress	
	Gratification	Pride + joy	
	Remorse	Shame + distress	
Attraction/ attribution	Love	Admiration + liking	Compound emotion
	Hate	Reproach + disliking	Extensions

Source: Elliott 1992, p. 31; 2016.

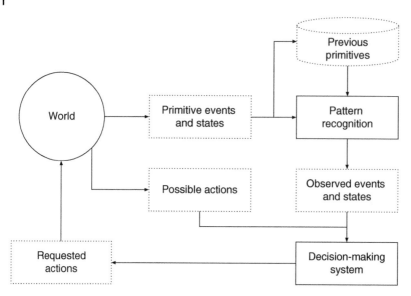

Figure 6.2 The primitive events and states originating from the world are used in pattern recognition and stored for later use; the decision-making system uses the observations made in pattern recognition to choose an appropriate action among the possibilities allowed by the world. Source: Kaukoranta et al. 2003.

we should find the optimum. The methods for this are classical such as hill climbing or simulated annealing, and they are usually based on heuristics. Often, it is sufficient to get a good enough result in a short time than use more resources to compute a better one. This reminds of the maxim attributed to General Patton: 'Better a good plan today than a perfect tomorrow.'

In interactive storytelling, optimization is suitable especially to the 'closed' storyworld where the story is more linear, under control, and less branching. Here, the designer has limitations on what are the possible actions or the limits of discourse like in the case of the conversation system of *Façade* (see Section 3.3.3).

Adaptation does not require *a priori* knowledge but tries to adapt to the feedback. It can be taught to find out the underlying dependencies of the variables, but usually there is no possibility for a human to abstract or retrieve this learnt knowledge from the system. Many of the artificial intellingence (AI) achievements in the 2010s were based on deep neural networks (DNNs), which – with the increase of processing power – became possible to solve. Often, these were simple, rule-based games such as chess, Go, or Jeopardy that offer clear feedback and make it possible for the algorithm to practice alone for countless repetitions to adapt to the rules.

With respect to interactive storytelling, adaptation would be an ideal way to use in open worlds when a character could adapt to a role and learn how to play it. The problems, however, are manifold. First, adaptation requires consistent and unambiguous feedback on what constitutes a 'good' action. Even if we would have that, the training time might not be long enough as a human-in-the-loop the character cannot endlessly iterate the same situation to serve adaptation. For instance, the video game *Black & White* (Lionhead Studios 2001) was promised to include a neural network that would allow the player's pet to learn from the player's feedback. The adaptation using a neural network, however, turned out to take too long and the developers had to resort back to a simpler non-adaptive solution.

A typical problem for computer-controlled characters is that they can jump from behaviour to behaviour, never settling long enough to be comprehended. Sengers (2002) labels this phenomenon as schizophrenia because the character's behaviour has been designed by solving sub-problems individually but they do not form a cohesive and holistic overall behaviour. Moreover, the character's task is to take actions that will *communicate* (which are not necessarily those that are 'correct').

We want to have characters whose behaviour looks convincingly human, not optimal. Regardless of the underlying method for decision-making, the character is bound to show certain behaviour in relation to the interactor, which can range from simple reactions to general attitudes and even complex intentions. As we can see in Figure 3.3 (p. 69), the data flow of the human interactor and the computer-controlled character resemble each other, which allows us to project human-like features onto the characters. This means that when it comes to decision-making, there is no need for perfection, but the characters can be – and should be – flawed and error-prone as we humans are.

Decision-making is a wide research area with different methods meeting different needs. We refer the readers to Smed and Hakonen (2017, Chap. 9) for a more detailed review of decision-making methods used in computer games.

6.2 Elemental Building Blocks

Murray (1997) emphasizes that immersion in a digital world can be enhanced by virtual objects behaving in an expected and realistic way, especially in reaction to the interactor's actions. By interacting with objects in a fictional world, these objects can become imbued with life and realism. In this way, interaction can enhance the feeling of immersion, bringing the world to life around the interactor – creating a positive feedback loop of immersion.

Apart from the characters, the storyworld is filled with other objects and mechanics. Here, we go through props, scenes, and events that the designer sets up and the interactor experiences.

6.2.1 Props

Props are things in the storyworld that can be used to make changes and that can be owned, but do not have agency of their own. Naturally, we can find objects that are difficult to classify this way: is a pet a prop or character? Clearly, it has its own will and can make changes to the world, but they are usually not on the same level as human-like characters are (of course, we could have a storyworld with animal characters). Also, we could imagine a spellbook that has its own will: sometimes, it refuses to open, other times it might escape its owner and find a new one.

Leaving these borderline cases aside, normal props are usable in advancing in the storyworld. In traditional games, objects usually serve a clear purpose. For example, if your inventory has an item that has not been used yet, it is highly likely that you will need it at some later point. This is not necessarily true in the storyworld: the interactor might decide to use an item to solve a situation, but it might very well be possible that they decide to do something else – or they might not even own the item due to their previous choices and storyline. Therefore, the designer has to be careful not to create a 'bottleneck' prop that provides the only possible solution. Unless the story is highly linear or branches only a little, the prop cannot be guaranteed to exist or to be in the interactor's possession or to have a clear indication where it should be used.

In an open world, we have to change our viewpoint on props. Now, a prop is a possibility for making a change – not the *requirement* for making a change. The prop (if discovered) calls the interactor to find out its possible uses, which can be seen as the prop's affordances. This resembles the game *NetHack* (DevTeam 2020), where any item can have different uses based on the

- verb (e.g. open, read, or zap);
- surroundings (e.g. dark or lit);
- internal state (e.g. weak, confused, or hallucinating);
- powers of observation (e.g. blind or infrared vision);
- personal characteristics or traits; and
- quality of the item (e.g. cursed, blessed, rusty, or burnt).

This would be an ideal situation where any combination would be covered, which is summarized in the *NetHack* players' maxim: 'The DevTeam thinks of everything'. One could imagine this as a multidimensional matrix with different attributes, where every entry would have a value. However, *NetHack* has been developed since 1987, and over these decades, by trial-and-error and countless iterations, a balance has been established. This resembles a combinatorial explosion of the branching narrative (see Section 4.1.2) in the sense that the combinatorial explosion will make the effort ever more onerous. However, as in *NetHack*, we could have shortcuts and broader classes of items that share similar qualities.

6.2.1.1 Schrödinger's Gun

Fictional universe is constrained only by what is revealed to the audience. *Chekhov's gun* is a narrative principle stating that everything presented in the story should be significant. This principle is related to the Russian short-story writer and playwright Anton Chekhov, who wants the author to remove everything that is irrelevant to the story to the extent that if there is a rifle hanging on the wall in the first chapter, it has to go off later in the story (otherwise, it should not have been mentioned in the first place). For example, point-and-click games adhere tightly to Chekhov's gun by highlighting only the active items on a scene. This allows the player to know that during the course of the story, something will be done with these items.

In *Assassin's Creed II* (Ubisoft Montreal 2009), the game mechanisms include an assortment of bombs that the player can throw. The player has to use these bombs in the sub-stories, where the game onboards the player with this mechanism. Otherwise, the player does not have to use the bombs at all as there are alternative ways to solve any future challenges. Chekhov's gun holds then for the whole game as the player has to use a bomb in onboarding, but – although the bombs are placed in the upcoming scenes – they are not necessarily used there, if the player opts against that.

Chekhov's gun can also be reverted as a *red herring*. In this case, the item is shown to the audience, leading them to assume that it will be used when the plot suggests it, but the surprise element is that the item is not used but the situation is solved by other means. For instance, in *Assassin's Creed II*, the bombs later on in the game cannot be considered red herrings, however, as the lack of their use cannot come as a surprise to the player who chooses not to use them.

In interactive storytelling, it is more accurate to extend the concept into *Schrödinger's gun* (Robertson and Young 2014). It combines the quantum physical concept of Schrödinger's cat (i.e. unobserved aspects of the world exist in multiple simultaneous states) with Chekhov's gun. The rationale here is that *only if* the rifle on the wall is observed by the interactor, it must go off at some later point; otherwise, it will remain in a 'superposition' as a possibility that was not realized by observation. For instance, in *Final Fantasy XII* (Square Enix 2006), the player never takes all the possible NPCs to the team at the same time. Often, as the game is played through, not all NPCs are even met once, although they exist in the potential of the story.

6.2.1.2 Internal Economy
In an interactive story, many props are mutable. They can be augmented by 'crafting', sold away, discarded, or even destroyed. We can recognize three broad categories for different kinds of props based on their level of significance:

- *Bulk resources* serve some purpose but are not significant (e.g. decorative items, ordinary coins, or bullets). These are resources that can be gathered, bought, sold, and used for crafting.
- *Individualized objects* are unique, for example, through a set of randomized or customized characteristics, which makes them memorable (e.g. a piece of clothing that has interactor-selected shapes and colour patterns). They are significant to the interactor but not necessarily to the story.
- *Quest items* are utterly significant for the unfolding of the story. They cannot be affected, except for their plot device intentions. This is to protect the structure of the story because if the interactor could destroy a key item for advancing the plot, they would eventually run into a dead end.

Props can be seen as *resources* that form an internal economy of the storyworld, which can also include entities (e.g. characters) and mechanics (Adams 2014, pp. 366–374). In the internal economy, the resources can have the following:

- *Sources*: Mechanics by which a resource or entity arrives in the storyworld (limited or unlimited)
- *Drains*: Mechanics that permanently drop resources out of the storyworld
- *Converters*: A mechanic (or entity) that turns one or more types of resources into another type of resource
- *Traders*: A mechanic governing trades of goods (i.e. reassignment of ownership)
- *Production mechanism*: Mechanics making resources conveniently available to the interactor

For a simple example of an internal economy, let us consider *Pac-Man* (Namco 1980). The game has six resources: pac-dots, power pellets, fruits, ghosts, lives, and points. The sources for pac-dots and power pellets are limited as they are placed in the beginning of a level; the sources for fruits and ghosts are unlimited as they either appear back in intervals (fruits) or re-appear whenever they have been drained (ghost). Being eaten by Pac-Man is the drain for pac-dots, power pellets, fruits, and ghosts. The source for lives is the beginning of the game, and reaching 10 000 points gives an extra life; the drain for lives is being eaten by a ghost. The source for points is eating pac-dots, power pellets, fruits, or ghosts; there is no drain for points.

Apart from designing, the internal economy is in a key position in balancing the storyworld. Adjusting the properties of sources and drains as well as other mechanics helps to fine-tune the difficulties. Also, the internal economy can be used to localize and remove possible deadlocks or livelocks.

6.2.2 Scenes

A scene is an environment or location where the story takes place. Scenes break up the physical space on a specific experience. In many ways, they resemble the idea of 'level' in video games, which also use different terms (depending on genre conventions) such as rounds, waves, stages, acts, chapters, scenarios, maps, and worlds (Rogers 2014, pp. 209–211). Consequently, scene design is close to level design, which focuses on arranging the architecture, props, and challenges and ensuring the right amount of challenges, rewards, and meaningful choices (Schell 2015, p. 381). To set a space in which the story takes place, we have to set the initial conditions of the scene, the set of challenges for the interactor, and the termination conditions of the scene. Moreover, we have to define the aesthetics and mood of the scene.

If the scene has a visual representation, we have to consider its physical layout as well. Figure 6.3 illustrates six common layouts (Adams 2014, pp. 445–449):

- *Open layout*: The interactor has almost entirely unconstrained movement (e.g. outdoors).
- *Linear layout*: The interactor has to experience the spaces in a fixed sequence (i.e. move to the next or previous space).
- *Parallel layout*: The interactor can switch from one path to another by choosing one of the parallel paths (e.g. the paths can offer different kind of challenges and stories).
- *Ring layout*: The interactor returns regularly back to the starting point for another round. The ring can include shortcuts that cut off a portion of the journey.
- *Network layout*: The interactor can explore freely the spaces that are connected to other spaces in a variety of ways (i.e. they do impose a particular sequence).
- *Hub-and-spoke layout*: The interactor is initially in a central hub that offers possibilities to choose from different spokes. Once the interactors have experienced the chosen spoke, they return back to the hub and make a new selection.

It is also possible to create a hybrid layout that combines aspects from these different layouts.

6.2.3 Events

An event is a specific change that happens once triggered by a condition. In contrast, a process is a sequence of changes that continues until it is stopped. Events can be caused by natural forces or some other sources (e.g. structural weakness in a building or an object).

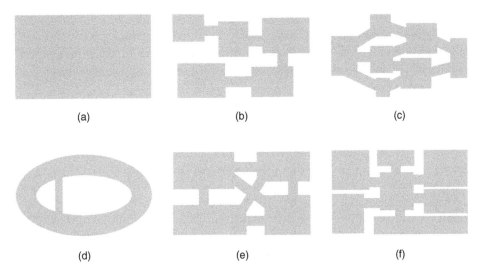

Figure 6.3 Layouts for a scene: (a) open, (b) linear, (c) parallel, (d) ring, (e) network, and (f) hub-and-spoke. Source: Adams 2014.

If we use an author-centric approach, events are a way to introduce dramatic changes (i.e. 'dramatic events'). Even in a pure character-centric approach, events could be set up beforehand by the designer to cause dramatic changes. For example, a tornado passing through a village is going to shake up the situation as some of the characters end dead or severely wounded, property destroyed or dislocated and lost. Dramatic events could even happen in a tight, regular rhythm like in *Minecraft* (Mojang Studios 2011) where night-time brings out dangers or in the story of *Odyssey* where Odysseus's crew loses every evening and morning two members to the cyclops Polyphemus. Not every event needs to have a dramatic afterthought. There can be mechanisms that cause events conditionally or based on time. They could be part of the storyworld and possibly later on used by the interactor.

Juul (2005, pp. 72–82) differentiates two types of games: games of emergence, which have just the rules and no preplanning, and games of progression, which allow certain events occurring in a predefined order. Taking these types to interactive storytelling, they would correspond to the character-centric and author-centric approaches. In the latter, events play a bigger role because predefined systems cause the interactor to experience the story in such a way that certain events are inevitably following other events. This progress can go through space (e.g. constraints on movement), time (e.g. scripted events), or story (e.g. tracking the progress through a plot).

6.3 Representation

In order to be understood, the story must be concretized into a representation. This representation can be anything that conveys the experience of the story to the interactor and, at the same time, serves as a means for the designer to express the story and vary it to reflect the interactor's reactions. With a traditional medium, the representation is typically fixed: paintings are visual; music is auditory; theatre plays are watched in theatres. With interactive storytelling, not only the representation may be multimodal but it can also be interactive. The interactor may be able to choose not to have audio input at all but, for example, rather to have speech and other auditory cues through subtitles. A game can allow the player to move around in the physical world with the game device to control the game, or instead the player may choose to control the game with a joystick and simulate the motion in the physical world.

In the case of visual representations, visual storytelling possibly has the most significant effect on human reception. Seeing and reacting to an image has much more success in provoking senses and being memorized longer than any other verbal or written information. In this matter, Panofsky (2003, pp. 306–310) states that the steps of understanding correspond to the forms of knowledge which presuppose historical experience.

Early semiotic work is known as connoisseurship, which is related to the interpretation of signs of authenticity and authorship. The designer holds the origin of the work of art and aims to characterize the existence, circulation, and discourses within a storyworld. The designer definitely beholds the attendance of certain events within the created world, along with changes, distortions, and their various modifications. Led by the designer's thought with conscious or unconscious desires, the contradictions can resolve in relations to the others, creating a specific meaning which the interactors have to find.

In visual representations, parts of the field are open for submitting the order of values in the context of the represented objects with potential signs. The changing nature of the image–sign relationship is an essential subject in the view of Schapiro (1969). One could say that semiotic approaches and theorems about each aspect of visual representations (an artwork, a sentence, a word, a letter) are the matters in discussion of interactive storytelling in the digital era (Merleau-Ponty 1964, p. 58).

Unlike verbal, the written text is under a continuous transformational process of perception since each generation has its own viewpoints and attitudes towards collected written material. That brings changes and movements in elements and makes differences in interrelations of the characteristics, which belong to the same elements of visual representations. Artwork stands for the subject, behind the work stands the sender whose expression stays within the spectators. Observers' interpretation forms the basis of the common meaning generated by the interaction between visual and verbal discourse. We can see clearly this approach in post-structuralism where the study of interpretation aims to the balance of taking a look at the past as an act of construction. According to Gadamer (2004), the true power of a visual representation is in its ability to shape the observer's understanding from what appearance suggests – an observer can receive several different stories, or even several different aspects of the same story, by observing one visual allegory. The power of a visual representation is in its ability to adjust the consciousness of the observer in which processes the idea of an artwork is a crucial aspect of the concept which its appearance suggests.

The role of art has always been a double to the real world, being compared and evaluated to how real it feels, or, in other words, how faithful it is to our senses of what real represents to an individual. Like any other form of art, narrative design and visual representations of either fictional or historical elements can be examined by using post-modern art theories. IDS systems (as well as digital games, in general) provide a new medium of expression where the interactor does not regard them as entertaining platforms but digital environments to gain new experiences.

Although narrative design is often thought as textual, it can also include visual or aural elements – or even omit the textual narrative and focus on other forms of storytelling. Let us look at and compare how some games present a complex narrative design to an interactor using different forms of storytelling. A common feature of these games is that they have a deep narrative design with a main protagonist that reflects the interactor's preferences in a gameplay – the interactor can decide the course of the narrative from aggressive/achievement-driven to more adventurous/story-driven experience.

To provide an open-world experience with a feel of free exploration in *Horizon Zero Dawn* (Guerrilla Games 2017), the narrative designer and the game designer have used a variety of traditional methods of literary and rhetorical allegories in revealing the story. Conversely, in games such as *Abzû* (Giant Squid Studios 2016) or *Journey* (Thatgamecompany 2012), the creators have focused fully on the visual storytelling methods with an almost complete absence of textual content in the game. In such an approach, semiotics theory (Schapiro 1969) and iconography (Panofsky 2003) have an essential role in creating the interactive narrative experience for the players, where even the symbolism of a colour or the type of light and the texture in a scene can provide necessary information to the interactor to progress in the game. Naturally, this makes high demands on the graphics team since their task is to translate the narrative design into a visual narrative by using all possible tools from semiotics, psychology, and symbolism theories. Moreover, this visual translation of the story-driven experience needs to be easily understood via a seemingly simple user interface design and clear indicators in the game environment that guide the player in the story progression.

The game *Life is Strange* (Dontnod Entertainment 2015) is based on more traditional storytelling methods, where the player makes clear choices from a given branching narrative. The story progresses as an episodic interactive narrative, which is also common in visual novels and interactive fiction. In these games, narrative designers focus on specific segments of the story that give a full loop and a sense of conclusion by the end of the game, and, at the same time, the story has enough of open-endedness that it can continue in another episode as a sequel, or even completely new game-titles that refer to the previously given narrative experience. Still, the follow-up game can usually be played and experienced without having played the previous game in a series, which is the case in adventure games such as *Tomb Raider* (Core Design 1996) or *Assassin's Creed* (Ubisoft Montreal 2007). The storyline binds all the games – and the big narrative construction that represents the game world and all its content – under one title. The introduction and tutorial parts of a game serve as an 'onboarding' to the given narrative framework for the players who are not already familiar with the preceding games in a series.

6.3.1 Visual

When developing visual language and style of the storyworld, the process of art creation slightly differs from traditional art production. Commonly, the artist starts with an idea and based on that idea chooses the methods and media used for art production. The creation of an art piece takes a certain amount of time, and alterations take place based on the artist's vision if it answers the message or idea that originated. In visualizing a storyworld, especially in concept art production, the artist is presented with the design documents and through discussions with the team gets familiar with the world, characters, atmosphere of the story they wish to tell. From the start, the process is guided by a team of designers where the artist's role is to depict the best possible visual representations of the design and aimed experience for the interactor. Furthermore, the artist must consider the platform and the technical requirements and limitations as they must be optimized to achieve a smooth experience.

The main role of concept art is to put the whole project in an understandable scope for the whole team. Besides being a great visual and marketing tool to present the project to the potential publishers, investors, or the community before even one line of code is made, it has a huge role in delivering the various aspects to the scope of development. It shows the environment, key features of the world, characters and the culture surrounding the world, the technical requirements to achieve the goals, the basis for animation type, and sound design that would fit in that world. Concept art plays an important role in the pre-production phase but can also take place during the development to test various features and changes.

Visual and audio cues are the main indicators that ensure correct communication between the platform and the interactor. These indicators and the visual representations are based on various design and technical requirements. Visual assets can also affect the interactor's experience of power, ambition, pride, anger, sorrow, or guilt as well as the moral context of the storyworld.

6.3.2 Audio

Music and audio design has a strong connection to the visual language and structure. It must reflect the visual cues and experience that the interactor has in order to enhance the emotional and sensory engagement with the storyworld. It is common that an audio designer joins the project at a later stage of development or that the audio is completely outsourced. Therefore, it is important that the vision and goal is communicated to the audio designer and the final decisions are approached as teamwork.

To discern the different types of audio, we can differentiate *diegetic* and *non-diegetic* sounds. Diegetic sounds refer to sounds created inside the storyworld such as sound effects and incidental sounds originating from the storyworld. Non-diegetic sounds do not arise directly from the characters' actions but the mood of the situation or theme of the scene. Musical soundtracks or laugh tracks are examples of non-diegetic sounds.

6.3.2.1 Diegetic

For most part, diegetic sounds are quite unproblematic as they reconstruct and resemble the sounds created by the corresponding real-world events. For interactive storytelling, the biggest challenge in this respect is to create sounds for the characters. Voice acting is a typical way to produce it in linear stories because it is possible to estimate the amount of assets required. Instead, true interactive storytelling would require generative sounds (e.g. using speech synthesis) because we cannot enumerate all the possible utterances that the characters might say.

This also holds for other types of assets, which can be either *prepared* (e.g. ready-made video clips) or *generative* (e.g. video generated in real time with the graphics engine).

Prepared assets require production-time knowledge of the content. They can be pieced together to offer variability (e.g. replacing the protagonist's name with a selection of prepared alternatives), but the variation is still numerable. Generative assets offer, instead, next to an infinite amount of variation. The burden is now on developing the generative methods, which – despite the best efforts – can appear to be lacking or their quality might not meet the public expectations. Often the question is finding a balance between these extremes. Some parts are better to have prepared while for others we have good enough generative methods.

This is an area where two things play an important role: technical innovations and imaginative design. New and improved technologies can bring generative methods closer to realism. Three-dimensional graphics is a good example of this because the increased polycount, faster shaders, and other improvements made possible by more effective hardware has reduced the need for including prepared video. On the other hand, speech generation (at the moment of writing) is still lagging much behind and would be hard to fool anyone as it lacks intonations, emotions, and other features of a real human voice.

This is where imaginative design can come to rescue. If the technology is not up to the level, a workaround is to modify the design to take the limitations as a part of the storyworld. If the synthetic voice is lacking emotion and character, why not design the world to be a dystopia where everyone is drugged out of their superfluous emotions and, because of that, talk monotonically.

6.3.2.2 Non-diegetic

Non-diegetic sounds and music can greatly affect the interactor's experience. Interactive media, however, poses a challenge that is not present in traditional media. While the soundtrack of a film is created specifically to suit the events of the scenes and the atmosphere, this is not always possible in interactive media where events do not necessarily repeat the same way every time. In interactive media, the dependency is actually reversed as the music and sound should adapt to the events and mood of the storyworld. Shortly put, we need *adaptive audio.*

When we are talking about adaptive audio, we mean non-diegetic sounds, usually music. In the simplest form, we can use cross-fading, where the volume of the currently playing song is lowered while the volume of the next song to be played is increased. This approach works quite well as long as the melodies of the songs match and no disturbing discord arises during fading. Another possibility is layering, where the instruments of the playing song are faded one by one and replaced by the themes and instruments of the next song until the song has changed to another. This approach requires that the different instruments are stored on their own tracks so that they can be individually faded out or in. Third option is to use transition matrices, where the music is broken down into appropriate phrases, between which the composer separately composes a suitable transition. The rows and columns of the matrix represent phrases and the entries of the matrix are the transitions between them. When the situation requires changing the music, the system looks at which phrase is being transitioned and what is the target phrase and, based on these, selects a suitable transition from the matrix. Understandably, this method – albeit producing musically intact transitions – is laborious.

Non-diegetic sounds play an important role in immersing the interactor into the storyworld. More than a soundscape, they also can provide cues on the possibilities for interaction and results of the taken actions. For instance, increasing heartbeat is typically indicating decreasing health. Also, the user interface can create non-diegetic sounds that verify that the selected action has been received (e.g. a click once a button has been pushed).

6.4 Summary

A storyworld comprises the objects and mechanics devised by the designer that create experience for the interactor. The storyworld aims at keeping the interactor interested in exploring but also making them act and realize themself. It involves passive entities, reactive entities, and autonomous entities. Passive entities are the setting or objects. Reactive entities are simple mechanisms such as a dispenser or a lift. Autonomous entities are those which seem to show their own will. In traditional games, we have seen many examples of the first two types, but interactive storytelling requires that the storyworld is populated with autonomous entities or agents or – as we call them – characters.

Characters form the most precious content of the storyworld as they keep us interested in the story and allow us to identify. Therefore, the characters aim at being as humanlike as possible, which does not mean that they have to *resemble* humans, but they can be cartoonish or otherwise caricatured. We are mostly interested in their behaviour: how they respond to the situation at hand, what kind of initiative they show, how they differ from other characters – what makes them unique and identifiable individuals.

Characters present the most difficult task both for implementation on the platform level and for the design. In order to have autonomous entities, the platform should offer mechanisms that make it possible to simulate the perception, process, and personality of a human being. A character should have the same power of perception as any other character in the storyworld (unless they have been granted with ESP or other paranormal abilities). Memory plays an important role in shaping the personality: someone might keep mulling over things from the past, whereas for another time makes the memories golden. This should be reflected in the model of memory. Personality, as we have seen, is a key to differentiate the characters. Simply put, we could have the same basic human model, but by tweaking the personality settings, we could create a diverse set of characters to populate the storyworld. Finally, decision-making actualizes the 'thought process' of a character.

We can only see the action of the character, not the computation that goes behind it. The same is true for human beings too: we do not know how our fellow beings come to the conclusion that made them act – we can only compare and extrapolate using our own self-awareness of our own thought process. Similarly, we should not have to know or care how a computer-controlled character came up with the decision, but can just imagine it. Human beings are interesting to us, and they are the measuring stick for a good story, which is why the platform should provide good and robust implementation for them.

The other building blocks of the storyworld include the props that characters are using, the scenes where things are happening, and the events that propel the story forward. As we have seen, each of them has its own role in making the storyworld alive and converting it an interesting place to be and to experience stories. For the interactor, the visual and audio representation makes this place concrete and affirms the story being told.

Exercises

6.1 Compare the topographical, operative, and presentational view with fabula, sjužet, and media/text presented in Section 2.1.3. What similarities do both of these classifications have and why? Where do they differ?

6.2 Excluding robots, NPCs, and characters, what other applications can you think of for autonomous agents? What kind of demands do they impose?

6.3 Why are the characters only aware of their mimetic components but cannot be aware of their illustrative or aesthetic components?

6.4 Chris Crawford says about the interaction cycle that it is a 'process between two or more active agents in which each agent alternately listens, thinks, and speaks' (see Section 1.1.3). Do you think this is an accurate description or is it lacking something?

6.5 Think of the limitations of a character's perception. What kind of filtering would it require? Devise a scheme to create a synthetic view out of the proto-view in this case.

6.6 Why should the character have both short-term memory (STM) and long-term memory (LTM)? Is there any benefit in doing this? How would forgetting work in the transformation from STM to LTM?

6.7 Read again Dautenhahn's classification of autobiographical memory (p. 150). Come up with examples of video game characters that would fit the different types. How well defined are the types? Is it easy to assign the characters into them?

6.8 Get acquainted with some RPG player attribute model (e.g. *Dungeons & Dragons*). Using the rules, create a character. Using the character, come up with your solution to the following situations:
(a) A friend is in danger of falling down from a cliff. How to help?
(b) A complex lock system blocks the exit. How to open it?
(c) You are on an open field and suddenly a thunderstorm gathers above you. How to react?

6.9 The matrix of Table 6.1 has become a popular meme. Find some examples and create your own version of a topic or person of your choice.

6.10 Take a Big Five personality test (you can find them easily online). Would the results define you as a character?

6.11 Take a group of people (e.g. 8–12) that you know well (e.g. your family, co-workers, or the cast of your favourite series). For each, write down the traits (2–5) that are the most important for you to recognize them (i.e. the essence of that person's uniqueness). Write them on, for example, separate papers and arrange them on the table into clusters (or use a digital cork table). Next, go through the list and try to find traits that are on the same scale (similar or mirroring). How many scales did you get? Could you reduce the number by combining similar ones? How do they compare with the scales of the model presented in this chapter?

6.12 How would you use the OCC model (or its simplification)? Think of different scenarios.

6.13 Let us try to apply the broad-and-shallow approach in the real world (see Section 3.3.3). For instance, think of doing the groceries. Devise a list of maximum ten discourse acts that maps all types of utterances related to this activity. Next, take a real-world discussion and assign it components with symbols 0–9 based on the mapping. Define 1–3 answers or reactions to each of them. Try out by programming or use a paper simulation to run an example. What do you observe?

6.14 Think of the following scenarios.
(a) Finding a suitable pair of trousers
(b) Learning to ride a bike
(c) Selecting a birthday present for a grandparent
(d) Getting a taxi
(e) Ordering a cocktail
(f) Giving a speech in a class reunion
For each item, think would you use an optimization or adaptation method to solve it.

6.15 Design a scenario which would include a Schrödinger's gun. What possible realizations it could take?

6.16 Consider the layout of a living area in a storyworld. Is it missing a toilet bowl or does it clearly have one? If there is not one, is this because it is a taboo to include it or because it could be taken as a Chekhov's gun?

6.17 Take the layouts illustrated in Figure 6.3 and give an example of how they could be realized as a scene or a set of scenes.

6.18 *Deus ex machina* (from Latin 'god from the machine') derives from ancient theatre, where the effect of the god's appearing in the sky, to solve a crisis by divine intervention, was achieved by means of a crane. As an event, is it different from ordinary events? If so, what makes it special?

6.19 Speech synthesis is not yet up to the quality of human voice actors. We mentioned that one way to work around technical limitations is to use imaginative design. Give an example how you could design the storyworld so that this limitation would actually be an integral part of it.

7

Perspectives

In previous chapters, we have covered the history and relevant background on interactive storytelling as well as introduced and explained concepts related to the four components – platform, designer, interactor, and storyworld. In this chapter, we offer different viewpoints on various topics that extend the previous chapters. This discussion focuses on possible changes and emerging trends that interactive storytelling might see in the near future.

7.1 Multiple Interactors

Interactive storytelling platforms are intentionally designed for single interactors. If we allow multiple interactors in the platform, we must also prepare for conflicts in the design. In distributed databases, the conflict is about maintaining consistency so that all users have the same view of the shared data. In multiplayer online games, the conflict is about maintaining both consistency and responsiveness so that all players have prompt access to relatively reliable game data (Smed and Hakonen 2017, pp. 256–258). A platform with multiple interactors takes the conflict to a new level because we have to create interwoven stories that are, at the same time, consistent, responsive, and compelling. A compelling storyworld requires that the events are dramatically interesting to all the interactors.

Two essential questions have to be addressed by multi-interactor platforms. The first and crucial challenge is how can we ensure that all interactors will stay in the focus of the story. The second one is about persistence: if the storyworld is persistent, how do we handle interactors entering and exiting at any time?

7.1.1 Multiple Focus

With one interactor, the focus of the generated story is clear, whereas with multiple interactors, the focus disperses, leading to a *too-many-heroes problem*, which asks how we can tell a story that would be compelling to multiple main characters (Smed 2014). Adams (2013, pp. 11–12) postulates that this could work in only epic stories with a massive amount of interactors, of which none is central. Most massive multiplayer online games, however, ignore this problem and offer the same story for all players. For example, *World of Warcraft*

Handbook on Interactive Storytelling, First Edition. Jouni Smed, Tomi 'bgt' Suovuo, Natasha Skult, and Petter Skult.
© 2021 John Wiley & Sons Ltd. Published 2021 by John Wiley & Sons Ltd.

(Blizzard Entertainment 2004) allows everyone to take turns in killing the Lich King and saving the world.

ˈIf we want to solve this problem, every character cannot be a hero, but someone also has to do the mundane work – even if we are in a storyworld. At the heart of this problem is that each human-controlled character (i.e. hero) needs a group of computer-controlled characters (i.e. extras) to support them. Therefore, one solution is that each new interactor also brings along new supporting characters. Another approach is to artificially limit the number of interactors in the storyworld so that we can provide each of them with a meaningful story.

One solution to the multiple-focus problem is that all the interactors in the same storyworld need not experience exactly the same story. In fact, most multiplayer games only sustain a shared plot but not a shared representation. If a player slays a monster, all the other players perceive this particular player slaying this particular monster. It is not so important if they see this occurring as a swing of a sword or a piercing of a sword. This principle could be further extended so that it is not necessary everyone to perceive that it was precisely this interactor who caused the monster to die, if it does not reveal something story-wise relevant about the interactor's character such as that they acted valiantly or cowardly.

Solving the multiple-focus problem is basically a design decision. If the platform allows multiple interactors, then the designer has to provide each of them enough content.

7.1.2 Persistence

Having multiple users, who can enter and exit at will, means that the system has to be persistent. Multiplayer online games can solve this problem by allowing a player to simply to materialize and vanish, but an interactive storytelling platform would have to also consider the ongoing stories and the presence of interactors. Again, this boils down to a design decision, and the chosen approach must be integrated seamlessly into the storyworld.

Let us think about what happens when an interactor logs out. One possibility is that the interactor's character just disappears from the storyworld, which is inconvenient and not believable unless it is included in the storyworld's internal logic. The designer would have to come up with an explanation, what happens when a character disappears (i.e. logs out in the real world) and why this can happen in the storyworld.

Second possibility is that the interactor's character becomes a computer-controlled character until the interactor logs back in. This character would continue to exist and act in the storyworld, while the real human interactor is not present and controlling it. The problem is now how to guarantee that something extraordinary does not happen to the character in the meanwhile. When the interactor is not present, the character cannot be subjected to big plot twists. For example, imagine the interactor coming back to the storyworld the next day and finding their character dead. Naturally, we can present a recap of the events that have taken place during the interactor's absence upon returning.

Third possibility is that the interactor gives tactical- (or even strategic-) level instructions to the character to follow during the absence (e.g. 'try to befriend this other character', 'stay home and do not answer the phone', or 'be happy and active') (Smed and Hakonen 2017, p. 284). However, many interactors might find this kind of a loss of control, even if it is only temporary, intrusive and confusing.

7.2   Extended Reality

Augmented reality (AR) and virtual reality (VR) gears have become considerably cheaper and user-friendly in the past few years, which is why they are expected to be ever more commonplace. Extended reality (XR) – which covers both AR and VR – will bring a new dimension to representation and immersion, but it will not change Murray's aesthetics categories discussed in Chapter 5, nor is it likely to bring new structural innovations. However, with improved representation and deeper immersion, we would be getting a step closer to the holodeck.

In comparison to other media for digital storytelling, XR poses a fundamental challenge of catching the interactor's attention and directing it to the right place at the right time. Conventional storytelling practices, from books to movies to most digital games, are presented on a two-dimensional screen, where the interactor receives the information as a separate entity from the story environment and participates as an avatar. In XR, the interactor becomes an active part of the storyworld, fully immersed in the social network of its fictional characters and interactive elements in a virtual environment.

In addition to the visual representation, sound plays a crucial role in guiding narratives in XR, since sound cues not only contribute to the level of presence the viewer experiences but also create a peripheral awareness of their surroundings by guiding the user through the narrative. As we saw in Section 6.3.2, prepared audio does not allow for immersive interaction, but audio elements should have interactive roles in the narrative as they can direct the interactors' attention (Bala et al. 2018; Nakevska et al. 2014). Sound should consider the plot and the interactive context of the user experience (UX) by allowing interactivity during viewing.

7.2.1   Visual Considerations

A key challenge is that the *field of view* is limited and the interactor cannot pay attention to the entire virtual scenery at once. The common filmmaking techniques – such as cinematography, sound, mise-en-scène and editing – are not suitable because the interactors are free to explore the scene by looking wherever they want (Fearghail et al. 2018; Ko et al. 2018); see Figure 7.1. Rather than having a window to a world, the viewer is present in it and can choose their own vantage point in the scene. This makes it hard to convey a narrative in XR. For example, the story could be carried onwards in traditional cinema by moving from a cut to cut, which allows the director to control the viewers' attention, whereas in XR the viewer might not be looking at all where the director wants.

Orientation of the viewer is important to make the viewer conceptualize the environment. It plays a crucial role especially when a cut takes place, since every cut requires the viewer to re-orientate themself in the new environment. Excessive or quick cuts can lead to disorientation in terms of both the environment and the narrative and can further impair the quality of immersion. Due to this reason, using the spatial nature of XR is essential for the directional approach, instead of being based on the time-based image sequence. The pacing and playing should be more like traditional theatre, with an emphasis on cinematography (Dowling et al. 2018). If the characters perform the same task for a long time or are

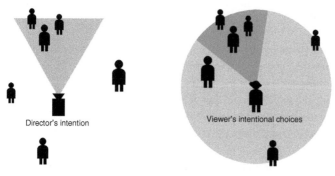

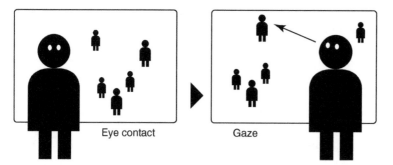

Figure 7.1 Traditional film environment in comparison to an XR environment. Source: Based on Ko et al. 2018.

Figure 7.2 Perception on directing the user's attention using eye contact and gaze. Source: Based on Ko et al. 2018.

silent, the viewers tend to explore the environment, which is a good moment to draw their attention to the narrative (Bala et al. 2016).

The viewer's attention is naturally drawn to the acting persons, and the attention in XR can be directed through the character's eyeline or through the character directly addressing the interactor (Fearghail et al. 2018; Ko et al. 2018); see Figure 7.2. Long takes, which are preferred in XR, are not used as often in traditional filmmaking. Instead, we can compare XR with immersive theatre, in which the actor's eye contact with the audience can be a means of strong non-verbal communication, and the actor's (i.e. the principal character in the scene) eye contact and gaze can be used to draw the viewer's attention from the scene to the narrative.

For many people, watching films is a *social experience*: they enjoy discussing the events of the presented material as they occur. In XR (and especially in VR), using devices requires that each person is using their own head-mounted display (HMD) to immerse themself within the scene. This means that the viewers get isolated from their surrounding environment during the experience. Even if viewers are watching the same content simultaneously, they will not get the same experience, due to the users' freedom to move their field of view to look where they want to. This is a drawback of XR systems because it separates the viewer from other people socially. Human interaction, such as pointing out interesting details or seeing what others are focusing on, does not work because you cannot see other people through the screens. Therefore, supporting social communication is crucial when developing XR applications (Rothe et al. 2018).

7.2.2 Developing a Language of Expression

The process of designing games based on a screen and given control inputs (e.g. a gamepad, mouse, or keyboard) has been evolving for decades. This evolution has created best practices that are often genre and platform specific. Enabling the players to physically interact inside a virtual game environment poses new challenges for implementing these conventional practices to produce completely new gaming experiences. UX design in XR is a collective experimental process that the developers are currently working on to find best practices for solving completely new challenges. Each new medium of immersive experience has faced a new set of challenges for which traditional practices previously used were unsuitable.

We can look back to the evolution of cinematic conventions and language more than a century ago. Beginning with the practices of stage theatre, directors and moviemakers found the solutions through decades of experimentation and what felt best to the audience. This is exactly what is happening with the XR game developers who are taking part in collaborative efforts through inclusiveness and discovery each day, sharing best practices in ongoing technical improvements.

XR still lacks defined and refined working methods for storytelling, and the most important element in the design process is prototyping and user testing (Rouse and Barba 2017). The work is still in its early phase, and best practices are taking shape (Skult and Smed 2020). Nevertheless, we can say already that this process will require – and create – a new language to allow the designers of interactive XR storytelling to express themselves.

7.3 Streaming Media

Streaming media has grown out to be the most important channel for transporting stories with service providers such as Netflix, Amazon Prime, and Disney+ providing more content and collecting viewers. In its core, it is based on traditional, one-way storytelling (see Figure 1.2, p. 4) although it is built upon technology that would allow more interaction.

7.3.1 Problems

The tentative trials on interactive television programmes (see Section 1.3.4), based mainly on branching stories, are ridden with problems: One of the biggest challenges is the mode of the programme, which is alternatively *lay back* or *lean forward*. In the lay-back mode, the spectator is a passive watcher, receiving authored content. In the lean-forward mode, the spectator is (inter)active, having agency, making choices, and possibly producing content themself. Whenever the mode changes, it interrupts the spectator's flow experience (see Section 5.3.3). The spectator's mind could repeatedly go through the same set of questions: 'Is it time again to find the remote control and quickly make a selection?', 'Can I watch now, or is there still something to choose?', 'Huh, was that all that I could choose here?', and 'I wonder when I can make changes again?'.

The *perspective* offered to the spectator can make them ask 'Am *I* in the story?' (i.e. 'Do I have an avatar?'). With respect to the first problem, a programme keeping the spectator mainly in the lay-back mode, the spectator is likely to be not so interested in having or customizing a personal avatar. If the programme offers more of the lean-forward mode, the spectator probably also wants to have more control of this aspect as well.

The programme can support *single or multiple simultaneous interactors*. If it focuses on a single interactor, it remains simple and manageable but, as an experience, it can be limited. Having multiple interactors creates technological and content-creational problems, which we discuss in detail in Section 7.1.

Regarding the content creation, producers have to decide which can be done *beforehand* and which *on-the-fly* (see also the discussion of prepared and generative assets in Section 6.3.2). If all the content is created beforehand, there will be a limited amount of it, which restricts how much the story can branch but also allows the content to have better production quality. Conversely, on-the-fly creation allows to have a seemingly infinite amount of the content, but the tight production schedule could reduce the quality of content (both technical quality and content-wise quality such as non-sequiturs on logically problematic situations).

For streaming media, *platform heterogeneity* can create problems. Especially in television sets and other devices where streaming media service is embedded, the minimum platform requirements might make it difficult to realize all the possible ideas.

Figure 7.3 summarizes the problems as questions regarding the experience, content, and technology of an interactive streaming media programme. Each production has to consider them and make their own decisions.

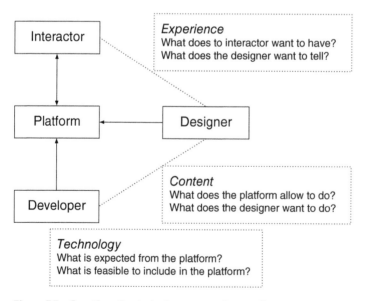

Figure 7.3 Questions for designing a streaming media programme.

7.3.2 Solution Proposals

To counter the problems presented in Section 7.3.1, we present here five ideas for a design. None of them has been realized on a larger scale, but we hope that they could act as catalysts to create novel approaches for the streaming media.

The first idea is to have *session-based episodes*, which clearly separates the lay-back and lean-forward modes. It is based on iteration, where the spectator is provided, for example, once a day or a week an episode to be watched in the lay-back mode. Having finished the episode, the spectator would then set parameters (e.g. goals) for the next episode (i.e. they would be in the lean-forward mode). These selections are used in creating the next episode. One could, quite rightly, draw parallels to webisodics (Section 1.3.2) or play-by-(e)mail games, which also follow the same iterative scheme. Session-based episodes would be easy to realize using existing platforms (in the simplest case, the content is basically just video), and they would even allow multiple interactors by having more rigorous time limits to make decisions. The challenge, however, would be that episodes require on-the-fly content, which means the platform must have a technical back end to support this.

The second idea aims at getting rid of the branching structure approach. One possibility is to use a *storypool*, which comprises (short) episodes of beforehand created content. Each episode in the storypool is labelled with a precondition and postcondition. The precondition defines, for example, using predicate logic the states of the storyworld that must hold in order the episode to be shown next. If there are more than one episode that would be possible to show next, selection is done randomly. After the selected episode has been shown, the state of the storyworld changes according to the postconditions. At this point, the spectators can make their own choices, which will also change the state of the storyworld. The next episode to be played is then selected similarly from the storypool based on the updated state of the storyworld. Although the storypool must initially have a sufficiently covering set of episodes, it is also possible to add new episodes into the storypool later. *Her Story* (Barlow 2016) can be seen as a simplistic example of this approach, but storypools are still largely untested and their construction might turn out to be too difficult in practice.

The third idea is based on emergent storytelling (see Section 3.2.2) and allows the spectators to create their *own reality TV shows*. The spectator first creates the cast and set-up for the show in a lean-forward mode. Once this is done, the spectator can watch the show in the lay-back mode but they can, at any time, change the mode to lean forward and add, delete, or make changes to the characters, scenes, props, or events. *The Sims* (Maxis 2000) can be a simple example of this approach, and Cavazza et al. (2002) demonstrated how this could work using cast and scenarios from the television sitcom *Friends*. The greatest challenge with this approach is that relying on emergence alone might not be enough to create an interesting show, but we would actually need to employ the ideas of a hybrid approach discussed in detail in Section 3.2.3.

The fourth idea is to use *parallel worlds or time loops* in creating the story. This can be called the *Groundhog Day* approach as it reverts to the initial situation and invites the spectator to choose a different path. Although this is basically a branching story, the difference is that here the depth of the story is limited, but it has more width (i.e. different parallel variations). This limits the possibilities of storyworld creation and interaction and makes it easier to produce the content beforehand. The video game *12 Minutes* (Antonio 2020) is a good example of what this kind of story could look like. The downside of this approach is it can be seen as a gimmick, and, therefore, falls out of fashion quite quickly.

The fifth idea is *avant garde* storytelling. Apart from financial and technological limitations, there is nothing to limit realization of weird or challenging ways to get the story to the audience. Limitations are possibilities for creative solutions and seeds for novel ways for creating interactive experiences – also in the streaming media.

7.4 Other Technological Prospects

Technological advances tend to have a rippling effect on the way software is designed. It can open new possibilities or change the way the existing ones are being used. Here, we have collected some other ideas that might be more important for interactive storytelling in the future.

7.4.1 Voice Recognition

Amongst the many technologies for interaction, voice recognition seems to offer the most interesting possibilities for interactive storytelling. There are already first examples of applications taking *Choose Your Own Adventure* gamebooks and converting them into audiobooks with speech control.

Broadly speaking, voice recognition provides the interactor with new ways to affect the storyworld. It is a more natural way to have conversation with a character as it removes the encumbrance of giving input by typing in utterances or selecting icons – regardless of whether the underlying model resembles the broad-and-shallow discussed in Section 3.3.3. Recalling Aristotle's narrative forms (see Section 2.1.1), the networks of social relationships are the key for the dramatic form, and – as in real life – these networks are created and maintained by discussing with the fellow characters.

7.4.2 Locating

Ruston (2014) divides the technology used in location-based narratives into location-aware technology (e.g. GPS, cell signal triangulation) and proximity detectors (e.g. Bluetooth, RFID, self-reporting). Location-aware technology is passive and automated but least intrusive and most immersive. Location can be used for the following:

- *Spatial annotation*: Provides information about a space and often involves a participatory component (e.g. uploading pictures)
- *Games*: Uses the real world as a game board and narratives to facilitate gameplay
- *Mobile narrative experiences*: Accessing a story with a mobile device while moving through a space

Location-based interactive storytelling is essential in many non-entertainment applications such as museum or exhibition guides, which connect elementally to a physical location. Here, the challenge for the design is superimposing the storyworld over the real world. The prime examples of location-based games such as *Ingress* (Niantic 2013) or *Pokémon*

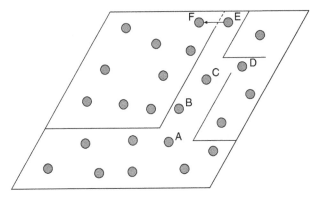

Figure 7.4 Storyworld events superimposed over the real world.

Go (Niantic 2016) have solved this by having a simple story that does not rely on the real-world topology. In *Ingress*, the two factions, the Enlightened and the Resistance, are having battle over the control over Exotic Matter (XM), which is connected to how much they control the sources of XM superimposed over the real world. The narrative stems then from the actions happening in the real world like history or news being written after the fact.

Let us consider how the paths in the real world could correspond to the storyworld by considering the example illustrated in Figure 7.4. A museum visitor can go to places (connected to story events) in any order but moving from A to D they have to go past B and C. It is unlikely that they will do this blindfolded but B and C will seep through and influence the experience. Also, the physical one-way barrier (e.g. turnstile) between E and F closes the possibility to return places A–E. The problem is similar to what we have encountered earlier in open storyworld (see Section 4.1.3) with the exception that here the design of the world cannot be altered to fit the story.

7.4.3 Artificial Intelligence

We have seen in the past few years an expansion of artificial intelligence (AI) methods. The development of AI has gone through a twisty path from AI winters, when the most promising approach at the time did not live up to the expectations. With the advent of increasing processing power of both general-purpose computing on graphics processing units (GPGPU) and cloud computing, AI methods, which were theoretical and applicable to small problems at best, are now at the reach of practically everybody. As a consequence, we have seen a promulgation of application areas.

One could well ask what does this mean to interactive storytelling. Throughout this book, we have witnessed many proposed analytical and theory-induced methods that have not really delivered interactive storytelling in its truest form. Could this current AI boom provide solutions that we have been trying to find otherwise?

Machine learning – and especially deep neural networks (DNNs) – is, at the time of writing, proposed as an all-around method for solving problems that are beyond the grasp of classical computer science. It seems a tempting approach for many problems, because one does not have to solve the problem but just make the DNN learn how to do it. All that is needed is an ample amount of material for learning and an evaluation function to measure how well the DNN is solving the given problem instance. We do have vast amounts of digitally encoded stories, free as the Gutenberg Project as well as proprietary. What could be easier, one can ask, than just feeding in all the data into a DNN and letting it learn how to generate stories in a similar manner than how AlphaGo learned to play Go better than any human being. Would this be a recipe for creating a digital storyteller who could adapt to any whims of the audience?

First examples of this are already in practical use, as we are writing this text. Generative Pre-trained Transformer 3 (GPT-3) introduced in February 2020 produces texts that are already hard to tell apart from text originating from a human. Could we now have 'new' interactive works by famous authors? What if we use the complete works of, say, Jane Austen or Lev Tolstoy as a corpus. Would we have an interactive storyworld as an early nineteenth-century genteel folks or late nineteenth-century Russians? Or could an author, instead of creating works, start to create intentionally a corpus for a storyworld which is then learned and used by a future derivant of GPT-3 or a similar method.

Or, simply put, has all the work presented in this book been in vain?

Let us formulate the argument as a *reductio ad absurdum* by supposing the contrary: Having a learning computer-controlled story generation system renders the analysis-based approach unsuitable. This means that effort required would be similar to training a human being to become a writer: reading texts – exemplar texts – and evaluating them, learning by doing, getting input, and so on, maybe even having an innate knack or talent for storytelling. If such a tool would turn out to be a masterful storyteller, we would not know much more of how it did it. Granted, we could observe new 'moves' that nobody has not imagined before such as has been the case of Alpha-Go. Unless that machine could analyse its own processes to abstract patterns, rules, recognize objects and relationships, we would not know anything more how storytelling works – and neither would it. It would be like a savant, capable of extraordinary feats without revealing the secrets within. And if it could, then it would provide us with possible new analyses or extend the old ones, as we have been already doing since the time of Aristotle (or before). This is clearly a contradiction with our premise, so the opposite must hold.

Only time will tell whether this scenario will take place and be a turning point for the research on interactive storytelling. Maybe this will be realized (first) on a small scale, for example, in the control of characters, whose behaviour gets more human-like. Nevertheless, telling and understanding stories is such a fundamental part of the human condition that having an adapting, reactive, and creative digital storyteller would prefigure the coming of true digital beings.

7.5 Ethical Considerations

When thinking about the ethical dimension of interactive storytelling, we have to realize that we are focusing on what human beings are doing. According to the classification that we have introduced in Section 1.1.1 – and used to organize the chapters of this book – we can take each of the partakers and look at them from this perspective one by one.

7.5.1 Platform

We expect the platform to be reliable, maintain our private information, and not be open for hacking. We should be able to trust that the information we share is treated respectfully and with care. The platform can be compromised by attacks using either technical or social weaknesses. For example, passwords can be stolen by cracking them (technical attack) or pretending to be the administrator and asking the players to give their passwords (social engineering attack). These demands on data security are typical for any kind of application nowadays.

We can extend this to include also what is done with the log data and profiles of the interactors. Apart from collecting data from the interactor's decisions, the platform can also record the player's decisions on advertisements (e.g. whether they decide to click it or skip it). Although this data is not related to the actual story, it is a valuable asset for the platform owner in terms of recognizing the most potential advertisers. Moreover, when this data is combined with the log data, the platform owner can try to modify the application to be more advertisement friendly – even to the extent of blurring the demarcation between the advertorial and actual content.

A special challenge would be profiling as the interactor makes many choices. A simple example is *The Walking Dead* (Telltale Games 2012), which computes morality of the player after each level. Imagine that this profile would cover much more of the interactor's personality.

The ethical problems present in the platform are related to how it is taking away the interactor's control of their resources such as money, time, attention, social capital, mental and physical energy, and security (Hyrynsalmi et al. 2020). When one uses an interactive storytelling application, one is willing to invest these resources: the interactor invests money to use the application, reserves time for experiencing the story, uses social capital to invite others to join in the platform, exerts mental and physical energy to progress in the story, and assumes to be secure in the real world whilst engaged in virtual risks in the storyworld.

7.5.2 Designer

As the creator of the storyworld, the designer has the burden of defining its ethical dimension. Adams (2014, pp. 159–162) lines out this ethical dimension so that the designer defines 'what right and wrong means within the context of that world'. Sicart (2009, p. 41) shares this view and asserts that the 'designer is responsible for most of the values that are embedded in the system and that play a significant role during the game experience'.

Broadly speaking, many of the same ethical considerations that apply to video games also apply to interactive storytelling. It would be possible to imagine how appealing such a storyworld could be for product placement or advertising. The characters could be harnessed for promoting products or services that are then needed in proceeding. Also, props could be based on real-world products. The line here is vague: It could be argued that this is just a way for monetization, and as long as it follows the judicial guidelines (e.g. promoting smoking is forbidden), it would be on the safe side. A counter argument would require these connections to be made visible as it might be hard to differentiate what is promotion and what is not. Of course, in the extreme, promotion by the characters might look like *The Truman Show*, where pushing the products becomes too intrusive to go unnoticed.

There is a short step from here to propaganda. One could easily imagine interactive storytelling as a tool for political, religious, or cultural propaganda. This is not uncommon as the controversy around games such as *America's Army* (United States Army 2002), *Quest for Bush* (Global Islamic Media Front 2006), and *Left Behind: Eternal Forces* (Inspired Media Entertainment 2006) have shown. Interactive storytelling might make this propaganda even more effective as it possibly immerses the interactor even deeper in the storyworld. It could be used to confirm already existing stereotypes, racist, misogynous, or other prejudices. In this sense, it is closer to social media than video games as its characters reacting to the interactor and situation can create a similar echo chamber effect. This could be even more pronounced if we have multiple interactors, who might even be able to hijack an existing platform to their use, which reminds how other Twitter users turned Microsoft's chatbot Tay in a short time into a proxy spewing out misogynous and racist hate speech.

7.5.3 Interactor

Having multiple human interactors also opens the door for ethical questions, the obvious one being cheating. Apart from technical cheating such as hacking software, this is about what belongs to the agreement the interactors are committed to. Cheating means achieving the goal by breaking the rules, but what are the goals and rules in a storyworld? Cheating that takes place inside the storyworld is just a part of the story, since every action within the storyworld – no matter how civil or rude – is part of the experience and should be valid. This kind of cheating can be called managed or explicitly possible. However, cheating that is not comprehended as a part of the interactors' agreement may ruin the experience, depending on if the cheat becomes acceptable as a way to broaden the conflict aspect of the storyworld. That is, the agreement may evolve, with mutual approval.

Multiple interactors can also bring about cyberbullying and other unethical behaviour that riddle, for example, multiplayer games and social media. Preventing this kind of behaviour can be hard to realize, but it should be a conscious aim of everyone taking part in the implementation, design, and use of an interactive storytelling application.

Modding blurs the line between the interactor and designer (see Section 3.1.4). It also makes the modder to face the same ethical questions as the designer.

7.5.4 Storyworld

By large, we can attribute events in the storyworld to the other three partakers who are obviously humans. Could there be ethical issues that stem from the computer-controlled creations alone?

As the systems become more complex, it is possible that there emerges a phenomenon that is ethically questionable. This might seem a highly hypothetical possibility, but we can imagine a scenario where the ethically problematic phenomenon cannot be explained away by the intentions of the platform developer, designer, or interactor. Could one talk then about the ethics of a computer-controlled character? Could this happen? Would we be able to recognize the behaviour of a character (e.g. a psychopathic character)?

Yes, we could – but then we have to frame the question *inside* the storyworld. As the character lives there, it does not know the existence of a world outside of it – the world of the humans who created it, populated it, and participate in it. It does not know what its gods are doing. We can only judge it within its own world and hold it responsible there.

7.6 Summary

Interactive storytelling has still many open questions. The most fundamental of them all is whether it is possible to realize it in the first place. All the models or proposed systems are lacking in one way or another. Perhaps the narrative paradox is something that cannot be solved but we have to content ourselves with compromises and clever workarounds. As we have discussed throughout in this book, it is not enough to solve single instances, but it requires a collaboration of different levels and partakers: We must have reusable platforms that allow the designers to focus solely on creating the storyworld without technical considerations so that the interactors can fully realize the freedom and agency given to them.

Inevitably, we will see improvements in many areas. Some of them will be theoretical – and we sincerely wish that this book has helped in its own way to come up with these advances. More obvious will be the technological steps – new devices and modes of interaction they enable – that provide new areas for interactive storytelling. Still, it is worth bearing in mind what the previous research is pointing at. Maybe the technological advances allow us to do more – maybe it will be easier to create conversing and interacting characters due to advances in AI; maybe there will be ever more immersive technologies that make it hard to distinguish reality from fiction. Whatever that is, we will still be sitting around the campfire where we started this book and waiting for the next storyteller to take their stand.

Exercises

7.1 Can you think of examples of stories with multiple main characters? List them and analyse what is common in the cases you found. Can those stories be extended to include interaction?

7.2 Multiple interactors bring the too-many-heroes problem. But how many heroes are actually too many? Can you pinpoint the amount, when an interactive storyworld would become unmanageable or too limiting?

7.3 Regarding persistence of a storyworld, the text proposes three possible solutions. How would you perceive them as an interactor?

7.4 Invent possible explanations for a storyworld where the interactors can appear and disappear at any time. Bear in mind that the duration of disappearance can be arbitrarily long. Try to keep the explanation as logical as possible.

7.5 One classical model for understanding the relationship of VR and AR is shared-space technologies (Benford et al. 1998), which is illustrated in Figure 7.5.

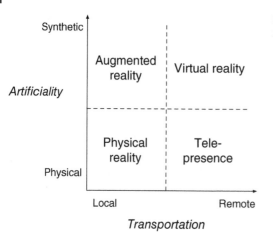

Figure 7.5 Shared-space technologies.
Source: Modified from Benford et al. 1998.

The transportation axis indicates the level to which the users leave behind their local space, and the artificiality axis the level to which a space is computer generated. By using these two dimensions, four types of technology can be classified: Physical reality resides in the local, physical world (i.e. the things are tangible and the participants are corporeal). Conversely, virtual reality allows the participants to be transported to a remote, synthetic world. In telepresence, the participants have and experience the presence at a real-world location remote from their physical location (e.g. remote-controlled drones with sensory feedback). In augmented reality, synthetic objects are overlaid on the local environment.

How would you see the role of interactive storytelling in each of the quadrants?

7.6 Stage a scene for VR (you can do it as well in the real world, if you do not have the possibility to use VR devices). Your task is to tell a story of a bank robbery gone wrong and the scene is the bank hall. The interactor steps into the scene and is in the middle of action.

Think how you can keep the interactor focused on the narratively important events while there are many other things unfolding simultaneously. How could you draw their attention to the intended direction? Would it still be possible for them to miss something essential – and if so, how to remedy that? If possible, try to enact the scene as a group.

7.7 The history of film provides a reference point to many so-called new media. For example, check the following films:
- *Georges Méliès: A Trip to the Moon* (1902)
- *Robert Wiene: The Cabinet of Dr. Caligari* (1920)
- *Sergei Eisenstein: Battleship Potemkin* (1925)
- *Buster Keaton: The General* (1926)
- *Charles Chaplin: City Lights* (1931)
- *Orson Welles: Citizen Kane* (1941)

Observe how the cinematic language develops. Alternatively, you could observe a similar kind of development in video games (especially within one genre). For example, you can try out the following games:

- *Space Invaders* (Taito 1978)
- *Zaxxon* (Sega 1982)
- *Elite* (Braben and Bell 1984)
- *Wing Commander* (Origin Systems 1990)
- *Eve Online* (CCP Games 2003)

You can also review story-driven games of the past years.
Based on your observations, how do you see the language of interactive storytelling developing in the (near) future?

7.8 Why is the branching story structure (see Section 4.1.2) so alluring choice for implementing interactivity into streaming media programmes?

7.9 Think about an interactive storytelling application using voice recognition. What kind of benefits could it provide to the interactor's experience?

7.10 Location-based interactive stories would have many application areas (e.g. museums or expos). The superimposing of the storyworld seems, however, problematic. Is it so? Can you think about alternatives? (*Hint*: You might want to recall or observe how children play outside and abstract their surroundings into the make-believe play.)

7.11 If we would have an AI that learns from a corpus of stories, it would quite likely need an evaluation function to rate their quality. How would you define this evaluation function (i.e. what would you rate as a good story)?

7.12 If the platform would use the interactor's decisions to create a model of their personality, how could that be used to make monetization more effective?

7.13 Sketch a design for a storyworld that would try to convert the interactor's stance one-sidedly on some controversial issue. How easy or difficult is it to include propaganda into the design?

7.14 Do you agree with our statement that cheating is not a problem in pure interactive storytelling? What about impure interactive storytelling, where there are game-like qualities like measurable goals, comparable objectives, or outright rules?

7.15 Come up with an example (no matter how hypothetical) where the computer-controlled characters would act unethically on their own accord (and not because of some intentional human intervention).

7.16 The future of interactive storytelling is full of promise. Let us think around and try to conduct a premortem to consider what if interactive storytelling never broke through. The idea of a premortem is simple: 'Imagine that we are a year into the future. We implemented the plan as it now exists. The outcome was a disaster. Please take 5 to 10 minutes to write a brief history of that disaster.' (Kahneman 2012, pp. 264–265). Make a premortem on the failure of interactive storytelling. What can we learn from it?

7.17   There might be other technological advances that we, the authors of this book, might have overlooked – or that might have become prominent after the publication of this book. What are they? What problems do they bring about? What kind of problems could they solve?

Bibliography

Aarseth, E.J. (1997). *Cybertext: Perspectives on Ergodic Literature*. Baltimore, MD: The Johns Hopkins University Press.

Aarseth, E. (2012). A narrative theory of games. *Proceedings of the International Conference on the Foundations of Digital Games*, pp. 129–133.

Abbott, H. (2002). *The Cambridge Introduction to Narrative*. Cambridge: Cambridge University Press.

Adams, E. (2004). The Designer's Notebook: Postmodernism and the 3 Types of Immersion Blog Entry. https://www.gamasutra.com/view/feature/130531/ (accessed 22 December 2020).

Adams, E.W. (2013). Resolutions to some problems in interactive storytelling. PhD thesis. University of Teesside Middlesbrough, UK.

Adams, E. (2014). *Fundamentals of Game Design*, 3e. San Francisco, CA: New Riders.

Advanced Stories Group (2019). *Advanced Stories Authoring and Presentation System*. http://advancedstories.net/.

Ahearn, L.M. (2001). Language and agency. *Annual Review of Anthropology* 30: 109–137. https://doi.org/10.1146/annurev.anthro.30.1.109.

Aristotle (1932). *Poetics: Aristotle in 23 Volumes*, vol. 23 (trans. W.H. Fyfe). London: William Heinemann.

Aylett, R. (1999). Narrative in virtual environments – towards emergent narrative. In: *Narrative Intelligence: Papers from the 1999 Fall Symposium* (ed. M. Mateas and P. Sengers), 83–86. Menlo Park, CA, USA: AAAI Press.

Aylett, R. and Louchart, S. (2007). Being there: participants and spectators in interactive narrative. In: *Virtual Storytelling. Using Virtual Reality Technologies for Storytelling. Proceedings of the 4th International Conference, ICVS 2007*, Saint-Malo, France (5–7 December 2007), vol. 4871, *Lecture Notes in Computer Science* (ed. M. Cavazza and S. Donikian), 117–128. Springer-Verlag.

Aylett, R., Lim, M.Y, Louchart, S. et al. (eds.) (2010). *Interactive Storytelling: 3rd Joint Conference on Interactive Digital Storytelling, ICIDS 2010*, Edinburgh, UK (1–3 November 2010), *Lecture Notes in Computer Science*, vol. 6432. Springer-Verlag.

Aylett, R., Louchart, S., and Weallans, A. (2011). Research in interactive drama environments, role-play and story-telling. In: *Interactive Storytelling: 4th International Conference on Interactive Digital Storytelling, ICIDS 2011*, Vancouver, Canada (November 28–December 1, 2011), *Lecture Notes in Computer Science*, vol. 7069 (ed. M. Si, D. Thue, E. Andre et al.), 1–12. Springer-Verlag.

Handbook on Interactive Storytelling, First Edition. Jouni Smed, Tomi 'bgt' Suovuo, Natasha Skult, and Petter Skult.
© 2021 John Wiley & Sons Ltd. Published 2021 by John Wiley & Sons Ltd.

Aylett, R., Vala, M., Sequeira, P., and Paiva, A. (2007). FearNot! – an emergent narrative approach to virtual dramas for anti-bullying education. In: *Virtual Storytelling. Using Virtual Reality Technologies for Storytelling. Proceedings of the 4th International Conference, ICVS 2007*, Saint-Malo, France (5–7 December 2007), *Lecture Notes in Computer Science*, vol. 4871 (ed. M. Cavazza and S. Donikian), 202–205. Springer-Verlag.

Bailey, P. (1999). Searching for storiness: story-generation from a reader's perspective. In: *Narrative Intelligence: Papers from the 1999 Fall Symposium* (ed. M. Mateas and P. Sengers), 157–163. Menlo Park, CA, USA: AAAI Press.

Bala, P., Dionisio, M., Nisi, V., and Nunes, N. (2016). IVRUX: a tool for analyzing immersive narratives in virtual reality. In: *Interactive Storytelling: 9th International Conference on Interactive Digital Storytelling, ICIDS 2016*, Los Angeles, CA, USA (15–18 November 2016), *Lecture Notes in Computer Science*, vol. 10045 (F. Nack and A.S. Gordon), 3–11. Springer-Verlag.

Bala, P., Masu, R., Nisi, V., and Nunes, N. (2018). Cue control: interactive sound spatialization for 360° videos. In: *Interactive Storytelling: 11th International Conference on Interactive Digital Storytelling, ICIDS 2018*, Dublin, Ireland (5–8 December 2018), *Lecture Notes in Computer Science*, vol. 11318 (ed. R. Rouse, H. Koenitz, and M. Haahr), 333–337. Springer-Verlag.

Balet, O., Subsol, G. and Torguet, P. (eds.) (2001). *Virtual Storytelling. Using Virtual Reality Technologies for Storytelling. Proceedings of the International Conference, ICVS 2001*, Avignon, France (27–28 September 2001), *Lecture Notes in Computer Science*, vol. 2197. Springer-Verlag.

Balet, O., Subsol, G. and Torguet, P. (eds.) (2003). *Virtual Storytelling. Using Virtual Reality Technologies for Storytelling. Proceedings of the 2nd International Conference, ICVS 2003*, Toulouse, France (20–21 November 2003), *Lecture Notes in Computer Science*, vol. 2897. Springer-Verlag.

Barber, H. and Kudenko, D. (2007). Dynamic generation of dilemma-based interactive narratives. In: *Proceedings of the 3rd Artificial Intelligence and Interactive Digital Entertainment Conference* (ed. J. Schaeffer and M. Mateas), 2–7. Menlo Park, CA, USA: AAAI Press.

Barthes, R. (1977). *Elements of Semiology*. New York, NY: Hill & Wang.

Bartle, R. (1996). Hearts, clubs, diamonds, spades: players who suit MUDs. *Journal of MUD Research*. 1 (1). http://mud.co.uk/richard/hcds.htm.

Bartle, R. (2005). Virtual worlds: why people play. In: *Massively Multiplayer Game Development 2* (ed. T. Alexander), 3–18. Hingham, MA: Charles River Media.

Bateman, C. and Boon, R. (2005). *21st Century Game Design*. Hingham, MA: Charles River Media.

Bates, J. (1992). Virtual reality, art and entertainment. *Presence* 1 (1): 133–138.

Benford, S., Greenhalgh, C., Reynard, G. et al. (1998). Understanding and constructing shared spaces with mixed-reality boundaries. *ACM Transactions on Computer-Human Interaction* 5 (3): 185–223.

Bevensee, S.H., Boisen, K.A.D., Olsen, M.P. et al. (2012). Project Aporia – an exploration of narrative understanding of environmental storytelling in an open world scenario. In: *Interactive Storytelling: 5th International Conference on Interactive Digital Storytelling, ICIDS 2012*, San Sebastián, Spain (12–15 November 2012), *Lecture Notes in Computer Science*, vol. 7648 (ed. D. Oyarzun, F. Peinado, R.M. Young et al.), 96–101. Springer-Verlag.

Bizzocchi, J. (2007). Games and narrative: an analytical framework. *Loading* 1 (1): 5–10. http://journals.sfu.ca/loading/index.php/loading/article/view/1.

Bizzocchi, J., Lin, M.B., and Tanenbaum, J. (2011). Games, narrative and the design of interface. *International Journal of Arts and Technology* 4 (4): 460–479. https://doi.org/10.1504/IJART.2011.043445.

Blair, D. and Meyer, T. (1997). Tools for an interactive virtual cinema. In: *Creating Personalities for Synthetic Actors: Towards Autonomous Personality Agents, Lecture Notes in Computer Science*, vol. 1195 (ed. P. Petta and R. Trappl), 83–91. Springer-Verlag.

Blonsky, M. (1985). *On Signs*. Baltimore, MD: Johns Hopkins University Press.

Boal, A. (1979). *Theatre of the Oppressed*. London: Pluto Press.

Bringsjord, S. (2001). Is it possible to build dramatically compelling interactive digital entertainment? *Game Studies* 1: (1). http://www.gamestudies.org/0101/bringsjord/.

Bringsjord, S. and Ferrucci, D. (1999). BRUTUS and the narrational case against Church's thesis. In: *Narrative Intelligence: Papers from the 1999 Fall Symposium* (ed. M. Mateas and P. Sengers), 105–111. Menlo Park, CA, USA: AAAI Press.

Brom, C., Pešková, K., and Lukavský, J. (2007). What does your actor remember? Towards characters with a full episodic memory. In: *Virtual Storytelling. Using Virtual Reality Technologies for Storytelling. Proceedings of the 4th International Conference, ICVS 2007, Saint-Malo, France (5–7 December 2007), Lecture Notes in Computer Science*, vol. 4871 (ed. M. Cavazza and S. Donikian), 89–101. Springer-Verlag.

Bruni, L.E. and Baceviciute, S. (2007). Narrative intelligibility and closure in interactive systems. In: *Virtual Storytelling. Using Virtual Reality Technologies for Storytelling. Proceedings of the 4th International Conference, ICVS 2007*, Saint-Malo, France (5–7 December 2007), *Lecture Notes in Computer Science*, vol. 4871 (ed. M. Cavazza and S. Donikian), 13–24. Springer-Verlag.

Cage, D. (2009). Writing interactive narrative for a mature audience Keynote speech. *Game Developers Conference Europe*, Cologne, Germany.

Campbell, J. (2008). *The Hero with a Thousand Faces*, 3e. Novato, CA: New World Library.

Cardona-Rivera, R.E., Sullivan, A. and Young, R.M. (eds.) (2019). *Interactive Storytelling: 12th International Conference on Interactive Digital Storytelling, ICIDS 2019*, Little Cottonwood Canyon, UT, USA (19–22 November 2019), *Lecture Notes in Computer Science*, vol. 11869. Springer-Verlag.

Carvalho, D.B., Clua, E.G., Pozzer, C.T. et al. (2017). Simulated perceptions for emergent storytelling. *Computational Intelligence* 33 (4): 605–628. https://doi.org/10.1111/coin.12088.

Castronova, E. (2005). *Synthetic Worlds: The Business and Culture of Online Games*. Chicago, IL: University of Chicago Press.

Cavazza, M. and Donikian, S. (eds.) (2007). *Virtual Storytelling. Using Virtual Reality Technologies for Storytelling. Proceedings of the 4th International Conference, ICVS 2007*, Saint-Malo, France (5–7 December 2007), *Lecture Notes in Computer Science*, vol. 4871. Springer-Verlag.

Cavazza, M., Charles, F., and Mead, S.J. (2002). Interactive storytelling: from computer games to interactive stories. *The Electronic Library* 20 (2): 103–112.

Chatman, S. (1978). *Story and Discourse: Narrative Structures in Fiction and Film*. Ithaca, NY: Cornell University Press.

Ciarlini, A.E.M., Casanova, M.A., Furtado, A.L., and Veloso, P.A.S. (2010). Modeling interactive storytelling genres as application domains. *Journal of Intelligent Information* 35 (3): 347–381. https://doi.org/10.1007/s10844-009-0108-5.

Colburn, R. (2020). An influencer's unraveling is playing out as an interactive horror story on Instagram. The A.V. Club. https://news.avclub.com/an-influencers-unraveling-is-playing-out-as-an-interact-1844718965 (accessed 22 December 2020).

Colby, B.N. (1973). A partial grammar of Eskimo folktales. *American Anthropologist* 75 (3): 645–662.

Crawford, C. (1984). *The Art of Computer Game Design*. Berkeley, CA: Osborne/McGraw-Hill.

Crawford, C. (2005). *On Interactive Storytelling*. Berkeley, CA: New Riders.

Crawford, C. (2011a). Storytron: plans for the future Web page. http://www.storytron.com/PlansForFuture.html (accessed 22 December 2020).

Crawford, C. (2011b). Storytron: what went wrong. http://www.storytron.com/WhatWentWrong.html (accessed 22 December 2020).

Crawford, C. (2013). *On Interactive Storytelling*, 2e. Berkeley, CA: New Riders.

Crawford, C. (2019). Erasmatazz. http://www.erasmatazz.com/ (accessed 22 December 2020).

Crawford, C. (2020). Siboot. http://siboot.org/ (accessed 22 December 2020).

CrossTalk (2020). CrossTalk. http://www.dfki.de/crosstalk/ (accessed 22 December 2020).

Csikszentmihalyi, M. (1990). *Flow: The Psychology of Optimal Experience*. New York, NY: Harper & Row.

Dautenhahn, K. (1998). Story-telling in virtual environments. *Working Notes Intelligent Virtual Environments, Workshop at the 13th Biannual European Conference on Artificial Intelligence (ECAI 1998)*.

Davis, M. and Travers, M. (1999). A brief overview of the Narrative Intelligence Reading Group. In: *Narrative Intelligence: Papers from the 1999 Fall Symposium* (ed. M. Mateas and P. Sengers), 11–16. Menlo Park, CA, USA: AAAI Press.

de Saussure, F. (1966). *Course in General Linguistics* (trans. W. Baskin). New York, NY: McGraw-Hill.

de Saussure, F. (2006). *Writings in General Linguistics*. Oxford: Oxford University Press.

Digman, J.M. (1990). Personality structure: emergence of the five-factor model. *Annual Review of Psychology* 41 (1): 417–440. https://doi.org/10.1146/annurev.ps.41.020190.002221.

Dowling, D., Fearghail, C.O., Smolic, A., and Knorr, S. (2018). Faoladh: a case study in cinematic VR storytelling and production. In: *Interactive Storytelling: 11th International Conference on Interactive Digital Storytelling, ICIDS 2018*, Dublin, Ireland (5–8 December 2018), *Lecture Notes in Computer Science*, vol. 11318 (ed. R. Rouse, H. Koenitz, and M. Haahr), 359–362. Springer-Verlag.

Eco, U. (1978). *Theory of Semiotics*. Bloomington, IN: Indiana University Press.

Eco, U. (1989). *The Open Work*. Cambridge, MA: Harvard University Press.

Elliott, C. (1992). The affective reasoner: a process model of emotions in a multi-agent system. PhD thesis. Evanston, IL, USA: Northwestern University.

Elliott, C. (2016). Emotion categories. https://condor.depaul.edu/~elliott/ar/papers/EmotionTable2016.html.

Episode Interactive (2020). Episode. https://www.episodeinteractive.com/ (accessed 22 December 2020).

Ermi, L. and Mäyrä, F. (2005). Fundamental components of the gameplay experience: analysing immersion *Proceedings of the 2005 DiGRA International Conference: Changing Views – Worlds in Play.* http://www.digra.org/wp-content/uploads/digital-library/06276 .41516.pdf (accessed 22 December 2020).

Expressive Intelligence Studio (2019). Prom Week. https://promweek.soe.ucsc.edu/ (accessed 22 December 2020).

Fairclough, C.R. (2004). Story games and the OPIATE system. PhD thesis. Trinity College Dublin, Ireland: University of Dublin.

Fairclough, C. and Cunningham, P. (2002). An interactive story engine. In: *Proceedings of the 13th Irish International Conference on Artificial Intelligence and Cognitive Science, Lecture Notes in Artificial Intelligence*, vol. 2464 (ed. M. O'Neill, R.F.E. Sutcliffe, C. Ryan et al.), 171–176. Springer-Verlag.

Falk, J.H. and Dierking, L.D. (2016). *The Museum Experience Revisited*. Abingdon, Oxon: Routledge.

Fearghail, C.O., Ozcinar, C., Knorr, S., and Smolic, A. (2018). Director's cut – analysis of aspects of interactive storytelling for VR films. In: *Interactive Storytelling: 11th International Conference on Interactive Digital Storytelling, ICIDS 2018*, Dublin, Ireland (5–8 December 2018), *Lecture Notes in Computer Science*, vol. 11318 (ed. R. Rouse, H. Koenitz, and M. Haahr), 308–322. Springer-Verlag.

Fendt, M.W., Harrison, B., Ware, S.G. et al. (2012). Achieving the illusion of agency. In: *Interactive Storytelling: 5th International Conference on Interactive Digital Storytelling, ICIDS 2012*, San Sebastián, Spain (12–15 November 2012), *Lecture Notes in Computer Science*, vol. 7648 (ed. D. Oyarzun, F. Peinado, R.M. Young et al.), 114–125. Springer-Verlag.

Field, S. (1984). *The Screenwriter's Workbook*. New York, NY: Dell Publishing.

Figueiredo, R. and Paiva, A. (2010). 'I want to slay that dragon!' – influencing choice in interactive storytelling. In: *Interactive Storytelling: 3rd Joint Conference on Interactive Digital Storytelling, ICIDS 2010*, Edinburgh, UK (1–3 November 2010), *Lecture Notes in Computer Science*, vol. 6432 (ed. R. Aylett, M.Y. Lim, S. Louchart et al.), 26–37. Springer-Verlag.

Fisher, W.R. (1984). Narration as a human communication paradigm: the case of public moral argument. *Communication Monographs* 51 (1): 1–22. https://doi.org/10.1080/03637758409390180.

Forster, E.M. (1962). *Aspects of the Novel*. Harmondsworth: Penguin Books.

Frasca, G. (2003). Ludologists love stories, too: notes from a debate that never took place. In: *Level Up: Digital Games Research Conference* (ed. M. Copier and J. Raessens). http://www .digra.org/wp-content/uploads/digital-library/05163.01125.pdf.

Freytag, G. (1900). *Freytag's Technique of the Drama: An Exposition of Dramatic Composition and Art*, 3e (trans. E.J. MacEwan). Chicago, IL: Scott, Foresman and Company. Originally published in German *Die Technik des Dramas*, 1863.

Gadamer, H.G. (2004). *Truth and Method*, 2e. London: Bloomsbury Academic.

Genette, G. (1980). *Narrative Discourse: An Essay in Method*. New York, NY: Cornell University Press.

Göbel, S., Braun, N., Spierling, U. et al. (eds.) (2003). *Technologies for Interactive Digital Storytelling and Entertainment. Proceedings of the 1st International Conference, TIDSE 2003*, Darmstadt, Germany (24–26 March 2003), *Computer Graphik Edition*, vol. 9. Fraunhofer IRB Verlag.

Göbel, S., Braun, N. and Iurgel, I. (eds.) (2006). *Technologies for Interactive Digital Storytelling and Entertainment. Proceedings of the 3rd International Conference, TIDSE 2006* Darmstadt, Germany (4–6 December 2006), *Lecture Notes in Computer Science*, vol. 4326. Springer-Verlag.

Göbel, S., Spierling, U., Hoffman, A. et al. (eds.) (2004). *Technologies for Interactive Digital Storytelling and Entertainment. Proceedings of the 2nd International Conference, TIDSE 2004*, Darmstadt, Germany (24–26 June 2004), *Lecture Notes in Computer Science*, vol. 3105. Springer-Verlag.

GOG.com (2019). Revisit rainy Los Angeles with the return of the classic Blade Runner. https://www.gog.com/news/revisit_rainy_los_angeles_with_the_return_of_the_classic_blade_runner (accessed 22 December 2020).

Gomes, P., Paiva, A., Martinho, C., and Jhala, A. (2013). Metrics for character believability in interactive narrative. In: *Interactive Storytelling: 6th International Conference on Interactive Digital Storytelling, ICIDS 2013*, Istanbul, Turkey (6–9 November 2013), *Lecture Notes in Computer Science*, vol. 8230 (ed. H. Koenitz, T.I. Sezen, G. Ferri et al.), 205–216. Springer-Verlag.

Hales, C. (2015). Interactive cinema in the digital age. In: *Interactive Digital Narrative: History, Theory and Practice* (ed. H. Koenitz, G. Ferri, M. Haahr et al.), 36–50. New York, NY: Routledge.

Hardy, B. (1968). Towards a poetics of fiction: 3) an approach through narrative. *Novel* 2 (1): 5–14.

Harrell, D.F. and Zhu, J. (2009). Agency play: dimensions of agency for interactive narrative design. In: *Intelligent Narrative Technologies II: Papers from the 2009 AAAI Spring Symposium* (ed. S. Louchart, M. Mehta, and D.L. Roberts), 44–52. Menlo Park, CA, USA: AAAI Press.

Hegel, G.W.F. (1967). *The Phenomenology of Mind*. New York, NY: Harper Torchbooks.

Heinonen, T., Kivimäki, A., Korhonen, K. et al.; Aristoteles (2012). *Aristoleen runousoppi: Opas aloittelijoille ja edistyneille*. Helsinki, Finland: Kustannusosakeyhtiö Teos (in Finnish).

Henrickson, L. (2018). The policeman's beard is algorithmically constructed. *3:AM Magazine*. https://www.3ammagazine.com/3am/the-policemans-beard-is-algorithmically-constructed/ (accessed 22 December 2020).

Herman, L. (2001). *Phoenix: The Fall & Rise of Videogames*. Springfield, NJ: Rolenta Press.

Heussner, T., Finley, T.K., Hepler, J.B., and Lemay, A. (2015). *The Game Narrative Toolbox*. Burlington, MA: Focal Press.

Ho, W.C. and Dautenhahn, K. (2008). Towards a narrative mind: the creation of coherent life stories for believable virtual agents. In: *Proceedings of the 8th International Conference on Intelligent Virtual Agents (IVA 2008), Lecture Notes in Computer Science*, vol. 5208 (ed. H. Prendinger, J.C. Lester, and M. Ishizuka), 59–72. Springer-Verlag.

Huizinga, J. (1955). *Homo Ludens: A Study of the Play-Element in Culture*. Boston, MA: The Beacon Press. Originally published in Dutch 1938.

Hyrynsalmi, S., Kimppa, K.K., and Smed, J. (2020). The ethics of game experience. In: *Game User Experience and Player-Centered Design* (ed. B. Bostan), 253–263. Cham, Switzerland: Springer Nature. https://doi.org/10.1007/978-3-030-37643-7_11.

Ibanez, J., Aylett, R., and Ruiz-Rodarte, R. (2003). Storytelling in virtual environments from a virtual guide perspective. *Virtual Reality* 7 (1): 30–42.

Inkle Studios (2020). Ink. https://www.inklestudios.com/ink/ (accessed 22 December 2020).

Itkonen, E. (2015). Influencing perceived agency: a study into user experiences in digital interactive storytelling. Master's thesis. University of Turku Turku, Finland.

Itkonen, E., Kyrki, J., and Smed, J. (2017). Studying interactive storytelling system Regicide: Part I. Agency. *Computers in Entertainment.* http://cie.acm.org/articles/studying-interactive-storytelling-system-regicide-part-i-agency/.

Iurgel, I.A., Zagalo, N. and Petta, P. (eds.) (2009) *Interactive Storytelling: 2nd Joint Conference on Interactive Digital Storytelling, ICIDS 2009*, Guimar aes, Portugal (9–11 December 2009), *Lecture Notes in Computer Science*, vol. 5915. Springer-Verlag.

Jacobsson, R. (1987). *Language in Literature.* Cambridge, MA: Harvard University Press.

Jakobson, R. (1960). Linguistics and poetics. In: *Style in Language* (ed. T.A. Sebeok), 350–377. Cambridge, MA: MIT Press.

Jenkins, H. (2004). Game design as narrative architecture. In: *First Person: New Media as Story, Performance, and Game* (ed. N. Wardrip-Fruin and P. Harrigan), 118–130. Cambridge, MA: MIT Press.

Jennings, P. (1996). Narrative structures for new media: towards a new definition. *Leonardo* 29 (5): 345–350. https://doi.org/10.2307/1576398.

Johnsson, S. (2013). Why no one clicked on the great hypertext story. *Wired.* https://www.wired.com/2013/04/hypertext/ (accessed 22 December 2020).

Juul, J. (1999). En kamp mellan spiel og fortælling: Et speciale om computerspil og interaktiv fiktion. Master's thesis. University of Copenhagen Denmark. Translated in English *A Clash between Game and Narrative: a thesis on computer games and interactive fiction.* https://www.jesperjuul.net/thesis/ (accessed 22 December 2020).

Juul, J. (2001). Game telling stories? *Game Studies.* 1: (1). http://www.gamestudies.org/0101/juul-gts/.

Juul, J. (2005). *Half Real: Video Games Between Real Rules and Fictional Worlds.* Cambridge, MA: MIT Press.

Kahn, K.M. (1979). *Creation of computer animation from story descriptions.* PhD thesis. Cambridge, MA, USA: Massachusetts Institute of Technology.

Kahneman, D. (2012). *Thinking, Fast and Slow.* London: Penguin Books.

Karlsson, B.F. and Furtado, A.L. (2014). Conceptual model and system for genre-focused interactive storytelling. In: *Proceedings of the 13th International Conference Entertainment Computing (ICEC 2014), Lecture Notes in Computer Science*, vol. 8770 (ed. Y. Pisan, N.M. Sgouros, and T. Marsh), 27–35. Springer-Verlag.

Kaukoranta, T., Smed, J., and Hakonen, H. (2003). Understanding pattern recognition methods. In: *AI Game Programming Wisdom 2* (ed. S. Rabin), 579–589. Hingham, MA: Charles River Media.

Kay, A., Goldberg, A., and Tesler, L. (1978). Position paper on: how to advance from hobby computing to personal computing. *ACM SIGPC Notes* 1 (2): 29–31. https://doi.org/10.1145/1164917.1164923.

Kelso, M.T., Weyhrauch, P., and Bates, J. (1993). Dramatic presence. *Presence* 2 (1): 1–15. https://doi.org/10.1162/pres.1993.2.1.1.

Klein, S., Aeschlimann, J.F., Balsiger, D.F. et al. (1973). Automatic Novel Writing: A Status Report. *Technical Report 186.* Madison, WI, USA: University of Wisconsin.

Klesen, M., Kipp, M., Gebhard, P., and Rist, T. (2003). Staging exhibitions: methods and tools for modelling narrative structure to produce interactive performances with virtual actors. *Virtual Reality* 7 (1): 17–29.

Knoller, N. (2010). Agency and the art of interactive digital storytelling. In: *Interactive Storytelling: 3rd Joint Conference on Interactive Digital Storytelling, ICIDS 2010*, Edinburgh, UK (1–3 November 2010), *Lecture Notes in Computer Science*, vol. 6432 (ed. R. Aylett, M.Y. Lim, S. Louchart et al.), 264–267. Springer-Verlag.

Knoller, N. (2012). The expessive space of IDS-as-art. In: *Interactive Storytelling: 5th International Conference on Interactive Digital Storytelling, ICIDS 2012*, San Sebastián, Spain (12–15 November 2012), *Lecture Notes in Computer Science*, vol. 7648 (ed. D. Oyarzun, F. Peinado, R.M. Young et al.), 30–41. Springer-Verlag.

Ko, D., Ryu, H., and Kim, J. (2018). Making new narrative structures with actor's eye-contact in cinematic virtual reality (CVR). In: *Interactive Storytelling: 11th International Conference on Interactive Digital Storytelling, ICIDS 2018*, Dublin, Ireland (5–8 December 2018), *Lecture Notes in Computer Science*, vol. 11318 (ed. R. Rouse, H. Koenitz, and M. Haahr), 343–347. Springer-Verlag.

Koenitz, H. (2014). Five theses for interactive digital narrative. In: *Interactive Storytelling: 7th International Conference on Interactive Digital Storytelling, ICIDS 2014*, Singapore, Singapore (3–6 November 2014), *Lecture Notes in Computer Science*, vol. 8832 (ed. A. Mitchell, C. Fernandez-Vara, and D. Thue), 134–139. Springer-Verlag.

Koenitz, H. (2015). Towards a specific theory of interactive digital narrative. In: *Interactive Digital Narrative: History, Theory and Practice* (ed. H. Koenitz, G. Ferri, M. Haahr et al.), 91–105. New York, NY: Routledge.

Koenitz, H. (2018). Narrative in video games. In: *Encyclopedia of Computer Graphics and Games* (ed. N. Lee). Switzerland: Springer International Publishing Cham. https://doi.org/10.1007/978-3-319-08234-9.

Koenitz, H. and Chen, K.J. (2012). Genres, structures and strategies in interactive digital narratives – analyzing a body of works created in ASAPS. In: *Interactive Storytelling: 5th International Conference on Interactive Digital Storytelling, ICIDS 2012*, San Sebastián, Spain (12–15 November 2012), *Lecture Notes in Computer Science*, vol. 7648 (ed. D. Oyarzun, F. Peinado, R.M. Young et al.), 84–95. Springer-Verlag.

Koenitz, H. and Eladhari, M.P. (2019). Challenges of IDN research and teaching. In: *Interactive Storytelling: 12th International Conference on Interactive Digital Storytelling, ICIDS 2019*, Little Cottonwood Canyon, UT, USA (19–22 November 2019), *Lecture Notes in Computer Science*, vol. 11869, 26–39 (ed. R.E. Cardona-Rivera, A. Sullivan, and R.M. Young). Springer-Verlag.

Koenitz, H., Ferri, G., Haahr, M. et al. (2015). Towards a ludonarrative toolbox. *Proceedings of DiGRA 2015: Diversity of play: Games – Cultures – Identities*.

Koenitz, H., Sezen, T.I., Ferri, G. et al. (eds.) (2013a). *Interactive Storytelling: 6th International Conference on Interactive Digital Storytelling, ICIDS 2013*, Istanbul, Turkey (6–9 November 2013), *Lecture Notes in Computer Science*, vol. 8230. Springer-Verlag.

Koenitz, H., Haahr, M., Ferri, G., and Sezen, T.I. (2013b). First steps towards a unified theory for interactive digital narrative. In: *Transactions on Edutainment X, Lecture Notes in Computer Science*, vol. 7775 (ed. Z. Pan, A.D. Cheok, W. Muller et al.), 20–35. Springer-Verlag.

Kyrki, J. (2015). Metrics for predicting user behavior and experience in an interactive storytelling system. Master's thesis. Turku, Finland: University of Turku.

Kyrki, J., Itkonen, E., and Smed, J. (2017). Studying interactive storytelling system Regicide: Part II. Morality. *Computers in Entertainment*. http://cie.acm.org/articles/studying-interactive-storytelling-system-regicide-part-ii-morality/.

La Farge, P. (2020). Luminous airplanes. https://www.paullafarge.com/luminous-airplanes.html.

Laurel, B.K. (1986). Toward the design of a computer-based interactive fantasy system. PhD thesis. Columbus, OH, USA: Ohio State University.

Laurel, B. (1991). *Computers as Theatre*. Reading, MA: Addison-Wesley.

Laurel, B. (2004). Response by Brenda Laurel. In: *First Person: New Media as Story, Performance, and Game* (ed. N. Wardrip-Fruin and P. Harrigan), 310–315. Cambridge, MA: MIT Press.

Laurel, B. (2014). *Computers as Theatre*, 2e. Upper Saddle River, NJ: Addison-Wesley.

Laws, R.D. (2002). *Robin's Laws of Good Game Mastering*. Austin, TX: Steve Jackson Games.

Lebowitz, M. (1984). Creating characters in a story-telling universe. *Poetics* 13 (3): 171–194. https://doi.org/10.1016/0304-422X(84)90001-9.

Lebowitz, M. (1985). Story-telling as planning and learning. *Poetics* 14 (6): 483–502. https://doi.org/10.1016/0304-422X(85)90015-4.

Liddil, B. (1981). Interactive fiction: six micro stories. *Byte* 6 (9): 436.

Louchart, S. (2007). Emergent narrative – towards a narrative theory of virtual reality. PhD thesis. Salford, UK: University of Salford.

Louchart, S. and Aylett, R. (2005). Managing a non-linear scenario – a narrative evolution. In: *Virtual Storytelling. Using Virtual Reality Technologies for Storytelling. Proceedings of the 3rd International Conference, ICVS 2005*, Strasbourg, France (November 30–December 2, 2005), *Lecture Notes in Computer Science*, vol. 3805 (ed. G. Subsol), 148–157. Springer-Verlag.

Louchart, S., Swartjes, I., Kriegel, M., and Aylett, R. (2008). Purposeful authoring for emergent narrative. In: *Interactive Storytelling: 1st Joint International Conference on Interactive Digital Storytelling, ICIDS 2008*, Erfurt, Germany (26–29 November 2008), *Lecture Notes in Computer Science*, vol. 5334 (ed. U. Spierling and N. Szilas), 273–284. Springer-Verlag.

Louchart, S., Truesdale, J., Suttie, N., and Aylett, R. (2015). Emergent narrative: past, present and future of an interactive storytelling approach. In: *Interactive Digital Narrative: History, Theory and Practice* (ed. H. Koenitz, G. Ferri, M. Haahr et al.), 185–199. New York, NY: Routledge.

Lyons, J. (1977). *Semantics*, vol. 1. Cambridge: Cambridge University Press.

Machado, I., Brna, P., and Paiva, A. (2004). 1, 2, 3… action! Directing real actors and virtual characters. In: *Technologies for Interactive Digital Storytelling and Entertainment. Proceedings of the 2nd International Conference, TIDSE 2004*, Darmstadt, Germany (24–26 June 2004), *Lecture Notes in Computer Science*, vol. 3105 (ed. S. Gobel, U. Spierling, A. Hoffman et al.), 36–41. Springer-Verlag.

MacIntyre, A. (1981). *After Virtue: A Study in Moral Theory*. London: Duckworth.

Magerko, B. (2014). The PC3 framework: a formal lens for analyzing interactive narratives across media forms. In: *Interactive Storytelling: 7th International Conference on Interactive Digital Storytelling, ICIDS 2014*, Singapore, Singapore (3–6 November 2014), *Lecture Notes in Computer Science*, vol. 8832 (ed. A. Mitchell, C. Fernandez-Vara, and D. Thue), 103–112. Springer-Verlag.

Mandler, J.M. and Johnson, N.S. (1977). Remembrance of things parsed: story structure and recall. *Cognitive Psychology* 9 (1): 111–151.

Marczewski, A. (2013). *Gamification: A Simple Introduction*. Andrzej Marczewski.

Mateas, M. (2002). Interactive drama, art and artificial intelligence. PhD thesis. Pittsburgh, PA, USA: Carnegie Mellon University.

Mateas, M. (2004). A preliminary poetics for interactive drama and games. In: *First Person: New Media as Story, Performance, and Game* (ed. N. Wardrip-Fruin and P. Harrigan), 19–33. Cambridge, MA: MIT Press.

Mateas, M. and Sengers, P. (1999). Narrative intelligence. In: *Narrative Intelligence: Papers from the 1999 Fall Symposium* (ed. M. Mateas and P. Sengers), pp. 1–10. Menlo Park, CA, USA: AAAI Press.

Mateas, M. and Sengers, P. (eds.) (2003). *Narrative Intelligence*. Amsterdam, The Netherlands: John Benjamins.

Mateas, M. and Stern, A. (2004). Natural language understanding in Façade: surface-text processing. In: *Technologies for Interactive Digital Storytelling and Entertainment. Proceedings of the 2nd International Conference, TIDSE 2004*, Darmstadt, Germany (24–26 June 2004), *Lecture Notes in Computer Science*, vol. 3105 (ed. S. Gobel, U. Spierling, A. Hoffman et al.), 3–13. Springer-Verlag.

Mateas, M. and Stern, A. (2005). Structuring content in the Façade interactive drama architecture. In: *Artificial Intelligence and Interactive Digital Entertainment* (ed. R.M. Young and J. Laird), 93–98. Menlo Park, CA, USA: AAAI Press.

Mäyrä, F. (2007). The contextual game experience: on the socio-cultural contexts for meaning in digital play *Proceedings of the 2007 DiGRA International Conference: Situated Play*. http://www.digra.org/digital-library/publications/the-contextual-game-experience-on-the-socio-cultural-contexts-for-meaning-in-digital-play/ (accessed 23 December 2020).

Medilab Theme (2020). Nothing for dinner. http://nothingfordinner.org (accessed 23 December 2020).

Medler, B. and Magerko, B. (2006). Scribe: a tool for authoring event driven interactive drama. In: *Technologies for Interactive Digital Storytelling and Entertainment. Proceedings of the 3rd International Conference, TIDSE 2006*, Darmstadt, Germany (4–6 December 2006), *Lecture Notes in Computer Science*, vol. 4326 (ed. S. Gobel, R. Malkewitz, and I. Iurgel), 139–150. Springer-Verlag.

Meehan, J.R. (1976). The metanovel: writing stories by computer. PhD thesis. New Haven, CT, USA: Yale University.

Meehan, J.R. (1977). TALE-SPIN, an interactive program that writes stories. *Proceedings of the 5th International Joint Conference on Artificial Intelligence*, pp. 91–98.

Merleau-Ponty, M. (1964). *Signs* (trans. R. McCleary). Evanston, IL: Northwestern University Press.

Mitchell, A. (2010). Motivations for rereading in interactive stories: a preliminary investigation. In: *Interactive Storytelling: 3rd Joint Conference on Interactive Digital Storytelling, ICIDS 2010*, Edinburgh, UK (1–3 November 2010), *Lecture Notes in Computer Science*, vol. 6432 (ed. R. Aylett, M.Y. Lim, S. Louchart et al.), 232–235. Springer-Verlag.

Mitchell, A., Fernández-Vera, C. and Thue, D. (eds.) (2014). *Interactive Storytelling: 7th International Conference on Interactive Digital Storytelling, ICIDS 2014*, Singapore, Singapore (3–6 November 2014), *Lecture Notes in Computer Science*, vol. 8832. Springer-Verlag.

Montfort, N. (2004). *Twisty Little Passages: An Approach to Interactive Fiction*. Cambridge, MA: MIT Press.

Murray, J.H. (1997). *Hamlet on the Holodeck: The Future of Narrative in Cyberspace*. Cambridge, MA: MIT Press.

Murray, J.H. (2004). From game-story to cyberdrama. In: *First Person: New Media as Story, Performance, and Game* (ed. N. Wardrip-Fruin and P. Harrigan), 2–11. Cambridge, MA: MIT Press.

Murray, J.H. (2005). The Last Word on Ludology v Narratology in Game Studies Keynote Talk at DiGRA 2005, Vancouver, Canada. https://inventingthemedium.com/2013/06/28/the-last-word-on-ludology-v-narratology-2005/ (accessed 23 December 2020).

Murray, J.H. (2011). Why Paris needs Hector and Lancelot needs Mordred: using traditional narrative roles and functions for dramatic compression in interactive narrative. In: *Interactive Storytelling: 4th International Conference on Interactive Digital Storytelling, ICIDS 2011*, Vancouver, Canada (November 28–December 1 2011), *Lecture Notes in Computer Science*, vol. 7069 (ed. M. Si, D. Thue, E. Andre et al.), 13–24. Springer-Verlag.

Murray, J.H. (2012). *Inventing the Medium: Principles of Interaction Design as a Cultural Practice*. Cambridge, MA: MIT Press.

Murray, J.H. (2017). *Hamlet on the Holodeck: The Future of Narrative in Cyberspace*, Updated edn. Cambridge, MA: MIT Press.

Nack, F. and Gordon, A.S. (eds.) (2016). *Interactive Storytelling: 9th International Conference on Interactive Digital Storytelling, ICIDS 2016*, Los Angeles, CA, USA (15–18 November 2016), *Lecture Notes in Computer Science*, vol. 10045. Springer-Verlag.

Nakasone, A., Prendinger, H., and Ishizuka, M. (2009). ISRST: generating interesting multimedia stories on the web. *Applied Artificial Intelligence* 23 (7): 633–679. https://doi.org/10.1080/08839510903205423.

Nakevska, M., Funk, M., Hu, J. et al. (2014). Interactive storytelling in a mixed reality environment: how does sound design and users' preknowledge of the background story influence the user experience? In: *Interactive Storytelling: 7th International Conference on Interactive Digital Storytelling, ICIDS 2014*, Singapore, Singapore (3–6 November 2014), *Lecture Notes in Computer Science*, vol. 8832 (ed. A. Mitchell, C. Fernandez-Vara, and D. Thue), 188–195. Springer-Verlag.

Norman, D.A. (2013). *The Design of Everyday Things*, revised and expanded edn. Cambridge, MA: MIT Press.

Nunes, N., Oakley, I., and Nisi, V. (eds.) (2017). *Interactive Storytelling: 10th International Conference on Interactive Digital Storytelling, ICIDS 2017*, Funchal, Madeira, Portugal (14–17 November 2017), *Lecture Notes in Computer Science*, vol. 10690. Springer-Verlag.

Ortony, A., Clore, G.L., and Collins, A. (1988). *The Cognitive Structure of Emotions*. Cambridge: Cambridge University Press.

Osborn, B.A. (2002). An agent-based architecture for generating interactive stories. PhD thesis. Monterey, CA, USA: Naval Postgraduate School.

Oyarzun, D., Peinado, F., Young, R.M. et al. (eds.) (2012). *Interactive Storytelling: 5th International Conference on Interactive Digital Storytelling, ICIDS 2012*, San Sebastián, Spain (12–15 November 2012), *Lecture Notes in Computer Science*, vol. 7648. Springer-Verlag.

Oz Project (2002). The Oz Project Home Page. https://www.cs.cmu.edu/afs/cs/project/oz/web/oz.html (accessed 23 December 2020).

Panofsky, E. (2003). *Iconography and Iconology: An Introduction to the Study of Renaissance Art*. Chicago, IL: University of Chicago Press.

Perlin, K. (2005). Toward interactive narrative. In: *Virtual Storytelling. Using Virtual Reality Technologies for Storytelling. Proceedings of the 3rd International Conference, ICVS 2005,* Strasbourg, France (November 30–December 2 2005), *Lecture Notes in Computer Science,* vol. 3805 (ed. G. Subsol), 135–147. Springer-Verlag.

Pervin, L.A. (2003). *The Science of Personality,* 2e. New York, NY: Oxford University Press.

Pixelberry Studios (2020). Choices: stories your play. https://www.pixelberrystudios.com/ (accessed 23 December 2020).

Plato (1925). *Phaedrus: Plato in Twelve Volumes,* vol. 9 (trans. H.N. Fowler). London: William Heinemann.

Pratten, R. (2011). *Getting Started with Transmedia Storytelling: A Practical Guide for Beginners,* 2e. CreateSpace Independent Publishing Platform.

Prince, G. (1980). Aspects of a grammar of narrative. *Poetics Today* 1 (3): 49–63. https://doi.org/10.2307/1772410.

Prince, G. (1987). *A Dictionary of Narratology.* Lincoln, NE: University of Nebraska Press.

Propp, V. (1968). *Morphology of the Folktale.* Austin, TX: University of Texas Press.

Queneau, R. (1981). *Contes et propos.* Paris: Gallimard.

Racter (1984). *The Policeman's Beard Is Half Constructed.* New York, NY: Warner Books.

Ren'Py (2020). Ren'Py. https://www.renpy.org/ (accessed 23 December 2020).

Rettberg, S. (2015). The American hypertext novel, and whatever became of it? In: *Interactive Digital Narrative: History, Theory and Practice* (ed. H. Koenitz, G. Ferri, M. Haahr et al.), 22–35. New York, NY: Routledge.

Riedl, M.O. (2004). Narrative generation: balancing plot and character. PhD thesis. Raleigh, NC: North Carolina State University.

Riedl, M.O. and Young, R.M. (2010). Narrative planning: balancing plot and character. *Journal of Artificial Intelligence Research* 39: 217–268. https://doi.org/10.1613/jair.2989.

Robertson, J. and Young, R.M. (2014). Finding Schrödinger's gun. In: *Proceedings of the 10th AAAI Conference on Artificial Intelligence and Interactive Digital Entertainment (AIIDE-14)* (ed. I. Horswill and A. Jhala), 153–159. Menlo Park, CA, USA: AAAI Press.

Rogers, S. (2014). *Level Up! The Guide to Great Video Game Design,* 2e. Chichester: Wiley.

Rothe, S., Montagud, M., Mai, C. et al. (2018). Social viewing in cinematic virtual reality: challenges and opportunities. In: *Interactive Storytelling: 11th International Conference on Interactive Digital Storytelling, ICIDS 2018,* Dublin, Ireland (5–8 December 2018), *Lecture Notes in Computer Science,* vol. 11318 (ed. R. Rouse, H. Koenitz, and M. Haahr), 338–342. Springer-Verlag.

Rouse, R. and Barba, E. (2017). Design for emerging media: how MR designers think about storytelling, process, and defining the field. In: *Interactive Storytelling: 10th International Conference on Interactive Digital Storytelling, ICIDS 2017,* Funchal, Madeira, Portugal (14–17 November 2017), *Lecture Notes in Computer Science,* vol. 10690 (ed. N. Nunes, I. Oakley, and V. Nisi), 245–258. Springer-Verlag.

Rouse, R., Koenitz, H., and Haahr, M. (eds.) (2018). *Interactive Storytelling: 11th International Conference on Interactive Digital Storytelling, ICIDS 2018,* Dublin, Ireland (5–8 December 2018), *Lecture Notes in Computer Science,* vol. 11318. Springer-Verlag.

Rumelhart, D.E. (1975). Notes on a schema for stories. In: *Representation and Understanding: Studies in Cognitive Science* (ed. D.G. Bobrow and A. Collins), 211–236. New York, NY: Academic Press.

Ruston, S. (2014). Location-based narrative. In: *The Johns Hopkins Guide to Digital Media* (ed. M.L. Ryan, L. Emerson, and B.J. Robertson), 318–321. Baltimore, MD: Johns Hopkins University Press.

Ryan, M.L. (2001). *Narrative as Virtual Reality: Immersion and Interactivity in Literature and Electronic Media*. Baltimore, MD: Johns Hopkins University Press.

Ryan, M.L. (2006). *Avatars of Story*. Minneapolis, MN: University of Minnesota Press.

Ryan, M.L. (2008). Interactive narrative, plot types, and interpersonal relations. In: *Interactive Storytelling: 1st Joint International Conference on Interactive Digital Storytelling, ICIDS 2008, Erfurt, Germany (26–29 November 2008), Lecture Notes in Computer Science*, vol. 5334 (ed. U. Spierling and N. Szilas), 6–13. Springer-Verlag.

Ryan, M.L. (2015). *Narrative as Virtual Reality 2: Revisiting Immersion and Interactivity in Literature and Electronic Media*. Baltimore, MD: Johns Hopkins University Press.

Ryan, J.O., Mateas, M., and Wardrip-Fruin, N. (2015). Open design challenges for interactive emergent narrative. In: *Interactive Storytelling: 8th International Conference on Interactive Digital Storytelling, ICIDS 2015, Copenhagen, Denmark (November 30–December 4 2015), Lecture Notes in Computer Science*, vol. 9445 (ed. H. Schoenau-Fog, L.E. Bruni, S. Louchart, and S. Baceviciute), 14–26. Springer-Verlag.

Sampson, SaG. (ed.) (1920). *Coleridge Biographia Literaria: Wordsworth Prefaces and Essays on Poetry*, Chapters I–IV, XIV–XXII, 1800–1815. London: Cambridge University Press.

Sanchez, S., Balet, O., Luga, H., and Duthen, Y. (2004). Autonomous virtual actors. In: *Technologies for Interactive Digital Storytelling and Entertainment. Proceedings of the 2nd International Conference, TIDSE 2004*, Darmstadt, Germany (24–26 June 2004), *Lecture Notes in Computer Science*, vol. 3105 (ed. S. Gobel, U. Spierling, A. Hoffman et al.), 68–78. Springer-Verlag.

Scenejo (2020). Scenejo. http://scenejo.interactive-storytelling.de/ (accessed 23 December 2020).

Schapiro, M. (1969). On some problems in the semiotics of visual art: field and vehicle in image-signs. *Semiotica* I: 223–242.

Schell, J. (2015). *The Art of Game Design: A Book of Lenses*, 2e. Boca Raton, FL: CRC Press.

Schiesel, S. (2005). Redefining the power of the gamer. *The New York Times*, Sect. E, p. 1. https://www.nytimes.com/2005/06/07/arts/redefining-the-power-of-the-gamer.html (accessed 23 December 2020).

Schoenau-Fog, H., Bruni, L.E., Louchart, S., and Baceviciute, S. (eds.) (2015). *Interactive Storytelling: 8th International Conference on Interactive Digital Storytelling, ICIDS 2015, Copenhagen, Denmark (November 30–December 4, 2015), Lecture Notes in Computer Science*, vol. 9445. Springer-Verlag.

Sengers, P. (1998). Do the thing right: an architecture for action-expression. In: *Proceedings of the 2nd International Conference on Autonomous Agents* (ed. K.P. Sykara and M. Wooldridge), 24–31. https://doi.org/10.1145/280765.280770. New York, NY, USA: Association for Computing Machinery.

Sengers, P. (2002). Schizophrenia and narrative in artificial agents. *Leonardo* 35 (4): 427–431.

Şengün, S. (2013). Silent Hill 2 and the curious case of invisible agency. In: *Interactive Storytelling: 6th International Conference on Interactive Digital Storytelling, ICIDS 2013, Istanbul, Turkey (6–9 November 2013), Lecture Notes in Computer Science*, vol. 8230 (ed. H. Koenitz, T.I. Sezen, G. Ferri et al.), 180–185. Springer-Verlag.

Si, M., Thue, D., André, E. et al. (eds.) (2011). *Interactive Storytelling: 4th International Conference on Interactive Digital Storytelling, ICIDS 2011*, Vancouver, Canada (November 28–December 1, 2011), *Lecture Notes in Computer Science*, vol. 7069. Springer-Verlag.

Sicart, M. (2009). *The Ethics of Computer Games*. Cambridge, MA: MIT Press.

Singer, B. (2012). H+ the digital series YouTube channel.

Skult, N. and Smed, J. (2020). Interactive storytelling in extended reality: concepts for the design. In: *Game User Experience and Player-Centered Design* (ed. B. Bostan), 450–467. Cham: Springer Nature. https://doi.org/10.1007/978-3-030-37643-7_21.

Smed, J. (2014). Interactive storytelling: approaches, applications, and aspirations. *International Journal of Virtual Communities and Social Networking* 6 (1): 22–34.

Smed, J. and Hakonen, H. (2006). *Algorithms and Networking for Computer Games*. Chichester: Wiley.

Smed, J. and Hakonen, H. (2008). Are We 'Users' of Interactive Stories? *Technical Report 909*. Turku, Finland: Turku Centre for Computer Science.

Smed, J. and Hakonen, H. (2017). *Algorithms and Networking for Computer Games*, 2e. Chichester: Wiley.

Smed, J., Suovuo, T., Trygg, N. et al. (2018). The digital campfire: an ontology of interactive digital storytelling. In: *Modern Perspectives on Virtual Communications and Social Networking* (ed. J. Thakur), 174–195. Hershey, PA: IGI Global. https://doi.org/10.4018/978-1-5225-5715-9.ch007.

Spierling, U. (2007). Adding aspects of 'implicit creation' to the authoring process in interactive stories. In: *Virtual Storytelling. Using Virtual Reality Technologies for Storytelling. Proceedings of the 4th International Conference, ICVS 2007*, Saint-Malo, France (5–7 December 2007), *Lecture Notes in Computer Science*, vol. 4871 (ed. M. Cavazza and S. Donikian), 13–25. Springer-Verlag.

Spierling, U. (2009). Conceiving interactive story events. In: *Interactive Storytelling: 2nd Joint Conference on Interactive Digital Storytelling, ICIDS 2009*, Guimar aes, Portugal (9–11 December 2009), *Lecture Notes in Computer Science*, vol. 5915 (ed. I.A. Iurgel, N. Zagalo, and P. Petta), 292–297. Springer-Verlag.

Spierling, U. and Hoffmann, S. (2010). Exploring narrative interpretation and adaptation for interactive story creation. In: *Interactive Storytelling: 3rd Joint Conference on Interactive Digital Storytelling, ICIDS 2010*, Edinburgh, UK (1–3 November 2010), *Lecture Notes in Computer Science*, vol. 6432 (ed. R. Aylett, M.Y. Lim, S. Louchart et al.), 50–61. Springer-Verlag.

Spierling, U. and Szilas, N. (eds.) (2008). *Interactive Storytelling: 1st Joint International Conference on Interactive Digital Storytelling, ICIDS 2008*, Erfurt, Germany (26–29 November 2008), *Lecture Notes in Computer Science*, vol. 5334. Springer-Verlag.

Spierling, U. and Szilas, N. (2009). Authoring issues beyond tools. In: *Interactive Storytelling: 2nd Joint Conference on Interactive Digital Storytelling, ICIDS 2009*, Guimar aes, Portugal (9–11 December 2009), *Lecture Notes in Computer Science*, vol. 5915 (ed. I.A. Iurgel, N. Zagalo, and P. Petta), 50–61. Springer-Verlag.

Stern, A. (2008). Embracing the combinatorial explosion: a brief prescription for interactive story R&D. In: *Interactive Storytelling: 1st Joint International Conference on Interactive Digital Storytelling, ICIDS 2008*, Erfurt, Germany (26–29 November 2008), *Lecture Notes in Computer Science*, vol. 5334 (ed. U. Spierling and N. Szilas), 1–5. Springer-Verlag.

Stern, A., Flanagan, M., Mateas, M. et al. (2003–2009). Grand text auto. http://grandtextauto .org.

Subsol, G. (ed.) (2005). *Virtual Storytelling. Using Virtual Reality Technologies for Storytelling. Proceedings of the 3rd International Conference, ICVS 2005*, Strasbourg, France (November 30–December 2, 2005), *Lecture Notes in Computer Science*, vol. 3805. Springer-Verlag.

Sullivan, A. and Salter, A. (2017). A taxonomy of narrative-centric board and card games. *Proceedings of the 12th International Conference on the Foundations of Digital Games (FGD'17)*. https://doi.org/10.1145/3102071.3102100.

Suovuo, T., Skult, N., Joelsson, T.N. et al. (2020). The game experience model (GEM). In: *Game User Experience and Player-Centered Design* (ed. B. Bostan), 183–205. Cham: Springer Nature. https://doi.org/10.1007/978-3-030-37643-7_8.

Suttie, N., Louchart, S., Aylett, R., and Lim, T. (2013). Theoretical considerations towards authoring emergent narrative. In: *Interactive Storytelling: 6th International Conference on Interactive Digital Storytelling, ICIDS 2013*, San Istanbul, Turkey (6–9 November 2013), *Lecture Notes in Computer Science*, vol. 8230 (ed. H. Koenitz, T.I. Sezen, G. Ferri et al.), 205–216. Springer-Verlag.

Swartjes, I. and Theune, M. (2006). A fabula model for emergent narrative. In: *Technologies for Interactive Digital Storytelling and Entertainment. Proceedings of the Third International Conference, TIDSE 2006*, Darmstadt, Germany (4–6 December 2006), *Lecture Notes in Computer Science*, vol. 4326 (ed. S. Gobel, R. Malkewitz, and I. Iurgel), 49–60. Springer-Verlag.

Swartjes, I. and Theune, M. (2009). Iterative authoring using story generation feedback: debugging or co-creation? In: *Interactive Storytelling: 2nd Joint Conference on Interactive Digital Storytelling, ICIDS 2009*, Guimarães, Portugal (9–11 December 2009), *Lecture Notes in Computer Science*, vol. 5915 (ed. I.A. Iurgel, N. Zagalo, and P. Petta), 62–73. Springer-Verlag.

Swartjes, I. and Vromen, J. (2007). Emergent story generation: lessons from improvisational theater. In: *Intelligent Narrative Technologies: Papers from the 2007 AAAI Fall Symposium* (ed. B.S. Magerko and M.O. Riedl), 146–149. Menlo Park, CA, USA: AAAI Press.

Swartjes, I., Kruizinga, E., and Theune, M. (2008). Let's pretend I had a sword: late commitment in emergent narrative. In: *Interactive Storytelling: 1st Joint International Conference on Interactive Digital Storytelling, ICIDS 2008*, Erfurt, Germany (26–29 November 2008), *Lecture Notes in Computer Science*, vol. 5334 (ed. U. Spierling and N. Szilas), 230–241. Springer-Verlag.

Szilas, N. (1999). Interactive drama: beyond linear narrative. In: *Narrative Intelligence: Papers from the 1999 Fall Symposium* (ed. M. Mateas and P. Sengers), 150–156. Menlo Park, CA, USA: AAAI Press.

Szilas, N. (2004). Stepping into the interactive drama. In: *Technologies for Interactive Digital Storytelling and Entertainment. Proceedings of the 2nd International Conference, TIDSE 2004*, Darmstadt, Germany (24–26 June 2004), *Lecture Notes in Computer Science*, vol. 3105 (ed. S. Gobel, U. Spierling, A. Hoffman et al.), 14–25. Springer-Verlag.

Szilas, N. (2007). BEcool: towards an author friendly behaviour engine. In: *Virtual Storytelling. Using Virtual Reality Technologies for Storytelling. Proceedings of the 4th International Conference, ICVS 2007*, Saint-Malo, France (5–7 December 2007), *Lecture Notes in Computer Science*, vol. 4871 (ed. M. Cavazza and S. Donikian), 102–113. Springer-Verlag.

Szilas, N. and Ilea, I. (2014). Objective metrics for interactive narrative. In: *Interactive Storytelling: 7th International Conference on Interactive Digital Storytelling, ICIDS 2014, Singapore, Singapore (3–6 November 2014), Lecture Notes in Computer Science*, vol. 8832 (ed. A. Mitchell, C. Fernandez-Vara, and D. Thue), 91–102. Springer-Verlag.

Tanenbaum, J. (2008). Being in the story: readerly pleasure, acting theory, and performing a role. In: *Interactive Storytelling: 1st Joint International Conference on Interactive Digital Storytelling, ICIDS 2008, Erfurt, Germany (26–29 November 2008), Lecture Notes in Computer Science*, vol. 5334 (ed. U. Spierling and N. Szilas), 55–66. Springer-Verlag.

Tanenbaum, J. and Tanenbaum, K. (2008). Improvisation and performance as models for interacting with stories. In: *Interactive Storytelling: 1st Joint International Conference on Interactive Digital Storytelling, ICIDS 2008, Erfurt, Germany (26–29 November 2008), Lecture Notes in Computer Science*, vol. 5334 (ed. U. Spierling and N. Szilas), 250–263. Springer-Verlag.

Tanenbaum, K. and Tanenbaum, J. (2010). Agency as commitment to meaning: communicative competence in games. *Digital Creativity* 21 (1): 11–17. https://doi.org/10.1080/14626261003654509.

Tarantino, Q. (1996). *Pulp Fiction*. London: Faber and Faber.

ten Brinke, H., Linssen, J., and Theune, M. (2014). Hide and sneak: story generation with characters that perceive and assume. In: *Proceedings of the 10th AAAI Conference on Artificial Intelligence and Interactive Digital Entertainment (AIIDE-14)* (ed. I. Horswill and A. Jhala), 174–180. Menlo Park, CA, USA: AAAI Press.

Theune, M., Rensen, S., op den Akker, R. et al. (2004). Emotional characters for automatic plot creation. In: *Technologies for Interactive Digital Storytelling and Entertainment. Proceedings of the 2nd International Conference, TIDSE 2004, Darmstadt, Germany (24–26 June 2004), Lecture Notes in Computer Science*, vol. 3105 (ed. S. Gobel, U. Spierling, A. Hoffman et al.), 95–100. Springer-Verlag.

Thorndyke, P.W. (1977). Cognitive structures in comprehension and memory of narrative discourse. *Cognitive Psychology* 9 (1): 77–110.

Thue, D., Bulitko, V., Spetch, M., and Romanuik, T. (2010). Player agency and the relevance of decisions. In: *Interactive Storytelling: 3rd Joint Conference on Interactive Digital Storytelling, ICIDS 2010, Edinburgh, UK (1–3 November 2010), Lecture Notes in Computer Science*, vol. 6432 (ed. R. Aylett, M.Y. Lim, S. Louchart et al.), 210–215. Springer-Verlag.

Thue, D., Bulitko, V., Spetch, M., and Wasylishen, E. (2007). Interactive storytelling: a player modelling approach. In: *Proceedings of the 3rd Artificial Intelligence and Interactive Digital Entertainment Conference* (ed. J. Schaeffer and M. Mateas), 43–48. Menlo Park, CA, USA: AAAI Press.

Tolkien, J.R.R. (1964). *Tree and Leaf*. London: Allen & Unwin.

Truyens, J. (2020). Neurocracy: using Wikipedia as an interactive narrative device. *Gamasutra*. https://www.gamasutra.com/blogs/JoannesTruyens/20200805/366900/(accessed 23 December 2020).

Turner, S.R. (1994). *The Creative Process: A Computer Model of Storytelling and Creativity*. Hillsdale, NJ: Lawrence Erlbaum.

Twine (2020). Twine. http://twinery.org/ (accessed 23 December 2020).

Tychsen, A., Smith, J.H., Hitchens, M., and Tosca, S. (2006). Communication in multi-player role playing games – the effect of medium. In: *Technologies for Interactive Digital Storytelling and Entertainment. Proceedings of the 3rd International Conference, TIDSE 2006*, Darmstadt, Germany (4–6 December 2006), *Lecture Notes in Computer Science*, vol. 4326 (ed. S. Gobel, R. Malkewitz, and I. Iurgel), 277–288. Springer-Verlag.

Universal City Studios (2020). Series: Your Story Universe. https://www .universalbranddevelopment.com/businesses/games-and-digital-platforms/series-your-story-universe (accessed 23 December 2020).

Uusi-Illikainen, T. (2016). Analysis of story and gameplay elements in visual novel games. Master's thesis. Turku, Finland: University of Turku. http://www.doria.fi/handle/10024/117684 (accessed 23 December 2020).

Vahlo, J. (2018). In gameplay: the invariant structures and varieties of the video game gameplay experience. PhD thesis. Turku, Finland: University of Turku.

VandenBerghe, J. (2012). The five domains of play. *Game Developer Magazine* 19 (5): 44–46.

Versu (2020). Versu. https://versu.com/ (accessed 23 December 2020).

Virtual Storyteller (2020). Virtual Storyteller. https://wwwhome.ewi.utwente.nl/~theune/VS (accessed 23 December 2020).

Wardrip-Fruin, N. (2009). *Expressive Processing: Digital Fictions, Computer Games and Software Studies*. Cambridge, MA: MIT Press.

Wardrip-Fruin, N. and Harrigan, P. (eds.) (2004). *First Person: New Media as Story, Performance, and Game*. Cambridge, MA: MIT Press.

Wardrip-Fruin, N. and Montfort, N. (ed.) (2003). *The New Media Reader*. Cambridge, MA: MIT Press.

Ware, S.G., Young, R.M., Harrison, B., and Roberts, D.L. (2012). Four quantitative metrics describing narrative conflict. In: *Interactive Storytelling: 5th International Conference on Interactive Digital Storytelling, ICIDS 2012*, San Sebastián, Spain (12–15 November 2012), *Lecture Notes in Computer Science*, vol. 7648 (ed. D. Oyarzun, F. Peinado, R.M. Young et al.), 18–29. Springer-Verlag.

Weallans, A., Louchart, S., and Aylett, R. (2012). Distributed drama management: beyond double appraisal in emergent narrative. In: *Interactive Storytelling: 5th International Conference on Interactive Digital Storytelling, ICIDS 2012*, San Sebastián, Spain (12–15 November 2012), *Lecture Notes in Computer Science*, vol. 7648 (ed. D. Oyarzun, F. Peinado, R.M. Young et al.), 132–143. Springer-Verlag.

Wei, H., Bizzocchi, J., and Calvert, T. Time and space in digital game storytelling. (2010). *International Journal of Computer Games Technology*. https://doi.org/10.1155/2010/897217.

Weizenbaum, J. (1966). ELIZA – a computer program for the study of natural language communication between man and machine. *Communications of the ACM* 9 (1): 36–45. https://doi.org/10.1145/365153.365168.

Wilensky, R. (1983). Story grammars versus story points. *Behavioral and Brain Sciences* 6 (4): 579–623. https://doi.org/10.1017/S0140525X00017520.

YouTube (2014). Chris Crawford's 'The Dragon Speech' (STFR) Video. https://www.youtube .com/watch?v=kaBte1cBi5U(accessed23December2020).

Zeman, N.B. (2017). *Storytelling for Interactive Digital Media and Video Games*. Boca Raton, FL: CRC Press.

Ludography

Activision, *Alter Ego*. Activision, 1986.

Arkane Studios, *Dishonored*. Bethesda Softworks, 2012.

Antonio L, *12 Minutes*. Annapurna Interactive, 2020.

The Astronauts, *The Vanishing of Ethan Carter*. The Astronauts, 2014.

Barlow S, *Her Story*. Sam Barlow, 2016.

Barlow S, *Telling Lies*. Annapurna Interactive, 2019.

Blizzard Entertainment, *World of Warcraft*. Blizzard Entertainment, 2004.

Bogost I, *Airport Insecurity*. Persuasive Games, 2005.

Bogost I, *Disaffected!*. Persuasive Games, 2006.

BioWare, *Mass Effect*. Microsoft Game Studios, 2007.

BioWare, *Star Wars: Knights of the Old Republic*. LucasArts, 2003.

Blank M and Lebling D, *Zork*. 1977.

Braben D and Bell I, *Elite*. Acornsoft, 1984.

Capcom Production Studio 4, *Phoenix Wright: Ace Attorney*. Capcom, 2001.

CCP Games, *Eve Online*. CCP Games, 2003.

CD Projekt Red, *The Witcher*. Atari, 2012.

The Chinese Room, *Dear Esther*. The Chinese Room, 2012.

The Chinese Room, *Everybody's Gone to the Rapture*. Sony Computer Entertainment, 2015.

Core Design, *Tomb Raider*. Eidos Interactive, 1996.

Crowther W, *Colossal Cave Adventure*. 1976.

CtrlMovie, *Late Shift*. Wales Interactive, 2017.

Cyan Worlds, *Myst*. Brøderbund, 1993.

DevTeam, *NetHack*. 2020.

Different Tales, *Wanderlust Travel Stories*. Walkabout, 2019.

Different Tales, *Wanderlust: Transsiberian*. Walkabout, 2020.

Dontnod Entertainment, *Life Is Strange*. Square Enix, 2015.

Epic MegaGames and Digital Extremes, *Unreal*. GT Interactive, 1998.

Firaxis Games, *Civilization IV*. 2K Games and Aspyr, 2005.

The Fullbright Company, *Gone Home*. The Fullbright Company, 2013.

Galactic Cafe, *The Stanley Parable*. Galactic Cafe, 2011.

Giant Squid Studios, *Abzû*. 505 Games, 2016.

Global Islamic Media Front, *Quest for Bush*. Global Islamic Media Front, 2006.

Guerrilla Games, *Horizon Zero Dawn*. Sony Interactive Entertainment, 2017.

ICOM Simulations, *Sherlock Holmes: Consulting Detective*. ICOM Simulations, 1991.

id Software, *Doom*. id Software, 1993.

id Software, *Quake*. GT Interactive, 1996.

Infocom, *The Hitchhiker's Guide to the Galaxy*. Infocom, 1984.

Inkle, *80 Days*. Inkle, 2014.

Inspired Media Entertainment, *Left Behind: Eternal Forces*. Inspired Media Entertainment, 2006.

Irrational Games, *BioShock Infinite*. 2K Games, 2013.

Irrational Games and Looking Glass Studios, *System Shock 2*. Electronic Arts, 1999.

King, *Candy Crush Saga*. King, 2012.

Konami Computer Entertainment Tokyo, *Silent Hill 2*. Konami, 2001.

Limbic Entertainment, *Tropico 6*. Kalypso Media, 2019.

Linden Lab, *Second Life*. 2003.

Lionhead Studios, *Black & White*. Electronic Arts, 2001.

Lionhead Studios, *Fable II*. Microsoft Game Studios, 2008.

LucasArts, *Indiana Jones and the Fate of Atlantis*. LucasArts, 1992.

LucasArts, *The Curse of Monkey Island*. LucasArts, 1997.

LucasArts, *Star Wars: The Force Unleashed*. LucasArts, 2008.

LucasFilm Games, *Maniac Mansion*. LucasFilm Games, 1987.

Ludeon Studios, *RimWorld*. Ludeon Studios, 2018.

Maxis, *SimCity*. Maxis, 1989.

Maxis, *The Sims*. Electronic Arts, 2000.

Mojang Studios, *Minecraft*. Mojang Studios, 2011.

Mountains, *Florence*. Annapurna Interactive, 2018.

Namco, *Pac-Man*. Namco, 1980.

Niantic, *Ingress*. Niantic, 2013.

Niantic, *Pokémon Go*. Niantic, 2016.

Ninja Theory, *Hellblade: Senua's Sacrifice*. Ninja Theory, 2017.

Origin Systems, *Wing Commander*. Origin Systems, 1990.

Quantic Dream, *Fahrenheit*. Atari, 2005.

Quantic Dream, *Heavy Rain*. Sony Computer Entertainment, 2010.

Quantic Dream, *Beyond: Two Souls*. Sony Computer Entertainment, 2013.

Quantic Dream, *Detroit: Become Human*. Sony Interactive Entertainment, 2018.

Red Barrels, *Outlast 2*. Red Barrels, 2017.

Remedy Entertainment, *Max Payne*. Gathering of Developers, 2001.

Rockstar Studios, *Red Dead Redemption 2*. Rockstar Games, 2018.

Rovio Entertainment, *Angry Birds*. Chillingo, 2009.

Sarepta Studio, *My Child Lebensborn*. Sarepta Studio, 2018.

Sega, *Zaxxon*. Sega, 1982.

Short E, *Galatea*. Emily Short, 2000.

Short E, *Blood & Laurels*. 2014.

SIE Santa Monica Studio, *God of War*. Sony Interactive Entertainment, 2018.

Sierra On-Line, *King's Quest*. Sierra On-Line, 1984.

Sierra On-Line, *Space Quest: Chapter I – The Sarien Encounter*. Sierra On-Line, 1986.

Sierra On-Line, *Police Quest: In Pursuit of the Death Angel*. Sierra On-Line, 1987.

Sierra On-Line, *Leisure Suit Larry in the Land of the Lounge Lizards*. Sierra On-Line, 1987.

Sierra On-Line, *Leisure Suit Larry Goes Looking for Love (in Several Wrong Places)*. Sierra On-Line, 1988.

Simogo, *Device 6*. Simogo, 2013.

Smoking Car Productions, *The Last Express*. Brøderbund, 1997.

Square, *Final Fantasy VII*. Sony Computer Entertainment, 1997.

Square Enix, *Final Fantasy XII*. Square Enix, 2006.

Sullivan Bluth, *Dragon's Lair*. ReadySoft, 1989.

Supergiant Games, *Bastion*. Warner Bros, Interactive Entertainment, 2011.

Taito, *Space Invaders*. Taito, 1978.

Thatgamecompany, *Journey*. Sony Computer Entertainment, 2012.

Team Bond, *L.A. Noire*. Rockstar Games, 2011.

Telltale Games, *The Walking Dead*. Telltale Games, 2012.

Tequila Works, *Groundhog Day: Like Father Like Son*. Sony Pictures Virtual Reality, 2019.

2K Boston, *BioShock*. 2K Games, 2007.

Ubisoft Montreal, *Assassin's Creed*. Ubisoft, 2007.

Ubisoft Montreal, *Assassin's Creed II*. Ubisoft, 2009.

Ubisoft Montreal, *Assassin's Creed Origins*. Ubisoft, 2017.

United States Army, *America's Army*. United States Army, 2002.

Valve, *Half-Life*. Sierra Studios, 1998.

Valve, *Counter-Strike*. Valve, 2000.

Valve, *Portal 2*. Valve, 2011.

Vicarious Visions, *Terminus*. Vatical Entertainment, 2000.

Wales Interactive, *The Complex*. Wales Interactive, 2020.

Westwood Studios, *Blade Runner*. Virgin Interactive, 1997.

Index

Handbook on Interactive Storytelling, First Edition. Jouni Smed, Tomi 'bgt' Suovuo, Natasha Skult, and Petter Skult.
© 2021 John Wiley & Sons Ltd. Published 2021 by John Wiley & Sons Ltd.